NEW — A PREVIOUSLY UNPUBLISHED BOOK
FROM WHITE TREE PUBLISHING 2011

THE SIMPLICITY OF THE INCARNATION
BY J STAFFORD WRIGHT

Foreword by J I Packer

"I believe in ... Jesus Christ ... born of the Virgin Mary." A beautiful stained glass image, or a medical reality? This is the choice facing Christians today. Can we truly believe that two thousand years ago a young woman, a virgin named Mary, gave birth to the Son of God? The answer is simple: we can.

The author says, *"In these days many Christians want some sensible assurance that their faith makes sense, and in this book I want to show that it does."*

In this uplifting book from a previously unpublished and recently discovered manuscript, J Stafford Wright investigates the reality of the incarnation, looks at the crucifixion and resurrection of Jesus, and helps the reader understand more of the Trinity and the certainty of eternal life in heaven.

This book was written shortly before the author's death in 1985. *The Simplicity of the Incarnation* is published for the first time, unedited, from his final draft.

ISBN: 9-780-9525-9563-2
160 pages 5.25 x 8 inches £7:95 and US $11:95
Available from bookstores and major internet sellers

ALSO FROM WHITE TREE PUBLISHING 2011
CHRISTIANS AND THE SUPERNATURAL
By J Stafford Wright

There is an increasing interest and fascination in the paranormal today. To counteract this, it is important for Christians to have a good understanding of how God sometimes acts in mysterious ways, and be able to recognize how he can use our untapped gifts and abilities in his service. We also need to understand how the enemy can tempt us to misuse these gifts and abilities, just as Jesus was tempted in the wilderness.

In this single volume of his two previously published books on the occult and the supernatural (*Understanding the Supernatural* and *Our Mysterious God*) J Stafford Wright examines some of the mysterious events we find in the Bible and in our own lives. Far from dismissing the recorded biblical miracles as folk tales, he is convinced that they happened in the way described, and explains why we can accept them as credible.

The writer says: *When God the Holy Spirit dwells within the human spirit, he uses the mental and physical abilities which make up a total human being . . . The whole purpose of this book is to show that the Bible does make sense.*

And this warning: *The Bible, claiming to speak as the revelation of God, and knowing man's weakness for substitute religious experiences, bans those avenues into the occult that at the very least are blind alleys that obscure the way to God, and at worst are roads to destruction.*

ISBN 13: 9-780-9525-9564-9
222 pages 5.25 x 8 inches £8.95 and US $12.95
Available from bookstores and major internet sellers

Bible People Real People

An Unforgettable A-Z of
Who is Who in the Bible

J STAFFORD WRIGHT

First published 1978 by Scripture Union
as *Dictionary of Bible People* in the UK and
Ravel's Dictionary of Bible People in the USA
©1978 J Stafford Wright

This new edition ©2011 C Stafford Wright

ISBN 9-780-9525-9565-6

Scripture quotations are from Revised Standard Version
of the Bible, copyright © 1946, 1952, and 1971 National Council
of the Churches of Christ in the United States of America. Used
by permission. All rights reserved.

Also where stated, from:

The New English Bible. Copyright © Oxford University Press and
Cambridge University Press 1961, 1970. Used by Permission.

The Authorized (King James) Version.
Rights in the Authorized Version are vested in the Crown.
Reproduced by permission of the Crown's patentee,
Cambridge University Press.

The Jerusalem Bible. Copyright © 1966, 1967, 1968.
Darton, Longman & Todd Ltd. and Doubleday & Company, Inc.

All rights reserved. Without limiting the rights under
copyright reserved above, no part of this publication may be
reproduced, stored in a retrieval system, or transmitted, in
any form or by any means (electronic, mechanical,
photocopying, recording or otherwise), without the prior
written permission of the copyright owner of this book.

PUBLISHED BY
WHITE TREE PUBLISHING
28 FALLODON WAY
BRISTOL BS9 4HX
UNITED KINGDOM

To my grandchildren

(Original dedication)

Publisher's Note
Putting Things In Order

Readers who are not confident with finding their way through the Bible should start here. In an over-simplified summary, the Bible is divided into two parts, the Old Testament and the New Testament – before the birth of Jesus and after the birth of Jesus. It is a collection of books that Christians believe is God's word to mankind, and the ultimate authority on God and on all matters of the Christian life and salvation.

The Old Testament begins with the creation by God of everything, including people, and tells us about God coping with those who want to live their lives in their own way. It goes on to the choosing of God's special people, and their trials and tribulations with their many enemies. We see the comings and goings of numerous kings, both good and bad, with warnings from God's prophets. The message throughout the Old Testament is one of rescue, teaching that the Messiah, the Anointed One, the Rescuer and Liberator, is coming. The account finishes around 400 BC.

The New Testament continues the theme of rescue from God's judgment with the birth of Jesus the Messiah, telling us in four Gospels (true Good News messages) of his life, death for the sins of the world, and resurrection, moving on to the founding of the first churches in the book of Acts, and the persecution of the apostles as they travel around the Mediterranean area. There are various letters (epistles) by the apostles to the young churches, instructing and encouraging them in the Christian faith. The New Testament ends with the book of Revelation with its mix of prophetic visions – for that time and for the future end of the world.

THE OLD TESTAMENT

The Old Testament contains a mix of history, poetry and prophecy. The first five books (Genesis to Deuteronomy) are traditionally by Moses, covering creation, Noah's flood, Abraham becoming the father of the Jewish people about 2000 BC, their subsequent captivity in Egypt – plus their escape led by Moses – and their wandering in the desert where they are given the Ten Commandments, entering the Promised Land forty years later.

In the next books we have the settling in the Promised Land, under the rule of judges. There seems to be constant warfare with the surrounding nations. David, who killed Goliath, takes over from Saul, who was the first king. David makes Jerusalem the centre of worship. His son Solomon, a famously wise man early in his life, foolishly causes disunity in the twelve tribes of Israel, and they divide into two groups after his death, leading to the kingdom of Israel in the north and the smaller kingdom of Judah in the south. The neighbouring countries of Assyria, Babylon and Persia invade in succession, taking vast numbers of prisoners. Accounts of these times are in the books of Samuel and Kings, and told from the priestly viewpoint in Chronicles.

Now here's the confusing bit. After a collection of songs (called Psalms) and other poetic and wisdom writings, we come to the books with the names of various prophets – some written by the prophets and some about them. The tricky part for the ordinary reader is slotting them into the historical events recorded in the books of Samuel, Kings and Chronicles. Although the prophets are grouped together in the Bible, the arrangement bears little relation to their date order. This book will help.

The prophets give messages of love and warnings from God to the kings and people of Israel and Judah, but very few of them want to hear. The prophets' books span a period in history of approximately 440 years, from about 840 to 400 BC, although there are differences of opinion as to their exact dates. The prophets give some amazing details of the coming Messiah, who hundreds of years later would bring healing and forgiveness, which leads us to:

THE NEW TESTAMENT

Jesus the Son of God is born in Bethlehem. This is the culmination of where the events in the Old Testament have been leading: to Jesus the Messiah, the Promised Saviour of the world. His mother Mary is made pregnant by the Holy Spirit of God, so Jesus was born both man and God. Teaching and performing miracles, Jesus works for three years until he is arrested, tried, and condemned to death on a Roman cross. End of story?

Certainly not. Jesus is alive again on the third day, but with a resurrection body that can pass through doors. Clearly the disciples and friends know who he is. St Paul tells us that over 500 people on just one occasion met with Jesus after his resurrection, and most of them were still living. Jesus' followers, the disciples, are overjoyed, and spend forty days with him as he teaches them once again and reminds them of all that has happened. After commissioning them to go around the world and tell everyone that he has died to take the punishment they deserve from God for their sins, Jesus goes back to heaven. Ten days later he fills his followers with power through the Holy Spirit. Christians believe that Jesus is present in their lives today.

Four writers tell the story of Jesus in their Gospels (accounts of Good News) at the start of the New Testament, and one of the Gospel writers, Luke, continues the story of the early church in the book of Acts. The disciples, now called apostles, travel around the Mediterranean area, preaching and forming Christian churches, with the majority ending their lives under torture and execution, refusing to denounce what they know to be true – that they have met the risen Jesus. Paul and others wrote letters to early churches, and we have a collection of these in the second half of the New Testament.

You can get out your Bible and browse through it while using this book. Bibles have an index in the front with the page numbers for all 66 books – 39 Old Testament and 27 New Testament – making it easy to look up the references given here. The Bible will make much more sense once you start reading it.

Introduction

If you think you already know the Bible from front to back and back to front, then *Bible People Real People* may hold a few surprises.

This book by my father was first published shortly before the availability of translations such as the New International Version, but the entries work well with all versions, old and new. New Testament names are indicated thus[NT]. Names unmarked are by default from the Old Testament.

A letter f after a Bible reference means that the next few verses beyond the reference should also be read, and ff means that you should keep reading further still, until the whole subject of the reference changes, which might be a chapter or more. Bible references are given in full the first time they appear in a paragraph (e.g. Daniel 3:4), but subsequent references in that paragraph usually have just the chapter and verse, (e.g. 6:12) until a new book is referred to.

I have added the occasional footnote where I felt it appropriate, to explain something in a little more detail.

Chris Wright
Bristol
2011

The Author's Word to the Reader

When Scripture Union* suggested I might write this book, I was asked for something with a light touch. I have interpreted this as meaning that the characters should appear as people 'of like nature with ourselves', as James says of Elijah, and less as figures who have stepped out of stained-glass windows to provide material for sermons. I have not intentionally been irreverent — certainly not in speaking of God — although I have written of some of the characters as a responsible journalist might treat them today. I have tried not to moralize, but occasionally could not resist a moral application.

The name Jehovah has been used here as the transliteration of the name of God, and not Yahweh or Jahveh. Custom often overrides correct linguistics, and here custom must take precedence. Jehovah is the God who speaks, who can be known and addressed in prayer, and who is the Father of whom the Lord Jesus Christ spoke. Yahweh is the god of the lecture rooms, the journals, and the conferences. He is not the God who speaks, but the god who is spoken about. He has not yet ascended into heaven, and I have never heard of anyone praying to him. He is a concept, and consequently one can argue about, so that one can criticize him without ever becoming involved with the fire of his presence. This book speaks of Jehovah as the true God who has revealed himself, and not as man's concept of deity.

---

* The original publisher.

I personally believe in the full inspiration of the Bible. God obviously chose his penmen with differing styles and outlooks, and did not use them as mindless writing machines. He chose the right men to convey his truth accurately, and the overriding of his Spirit within them ensured that they included what God wished to be said, and omitted what he did not wish to be kept permanently on record (2 Peter 1:21; 2 Timothy 3:16).

However, since almost the whole of my ministry until my retirement was spent in theological colleges, lecturing for external examinations which required knowledge of assumptions and conclusions often different from my own, I have encountered most of the modern objections to the straight records of the Bible. So my mind works like this — and you will find it in this book: It is not sufficient to say, 'The Bible says it', but nowadays one must add, 'The Bible says it, and it can be shown to make good sense intellectually, even though others offer critical alternatives'. Hence, sometimes I have gone out of my way in this book to bring out some things in terms which I believe answer critical objections, without arguing them point by point. This sometimes governs the length of treatment of an individual name.

There are some detailed pieces of information that a reader of the Bible needs to know, and these have been introduced where they seemed most appropriate.

All important and some unimportant names have been dealt with. Anyone who simply appears in a genealogy or some other list is omitted, unless some special comment is needed on the name. To save space and repetition, reference is often made to another entry, which is shown in **bold**. I have tried to be consistent with dates, but scholars still differ over some of them.

There is one deliberate mistake in the book. This is the switch of two consecutive names, which breaks the alphabetical order. I mention it here in case some zealous reader, who believes in going through books with a fine tooth comb, should feel moved to waste a stamp by writing to point out this grievous error. Far be it from me to divulge the secret, but if you discover it you will see the reason for the change of order.

Please excuse the snippets of serendipity which sometimes come at the end of an article. As you use the book, you will acquire pieces of useless information in addition to the more serious items you are looking for, e.g. Magog. You may even find a few original ideas, with which you are not bound to agree. For example, I had an idea about Samson and the gates of Gaza, and wrote to the mayor of Gaza for a vital piece of information. He kindly replied, and his letter showed that my idea could be correct, so that poor Samson did not have to carry the city gates forty miles [64 km] on his back.

J Stafford Wright
Bristol

Who was Who – from A to Z

AARON. *Meaning unknown*
Son of Amram and Jochebed, and great-grandson of Levi. Elder brother of Moses (Exodus 6:20; 7:7). In confronting Pharaoh with Moses he was the more spectacular figure, since he was a persuasive talker (4:14) and since God used him and his stick to initiate signs and plagues (7:8-20). When the Israelites left Egypt, Moses took the lead, since it was he who received direct communications from God, which he then passed to Aaron (e.g. 16:32-34). Also Moses was the more decisive of the two. He helped Moses in prayer during the battle against Amalek (17:8-13), and shared with others in the fellowship meal when God was seen in his glory (24:9-11).

When left in charge, Aaron mistook popular demand, and an unusual coincidence, as guidance for making a golden calf to represent God – with disastrous results (Exodus 32:1-6, 23-25). God had already designated Aaron as the future high priest (28:1), thus giving him a safe routine position that followed an important pattern of ritual and sacrifice, which foreshadowed the work of Christ (e.g. Hebrews 9).

Aaron and Moses' sister Miriam clashed with Moses, nominally in a family quarrel over Moses' new wife, but actually in an attempt to break Moses' sole authority as a prophet (Numbers 12). He suffered himself similarly when Korah, Dathan, and Abiram disputed his own sole rights as high priest (chapter 16). Further demonstrations by the people were followed by a fatal plague, which was only stopped by Aaron's intercession (16:41-

50). His position was confirmed through the miraculous growth of flowers and almonds on his stick (chapter 17).

With Moses, Aaron was not allowed to enter the Promised Land after they boasted that they would produce water from the rock and did not give glory to God (Numbers 20:1-13). (See **Moses**.) Aaron died on Mount Hor, aged 123, after handing on his priestly regalia to his eldest son, Eleazar (20:22-29; 33:39).

ABED-NEGO. *Servant of Nebo*
One of Daniel's three friends, taken to Babylon by Nebuchadnezzar in 605 BC (Daniel 1:1-7). His Jewish name, Azariah (Jehovah has helped), was changed for official purposes to 'Servant of Nebo', a Babylonian god (1:7). After a test, in which the friends insisted on a vegetarian diet to avoid meat that had not been correctly killed, i.e. not *kosher* (Leviticus 10-16) or that had been offered to some idol (1 Corinthians 8), they were made court advisers (Daniel 1:8-20). Later they refused to worship Nebuchadnezzar's golden image, which on its plinth was some 90 feet (27.5 metres) high, over half the height of Nelson's Column in Trafalgar Square, London. They were thrown into a blazing kiln, but miraculously remained unharmed (Daniel 3).

The Greek (Septuagint) version of Daniel contains a song that the three were supposed to have sung in the fire. It occurs with other material after Daniel 3:23, but is printed separately in the Apocrypha. It forms the Benedicite in the Anglican Book of Common Prayer, with the closing verse, which has puzzled young and old worshippers, calling on Ananias, Azarias and Misael to bless the Lord. These are the Greek equivalents of their Jewish names.

ABEL. *Suggested meanings are Breath, Shepherd, or Son*
Second son of Adam and Eve (Genesis 4). A shepherd. Domestication of animals came in with the Neolithic or New Stone Age after about 9000 BC. Abel was murdered by his brother Cain after his offering had been pleasing to God and Cain's rejected. Some think Abel was accepted because he brought an animal

sacrifice as atonement (see **Cain**). The New Testament emphasizes his faith (Hebrews 11:4) and righteousness (Matthew 23:35).

ABIATHAR. *The Great One is Father,* or *The Father is plentiful*
A high priest descended through Eli (1 Kings 2:27). He escaped when Saul's spy, Doeg, massacred his father Ahimelech and eighty-five other priests (1 Samuel 21 and 22). He joined David with the high priestly ephod, which was the top garment containing the Urim and Thummim (Exodus 28:1-35), the jewels by which the Yes or No decision of God could be obtained, probably by using them as sacred lots after prayer (1 Samuel 14:41 in modern translations; 23:6-12). He shared the high priesthood with Zadok 15:24).

Perhaps Zadok had been appointed by Saul after the murder of Ahimelech, and David retained both as a gesture of peace, possibly making one responsible for the ark of the covenant in Jerusalem and the other for the tabernacle which at this time was at Gibeon (2 Chronicles 1:3). He had a son, Jonathan (2 Samuel 15:27).

Abiathar and Zadok stayed in Jerusalem as David's secret agents during Absalom's rebellion and occupation of the city, but used their sons as undercover messengers (2 Samuel 15:24-37). At the end of David's reign Abiathar joined the revolution to put Adonijah on the throne, while Zadok supported Solomon and David (1 Kings 1). Consequently Solomon deposed Abiathar in favour of Zadok (2:26-27).

There is a problem in Mark 2:26, where apparently Mark quotes Jesus as saying that the incident of David and the shewbread took place when Abiathar was high priest, whereas 1 Samuel 21:1 says that it was in the time of Ahimelech. It we look for an alternative to the explanation that either Jesus or Mark had a lapse of memory, there are two reasonable suggestions. One is to blame a copyist for a desire to display his memory of Old Testament history, only unfortunately his memory was at fault. There is a similar probability of this in Matthew 27:9 (see

Zechariah 4).

The other helpful suggestion is a different translation of the Greek. The two words 'Abiathar highpriest' are in the genitive case governed by the preposition *epi*, and there is no doubt that this can be translated 'when Abiathar was highpriest'. But the same construction occurs in Mark 12:26, where it is translated 'in the passage about the bush'. When there were no chapter numbers, reference had to be made to some keyword, so that the reader could look it up if he wished. There is no reason at all why Christ's words should not be translated, 'in the section dealing with Abiathar the highpriest' in the Davidic records. The Abiathar section naturally begins with Ahimelech. (See **Ahimelech**.)

ABIGAIL. *My Father rejoices*
1. David's sister, mother of Amasa by an Ishmaelite husband (1 Chronicles 2:17).
2. Wife of a wealthy sheep farmer, Nabal. After her husband died of a stroke, brought on by her lavish present to David and his men, she became David's second or third wife (1 Samuel 25). Her son Chileab (2 Samuel 3:3), also called Daniel (1 Chronicles 3:1) is not mentioned elsewhere.

ABIHU. *He (God) is Father*
Son of Aaron (Exodus 6:23), who was included in the group who had the vision of God on Sinai (24:1,9). He and his brother Nadab died when they experimented with a fancy form of worship (Leviticus 10:1-7). Since God immediately warns Aaron against taking alcohol before conducting worship, it is likely that Nadab and Abihu were drunk at the time.

ABIJAH. *Jehovah is Father*
Nine people have this name, but only four are significant.
1. Son of Samuel, who as judge took bribes to pervert the course of justice (1 Samuel 8:1-3).
2. A descendant of Aaron, responsible for duties in the tem-

ple worship (1 Chronicles 24:10). An ancestor of John the Baptist (Luke 1:5).

3. Son of Jeroboam I, who died in infancy, the only one in a bad family who had a peaceful death (1 Kings 14, especially verse 13).

4. Son of Rehoboam and grandson of Absalom (2 Chronicles 13), but his personal life was flamboyant (13:21) and uncontrolled (1 Kings 15:3). His variant name Abijam (15:1), probably meaning Father of the People, may be his own preferred title although most commentators treat it as a copyist's error.

ABIMELECH. *The (divine) king is my father*
1. King of Gerar, south of Gaza. Abraham spent some time there (Genesis 20), and claimed that Sarah, his wife, was his sister. She was in fact his half-sister (20:12). He was afraid that if the king wanted to take Sarah into his harem, as indeed happened, he would first kill him. Abraham made this his policy on other occasions (20:13; see 12:11-19). Abimelech justifiably rebuked Abraham, but remained friendly. The two made a pact over the ownership of the wells of Beersheba (21:25-34).

2. Probably his own son, who had more or less the same experience with Rebekah and Isaac (Genesis 26). Sons sometimes follow their fathers' bad examples. This Abimelech is called 'king of the Philistines' (26:1). Although the Philistines, largely from Crete, did not invade Palestine until much later, they evidently had outlying colonies to produce corn for their island centre. Hence they had come to worship the Canaanite corn god Dagon as early as Samuel's day (1 Samuel 5).

3. Son of Gideon, who set himself up as the first king of Israel after murdering his brothers (Judges 9). He captured Shechem after a quarrel with the Shechemites who had helped him to power, but was fatally injured by a millstone thrown from the tower when he attacked nearby Thebez.

ABINADAB. *My Father is generous*
A citizen of Kiriath-jearim, or Baale-Judah, ten miles west of

Jerusalem, whose family housed the ark of the covenant after the Philistines captured Shiloh (1 Samuel 7:1-2). The twenty years mentioned here are the period between verse 2 and the next major event in the rest of the chapter, but the ark remained there until David's day.

ABIRAM. *The Father is exalted*
A Reubenite who with Korah and Dathan led a demonstration against the supremacy of Moses and Aaron (Numbers 16). He and Dathan shirked the test of going before God with incense (chapters 12-14), but did not escape the earthquake rift which swallowed them up with all their property (chapters 23-33).

ABISHAG. *My father a wanderer*
A girl from Shunem in the north who nursed David in his old age but did not have sexual relations with him (1 Kings 1:1-4). After David's death, Solomon refused his brother Adonijah's request to marry her, perhaps because her association with David might give him a claim to the throne (2:13-25). One reasonable interpretation of the Song of Solomon is that Solomon tries to win a country girl for his harem, but ultimately allows her to return to her shepherd lover. She is called a Shulammite (6:13), probably the equivalent of Shunamite, and it is pleasing to identify her with Abishag.

ABISHAI. *Meaning uncertain*
David's nephew by his sister, Zeruiah, and brother of Joab (2 Samuel 2:18). In David's outlaw days he was leader of the band of the Thirty, but did not have the chance of promotion to the inner Three (23:18). It seems that places in the Thirty and the Three were filled when an enrolled member died.

Fanatically loyal to David, he urged him unsuccessfully to murder Saul (1 Samuel 26:6-9) and himself helped to murder Abner (2 Samuel 3:30). Similarly he demanded the right to execute Shimei when he cursed David (16:9), and evidently connived in the murder of his cousin Amasa (20:10). At some point he risked his life to rescue David from a powerful Philistine (21:15-22. See **Goliath**). He was also a good general, joint commander with David against Edom (2 Samuel 8:13. See too 1 Chronicles 18:12), and with Joab against Ammon (2 Samuel 10:9-14) and rebellious Absalom (18:2). He and Joab clearly believed that David was too mild and needed to be saved from himself (3:39)

ABNER. *Father is a lamp*
Saul's cousin (1 Samuel 14:50-51, see 9:1), and general (17:55; 26:5-16). He somehow escaped when Saul and Jonathan were killed in the great battle of Gilboa, and became the king-maker, setting up Saul's son Ishbaal as a rival to David (2 Samuel 2:8). After a particularly bloody tournament between champions of the rival kingdoms, Abner killed the impetuous young Asahel in self-defence (2:12-23), an act which eventually cost him his life at the hands of Asahel's brothers, Joab and Abishai (3:26-30). When Ishbaal rounded on him for taking one of the royal concubines, he decided to better himself by turning the whole kingdom over to David. Joab concluded he was playing a double game, and made this the excuse to take his revenge for Asahel's death (2 Samuel 3).

ABRAHAM. *Father of a multitude*
Name lengthened from Abram (The Father is exalted, or loving) to Abraham, and given the significance of 'Father of a multitude' (Genesis 17:5) as a perpetual reminder of the promises of God. This is not an etymological derivation, but God is not tied to lexicons. His date is variously placed between 2000 and 1600 BC.

His father, Terah, moved from Ur in south Babylonia to Haran in the north (Genesis 11:31). At seventy-five, Abraham was told by God to move to Palestine as the future land of his many descendants (12:1-3). He never owned land, except later his wife Sarah's tomb, but moved from place to place (Hebrews 11:8-10, 13-16), and built altars at Canaanite sanctuaries, evidently to claim them for Jehovah (Genesis 12:4-9). His journeys included

Egypt and Gerar (see **Abimelech**).

He not only accumulated flocks and herds (Genesis 13:2-7), but had several hundred retainers, from whom he raised an army of over 300 to rescue his nephew Lot, who had been captured in a raid (Genesis 14, see also **Melchizedek**). God promised that he would be honoured as a blessing to the world, and also promised him a multitude of descendants (12:2-3). Later he sealed this by a visible acceptance of a sacrifice (Genesis 15). Abraham tried to bring the fulfilment by following a recognized custom and taking his wife's maid, Hagar. She thus became the mother of Ishmael (Genesis 16). God, however, made it possible for Sarah to bear Isaac in her old age (Genesis 18 and 21). This naturally led to friction in the home, and Hagar and Ishmael had to leave (Genesis 21).

Hitherto, Abraham had taken God's promise by faith (Genesis 15:6), but now he was called to demonstrate this faith. God told him to offer Isaac in sacrifice on one of the mountains (Genesis 22), although he had previously promised that Abraham's descendants would come through Isaac (21:12). Isaac was not yet married. Abraham obeyed implicitly up to the last moment, when God stopped him. Clearly he believed that, if Isaac died, God would raise him from the dead so as to fulfil his promise (Hebrews 11:17-19). His act of total obedience justified him in the eyes of the world as a man with the inner faith that God looks for (James 2:21-24. NB: 'You see' verses 22 and 24). (See **Isaac**.)

After the death of Sarah and her burial in a cave bought from the Hittites (Genesis 23), Abraham sent his servant to Haran to find a wife for Isaac from his own relatives (Genesis 24). Abraham married again, and had other children, but willed everything to Isaac (25:1-6). He died aged 175 (25:7).

In the New Testament, Abraham's faith is singled out for special attention. He believed God and his promise, and was thereupon accounted righteous, even before he had demonstrated the reality of his faith. The same principle holds good in Christ (Romans 4). Since the Abrahamic promise included the blessing of all nations through his greatest descendant, Jesus Christ, Gentiles now become the children of Abraham without becoming Jews, but solely in and through Jesus Christ (Galatians 3-4; especially 3:16,29).

ABSALOM

Third son of David by Maacah, daughter of king of Geshur (2 Samuel 3:3). Extremely good-looking (14:26), a favourite of his father, and popular (13:39; 15:6). He killed his half brother Amnon for assaulting Absalom's sister, and took refuge at his grandfather's (2 Samuel 13). David foolishly only half forgave him, and although he allowed him to come back he refused to see him for two years (2 Samuel 14). Absalom was embittered and began to win over the ordinary people to himself, until he felt strong enough to stage a revolution (2 Samuel 15).

David abandoned Jerusalem and took his loyal troops over Jordan (2 Samuel 15 and 16), but Absalom forced him to fight. In the battle Absalom's mule took him under the low branches of an oak, in which his head became tightly wedged. Here he was found and killed by Joab and his men, to the great distress of David (2 Samuel 18). Absalom was married and had at least one daughter (2 Chronicles 11:20-21), but having no son to carry on his name he erected a memorial pillar to commemorate himself (2 Samuel 18:18).

ACHAN

A man of Judah, whose greed caused a setback to the success of the Israelite entry into Palestine. No individual was to make a profit out of the spoils of Jericho, which were to be placed in the tabernacle or destroyed. They were to be a kind of First Fruit dedication to the Lord. Achan made off with silver and gold and an attractive coat, and hid them in his tent. The next battle proved a fiasco, and God showed that the nation was tainted until the criminal was found. Achan's name was drawn by lot, and he confessed. He was stoned, and his possessions destroyed. A careful reading of Joshua 7:25-26, suggests that while his family were brought out as witnesses, he alone was put to death, and his tomb alone is mentioned.

ACHISH

King of Gath, a Philistine city. Although the Philistines constantly dominated Israel, David took refuge with Achish when Saul put his life in danger. The Gittites were suspicious of his motives, and David evaded arrest by pretending to be mad (1 Samuel 21:10-15). Later David went back to Achish, this time with 600 fighting men, and offered him his services (1 Samuel 27). He was allowed to settle in Ziklag and while pretending to be raiding Judah's territory he was actually destroying Canaanite 1 Samuel 27:8-12). Achish was so far deceived as to enlist David and his men against Saul. Once again other Philistines intervened, and David and his men had to be sent back (1 Samuel 29).

In estimating Achish as a foolishly trustful man, we must remember that he may have been gambling on using Saul's most powerful enemy to gain the final victory over Israel. David's behaviour can hardly be commended, and only the suspicion of the Philistine officers saved him from a very difficult situation in the battle on Mount Gilboa.

Another Achish is mentioned in the time of Solomon (1 Kings 2:39-40.)

ADAH

Wife of **Lamech**, mother of **Jabal** (4:19-20). (See both names.) Another was the Hittite wife of Esau (Genesis 36:2). Unlike his grandfather, father and brother, Esau preferred to 'keep up with the Joneses'.

ADAM

His name means *Man,* and the word is translated *man* some 500 times in the Old Testament.

As an individual, we read of his creation in Genesis 2:7, and follow through the story of his responsibility and his fall in chapters 2 and 3.

Many people regard the whole story as symbolic or parabolic of the fall of every man into self-centredness. But apart from the precise geographical statements, a Christian is bound to ask whether the record throws any light on how the first fully human being came into existence, capable of knowing God and of forming moral judgments.

The record certainly links man's body to other animal bodies, since both have a similar composition. Both come from the earth (Genesis 1:24; 2:7), and both return to dust (3:19; Psalm 104:29). Every creature that is made to live in this world has to have a body, and there are naturally strong resemblances between them. But the theory of evolution, as a complete explanation of life as it is, has so many gaps that it cannot account for the unbridgeable gulf between the rest of the animal world and man who is capable of conceptions of goodness, truth, beauty, and of God himself. Adam was made in the image and likeness of God, not in physical likeness, but in the possession of spiritual personality.

A problem arises when we theorize about the relationship of Adam in Genesis 2 to the manlike beings whose remains, tools and art stretch back for very many thousands of years. It is perfectly possible that Genesis 1 refers to these manlike beings, and that they were true men (the Hebrew is *Adam)* in the image of God (Genesis 1:26-27). Otherwise Genesis 1 could be a general account of the creation of mankind as the climax to the mineral, vegetable, and animal world, while Genesis 2 is a particular account of how the first true man was created.

It is generally agreed that the genealogies in Genesis 5 and 11 are not intended to be so complete as to bring Adam as late as 4000 BC, but it would be absurd to take the biblical story of Genesis 2 and 3 back tens of thousands of years (see **Melchizedek**). So an interesting alternative is to regard Adam as the first of the New Stone Age men, who were cultivators instead of mere hunters and food gatherers.

It is noteworthy that cultivation and domestication of animals are thought by anthropologists to have begun in Asia Minor at some time after 9000 BC. The Bible story stresses cultivation

(Genesis 2:15) and contact with the animal world (2:19; 4:2), and places Eden in Asia Minor (2:10-14). Unless this is pure coincidence, it is sensible to take the Bible story as more than myth (see also **Cain**).

Archaeology shows that after thousands of years during which manlike beings had been on earth, there was a sudden leap forward in civilization in the New Stone Age. We know that the previous manlike beings were not cultivators, but only hunters and food gatherers. They were able to express ideas in superb cave and rock art. We do not know whether they had the gift of language, although obviously, like the animals, they must have had communications by sound and gesture, with perhaps drawing and painting to supplement.

We take language as obvious, although the concept of communication by words is not innate, but needs to be taught. We cannot say whether these beings had any concept of God. Occasional burial of the dead is no proof that they believed in an afterlife. It may be that they lacked something equivalent to a soul, or that they were without the capacity for proper personality (including the knowledge of God) which was given to Adam.

Adam certainly was given the knowledge of God and the power to obey him. It is a fair supposition that, so long as his life was centred in God, his body resisted the seeds of death, which fossil remains show to have been in the rest of the animal and hominid world. His sin affected the whole of humanity, and Romans 5:14 and 1 Corinthians 15:22 speak of death, physical and spiritual, as stemming from Adam's transgression.

Anyone who holds that pre-adamites survived the Flood, can say that Adam was constituted the head of all beings who henceforth could be counted as human. All were given the capacity to know God, although they may still have needed to be taught the truth through the Adamites. All, as humans, were put 'in Adam', though not necessarily by physical descent, just as Christians are put 'in Christ' without being descended from him (1 Corinthians 15:22).

ADONIBEZEK. Name variously interpreted as *Lord of Bezek, Bezek is my lord, Lord of Lightning*
King of Bezek, in south Palestine. He was captured by the forces of Judah and Simeon, who decided to give him a taste of his own medicine. He had specialized in collecting rival kings and treating them like dogs at his table, after cutting off their thumbs and big toes. Adonibezek was similarly mutilated and taken to Jerusalem, and he took it as God's just recompense, although it is not said that the Israelites acted according to a divine command (Judges 1:3-7).

ADONIJAH. *Jehovah is my Lord*
Fourth son of David (2 Samuel 3:2-5). Since his elder brothers, Amnon and Absalom, and presumably the otherwise unknown Chileab, were dead, he expected to succeed David.

Adonijah had been a spoilt and handsome son (1 Kings 1:6), and shortly before David's death he persuaded Joab and Abiathar to arrange his coronation. Bathsheba, the mother of Solomon, reminded David that the throne had been promised to Solomon, and David roused himself enough from his sickbed to commission Zadok and Nathan to crown Solomon king. Adonijah was immediately deserted by his supporters and took refuge at the altar. Solomon told him not to be afraid so long as he was loyal to the crown.

After David's death, Adonijah persuaded Bathsheba to ask Solomon to give him Abishag for his wife (see **Abishag**). Since she had been close to David in his last illness, and some would have thought she had been as a wife to him, her marriage to Adonijah might have given him a fresh claim to the throne. Solomon evidently took the request in this way, and promptly executed Adonijah (1 Kings 2:19-25).

ADONIRAM. *My lord is exalted*
Probably identical with Adoram. Both names are given to the superintendent of the labour force under David (2 Samuel 20:24), Solomon (1 Kings 4:6; 5:14) and Rehoboam (12:18). The

labour force was made up of Canaanites (9:20-21), with supervisors drawn from the various tribes (11:28). The Israelites paid taxes and supplied provisions for Solomon and his projects (4:7-28), but were used for forced labour only in building the temple, so that all might have a share in this grand work (9:22; 5:13-18).

ADONIZEDEK. Probably *My lord is righteous*
The *-zedek* ending may have been characteristic of the kings of Jerusalem (compare Melchizedek). He and four other kings attacked the Gibeonites, who had made peace with Joshua. Joshua went to the aid of the Gibeonites, and the ensuing battle and rout was marked by a shower of stones from the sky and the strange prolongation of daylight in answer to the command (not even a prayer) of Joshua (see **Joshua** for more on these stones). Adonizedek and the other four kings hid in a cave. Joshua brought them out, and after a dynamic symbolism of subjugation he put them to death, afterwards hanging their bodies on nearby trees (Joshua 10).

ADRAMMELECH
Son and murderer of Sennacherib, king of Assyria (2 Kings 19:37). The fact of the murder is borne out by the Babylonian records, though the son is not named there.

AGABUS[NT]
A Christian prophet, based on Jerusalem. He travelled to Antioch to give warning of an approaching famine which would hit the whole empire (Acts 11:27-28). The disciples did not sit down under the inevitability of the prediction, nor did they begin to hoard food for themselves, but now and later they contributed to the hard-up church in Jerusalem (Acts 29-30). Agabus appears a second time in Caesarea, giving a symbolic demonstration of Paul's arrest when he returned to Jerusalem (21:10-11). Paul noted the warning, but did not regard the prophecy as God's command to desist.

AGAG
King of the Amalekites, taken prisoner by Saul, together with everything that the Israelites could find of value. Samuel had recognized Amalek as a menace in the past and this was still true. Speaking as a prophet, he had told Saul to destroy Amalek without taking any personal gain for himself. However difficult we find the command, we may assume that Amalek was still anxious to invade and wipe out Israel, and the fact that none of the Israelites were to benefit personally puts the nation in the position of commissioned executioners.

Saul's sin was in using his commission for personal gain, and when he brought back the spoils and Agag as his prize, he was told by Samuel that his disobedience meant his rejection as king. Agag supposed that his own survival was assured, but Samuel executed him as a criminal whose deeds deserved capital punishment (1 Samuel 15).

The general reference in Numbers 24:7 is probably to an earlier king of Amalek.

AGRIPPA[NT]
See **Herod**.

AGUR
An unknown writer of Proverbs 30. What a delightful man he was, humble, reverent, and a pungent observer of animals and men!

AHAB
King of Israel and son of Omri, who was founder of a new line in the northern kingdom. Reigned c. 870-850 BC. A great warrior, continually fighting with Syria (e.g. 1 Kings 22:1), but, according to Assyrian annals, allying with Benhadad of Syria and others to resist the Assyrian invasion at Qarqar (854 BC). He built cities, and also a palace finely decorated with ivory work (1 Kings 22:39). He was eventually killed in a battle to recapture Ramoth-gilead from Syria (1 Kings 22). The Bible is chiefly concerned

with his moral and spiritual character. He married Jezebel of Sidon, and was dominated by her wishes (1 Kings 21:25), including the stamping out of the worship of Jehovah in favour of Baal, in which she met the resistance of Elijah.

Ahab built her a temple (1 Kings 16:32), and allowed her to fill the court with her pet prophets (18:19). But he must have offered some resistance when their son was born since he gave him a Jehovah name, Azariah. His weakness was shown when he allowed Jezebel to have Naboth put to death so that he might occupy his vineyard. As an Israelite Ahab had a respect for persons and property which was quite different from the Sidonian absolute tradition (1 Kings 21). (See also **Jezebel, Elijah**.)

AHASUERUS
An example of the extreme difficulty of transliterating some names from one language to another. The king's name in Persian is Khshayarsha. The Hebrew equivalent, transliterated into English, is Ahasuerus. The Greek rendering is Xerxes. Two Bible references are almost certainly to Xerxes I (485-465 BC). Ezra 4:6 mentions a complaint made by enemies of Judah in his reign. The section 4:6-23 is an inset deliberately mentioning later attempts to frustrate the Jews in addition to that which took place immediately after the return in 536 BC. Xerxes I is almost certainly the king in the book of Esther. His delay in marrying Esther (Esther 1:3; 2:16) was occasioned evidently by his abortive invasion of Greece.

An otherwise unknown Ahasuerus was the father of Darius in the book of Daniel (Daniel 9:1. See **Darius**).

AHAZ. *He has grasped*
If, as some suppose, his name is an abbreviation of Jehoahaz, then Jehovah is the one who has grasped him. King of Judah (c. 735-715 BC), but without the fine qualities of his grandfather, Uzziah. Astonishingly enough, he was attracted by a fancy altar at defeated Damascus, and had a replica made for himself as a

substitute for one of the altars in the temple (2 Kings 16:10f). Isaiah was his contemporary, and some of the early chapters of Isaiah show the low state of people in authority and consequently of the land as a whole.

In particular, 2 Kings 7 describes the challenge to Ahaz when his land was invaded by Israel and Syria. Ahaz decided to call on Assyria for help (compare 2 Kings 16:7f). Isaiah gave him God's command to trust quietly in Jehovah, and offered him a miraculous sign from heaven or from the world of the dead (verse 10). Ahaz, wanting his own way, refused to suggest a sign. So Isaiah offered the Lord's own sign (verse 14), which to match the others must involve a miracle. This is the promise of the virgin birth, for although the Hebrew word can signify simply a young woman, it is never used in the Old Testament of anyone who is not a virgin or presumed virgin.

Although Ahaz may have interpreted the sign as meaning that the enemy would withdraw before a forthcoming marriage had produced a child of an age of moral responsibility, verse 17 shows that the sign is a message of judgment for Ahaz. In bringing in Assyria, Ahaz was bringing disaster for his own land. This and similar requests for help down the ages made Israel a subjugated and impoverished nation. Hence, when the virgin's promised child, Jesus the Messiah was born, he was not born on the throne in a flourishing community, but in a family where he must be brought up simply (2 Kings 15, compare 21 for the simple diet). For the simplicity of Christ's birth and upbringing see also 11:1; 53:2.

AHAZIAH. *Jehovah has grasped*
1. Son of Ahab. Only famous for falling out of the palace window, and sending to Baal-ze-bub for a private consultation. Elijah intercepted the messengers and asked why the king had not consulted Jehovah. Elijah foretold Ahaziah's death. Moab, then a tributary state paying a form of tax as acknowledgment of defeat, revolted during Azahiah's two-year reign (2 Kings 1).
2. Son of Jehoram of Judah by the powerful queen Athaliah

(2 Kings 8:25-26) (see **Athaliah**). On a visit to Jehoram of Israel, Ahaziah was caught up in Jehu's revolution, and Jehu ordered his death as well as Jehoram's. The two accounts of his death in 2 Kings 9:27-28 and 2 Chronicles 22:9 are often regarded as irreconcilable, but one can visualize a situation that would bring them together:

After Jehu had killed Jehoram at Jezreel, Ahaziah escaped in his chariot to Samaria (2 Chronicles 22:9), where there were 70 members of the royal family in a well-defended city (2 Kings 10:1). They were however not prepared to resist Jehu (10:5), and refused to give Ahaziah sanctuary when the emissaries of Jehu came to escort him back to Jehu (2 Chronicles 22:9). When Ahaziah had nearly reached Jezreel again, he turned his chariot and made off at top speed. Jehu and some of his charioteers followed him, with the command to shoot to kill. They managed to hit him, but his charioteer outstripped them, and brought the dying king to Megiddo. Jehu's men gave his servants permission to take him back to Jerusalem for burial.

AHIJAH (sometimes **Ahiah**). *Jehovah is my brother*
Six bear this name, but only one has more than a bare mention. This is a prophet who towards the end of Solomon's reign told Jeroboam that he would become king of ten of the tribes of Israel after the death of Solomon. He demonstrated this by a typical prophetic parable, tearing his new coat into twelve pieces and giving ten to Jeroboam (1 Kings 11:29ff).

When Ahijah was old and blind, Jeroboam sent his wife in disguise to consult him about his son's illness. Ahijah knew from God that this was the queen, and poured out God's message of judgment on Jeroboam and his house for deliberately introducing idolatry into his kingdom (1 Kings 14). He was probably one of the recorders whose histories were available for historians like the writers of Kings and Chronicles (2 Chronicles 9:29).

AHIKAM. *My brother has risen*
A trusted member of Josiah's court, sent with others to consult

Huldah the prophetess (2 Kings 22:12-13). In the reign of Jehoiakim, Ahikam saved Jeremiah from being put to death (Jeremiah 26:24). He was the father of the later governor, Gedaliah (2 Kings 25:22).

AHIMAAZ. *Anger is my brother*
Only one of the three of this name has more than a mention. Son of Zadok, who with Jonathan son of Abiathar was David's spy near Jerusalem during Absalom's rebellion (2 Samuel 15:36). They were betrayed by a boy, but escaped by hiding in a well and managed to get to David with the vital information that he needed (17:17-21). After Absalom's death, Ahimaaz managed to outrun the official messenger and tried to break the news to David as gently as possible before the other runner, a foreigner, arrived and blurted out the truth (18:19-33).

AHIMELECH. *Brother of a king*
Priest in charge of the ark of the covenant at Nob. When David was escaping from Saul, he pretended that he and his small band of men were on an official assignment, and persuaded Ahimelech to let them have the dedicated bread which normally only the priests might touch, and also the sword of Goliath which was stored behind the vestments (1 Samuel 21).

When the news reached Saul through Doeg, one of his herdsmen who had been present at the time, Saul summoned Ahimelech and his fellow priests, and in spite of their genuine plea of ignorance of David's falsehood, he massacred them all, except for Abiathar, who escaped and joined David. His grandson, the son of Abiathar, also had the name of Ahimelech (2 Samuel 8:17; 1 Chronicles 24:6).

AHITHOPHEL.
If, as seems likely, his name means *Brother of folly,* this must either have been a playful nickname, or having been given the name for some reason by his parents he was spurred on to show that he was very far from foolish, becoming one of the wisest

men in David's court (2 Samuel 16:23). There was evidently a class of Wise men and Wise women, as well recognized as the class of prophets and priests (e.g. 2 Samuel 14:2; Jeremiah 18:18), and ultimately they were the treasurers of what we call the Wisdom Literature (e.g. Proverbs, Ecclesiastes).

Ahithophel's wisdom did not keep him loyal to David, and he was unwise enough to believe that the future lay with Absalom when he rebelled (2 Samuel 15:12). Unfortunately for him, David had another wise man, Hushai, who infiltrated into Absalom's ring of advisers, and argued successfully against Ahithophel's excellent plans to attack David immediately (2 Samuel 17).

Ahithophel had the weakness of some men at the top: he could not stand loss of face. His suicide showed that he was better in advising others than in solving a personal crisis (2 Samuel 17:23). His successors as counsellors after David's return are named in 1 Chronicles 27:34.

ALEXANDER[NT]

Several in the New Testament have this name, but nothing is known of them apart from the single mention. We may note:

1. A Jew in Ephesus who tried to stop the Demetrius riot. His selection by the Jews and the crowd suggests that he was the Jewish liaison man in the city (Acts 19:33). It has been suggested that he wished to dissociate the Jews from the Christians, a rather cowardly act, since as a Jew he should have been as strong an objector against Diana and her images as were the Christians.

2. A misguided teacher of Christian faith and morals (1 Timothy 1:19-20). He and his associate Hymenaeus are 'delivered to Satan' by Paul (see **Hymenaeus**). There is a similar phrase in 1 Corinthians 5:5. It certainly includes excommunication, but the full expression in 5:5 suggests that God allowed Satan to attack them with all kinds of physical troubles (see Job 1; 2), so that they might turn back to God. Satan naturally hoped to destroy them.

3. A coppersmith in the Ephesus area, a strong opponent of Paul and his preaching (2 Timothy 4:14-15). The RSV follows the better manuscript reading, 'the Lord will requite' rather than the KJV, 'the Lord reward' (i.e. a simple future rather than a wish). He might possibly be the same man as 1 or 2.

4. Son of Simon of Cyrene (Mark 15:21). See **Simon, Rufus**.

ALEXANDER THE GREAT (356-323 BC)
The Macedonian/Greek conqueror of Persia. Although not named in the Bible, he is probably the 'great horn' of Daniel 8. At his death his empire was divided between his four generals (Daniel 8:21-22).

ALPHAEUS [NT]
The name of the father of Matthew/Levi (Mark 2:14) and also of the father of James (Mark 3:18). There is no indication that Matthew and James were brothers. (See also **Cleopas**)

AMASA
Like Joab, Amasa was David's nephew (2 Samuel 17:25). Absalom made him his general, but he lost the battle to Joab (2 Samuel 18). David could not forgive Joab for killing Absalom, and made Amasa general of his own army in his place (19:13). This was a fatal misjudgment in dealing with a man like Joab, and when Amasa showed his incompetence, Joab murdered him as he had previously murdered Abner (20:4-10).

AMAZIAH. *Jehovah is mighty*
King of Judah (c. 800 BC) after his father Joash had been murdered. He punished the murderers but spared their children. His reign is recorded in 2 Kings 14 and 2 Chronicles 25. Although he conquered Edom, after refusing the help of mercenaries from Israel, he brought back some Edomite gods for his own use, and consequently was rebuked by a prophet. His dispute with the prophet has all the marks of a man with a guilty conscience (2 Chronicles 25:15f).

Looking round for fresh fields to conquer, Amaziah challenged Jehoash of Israel, and was hopelessly defeated. His

Edomite gods were of little help to him as Jehoash helped himself to what he wanted in the palace and temple. Amaziah's people turned on him, and although he managed to slip out of Jerusalem, they caught him at Lachish and put him to death.

AMON

Son of Manasseh. Manasseh was a connoisseur of idolatry, and probably named his son after the Egyptian god Amon. Amon reigned two years in Jerusalem (642-640 BC), and followed in the steps of his father. He was assassinated by his servants (2 Kings 21:19f; 2 Chronicles 33:21-25).

AMOS

A foreign missionary, coming from Tekoa in Judah to speak to the northern kingdom of Israel (c. 750 BC). As a former shepherd (Amos 1:1; 7:14), his language shows that he had come to realize while out in the wilds the greatness of God as creator, (e.g. 4:13; 5:8-9). But he did not divorce creation from revelation, and although he condemned other nations for atrocities that shocked the common conscience of mankind (1:3–2:3) he denounced Israel and Judah for flying in the face of the special revelation that God had given them (e.g. 2:4–3:2). To be the chosen people did not mean that they were chosen to behave as they wished (e.g. 3:2; 5:18-24). Since he selected Bethel as one of his preaching centres, the high priest of the golden calf (1 Kings 12:28-30) reported him to the king, and presumably he was expelled as an undesirable alien (Amos 7:12-13).

Some have thought that in Amos 7:14-15 Amos dissociates himself from the earlier prophets. There is no evidence that these earlier prophets were in any way inferior, and indeed Amos speaks of them as called by God (Amos 2:11). What he means is that he was not brought up in one of the prophetic schools of 'sons of the prophets' (e.g. 2 Kings 4:38), but was called while looking after the flocks and herds.

AMRAPHEL

King of Shinar. One of four kings who invaded Palestine and captured Lot among others (Genesis 14:ff). Formerly identified with the great Hammurabi, king of Babylon, c. 1790 BC, but this is now thought unlikely. He is otherwise unknown. Shinar may be Singar in Upper Mesopotamia.

ANANIAS NT

1. An early disciple, who with his wife Sapphira made a show of giving the whole of the proceeds of a sale to the church funds. In fact they gave only a proportion. Their deception and boast were challenged by Peter, and both independently were punished by death. Their story shows that the Christian community in Jerusalem did not expect everyone to sell all that they had, since Peter tells Ananias that he was free to sell or not sell his land, and free to hand over whatever proportion he felt right (Acts 5:4). An interesting theological point is that Peter says that the lie to the Holy Spirit is a lie to God, thus showing the Deity and the personality of the Holy Spirit (verses 3-4).

2. A disciple at Damascus who was sent by God to lay hands on Paul after his conversion, so that his sight might be restored (Acts 9:10-19).

3. High priest and Chairman of the Council that tried Paul after his arrest in Jerusalem (Acts 23:2). A hot-tempered bigot, Ananias ordered the guards to hit Paul in the face when he made his plea of innocence. When the Romans broke up the court and smuggled Paul away to Caesarea, Ananias followed with a good barrister, but was unsuccessful in his attempt to make the governor hand over the prisoner (Acts 24:ff). The Jewish historian, Josephus, shows him to have been a quarrelsome, violent and greedy man. In the end he was murdered by his own people in AD 66.

ANDREW NT

One of the Twelve. Originally a disciple of John the Baptist, Andrew heard John's testimony to Jesus as the Lamb of God, and immediately followed him. Next day he brought his brother, Simon Peter, to Jesus (John 1:35-42). Thereafter he appears as the quiet introducer, e.g. of the boy with the loaves and fishes (6:8) and of the Greeks who wished to see Jesus (12:20-22). He is not mentioned after Acts 1:13 where he is listed among the disciples in the upper room.

There is a fairly strong tradition that he was crucified at Patrae in Achaia, but no suggestion earlier than the 13th century that his cross was the X shaped type that is now known as Saint Andrew's cross. This cross appears on Scotland's flag, since the story goes that Saint Andrew became Scotland's patron saint after a missionary, Regulus, brought with him the arm of Andrew as a sacred relic in the 8th century.

ANDRONICUS [NT]

He and Junias create a problem by being greeted as Paul's kinsmen, and as men of note among the apostles (Romans 16:7). Although the Greek word for kinsmen regularly refers to relatives, it is unlikely to have this meaning here, since four others have the same description in this chapter (verses 11,21). Hence the term describes fellow Jews, as in Romans 9:3. Their other description as 'men of note among the apostles' might mean that the apostles regarded them with respect, but more likely means that they ranked as apostles. Although this term was first used of the Twelve (Luke 6:13), others like Barnabas (Acts 14:14) and James, the Lord's brother (Galatians 1:19) are also called apostles. The wider title must indicate some special commission given to certain early disciples, and Paul specially says that Andronicus was in Christ before he was.

ANNA [NT]

A widow of 84, whose husband had died after only seven years of marriage (Luke 2:36-38). She was of the tribe of Asher, a fact that shows that not all of the northern tribes were lost in exile. She had the gift of prophecy, and testified to the future of the infant Jesus.

ANNAS NT

High priest from AD 6-15. The Romans then deposed him, but like bishops today he retained his title, while five of his sons and his son-in-law, Caiaphas kept the high priesthood in the family. It is not surprising that when Jesus was arrested he was taken first to the dominant Annas for a preliminary hearing (John 18:12-24).

Annas tried to retrieve the disaster of the resurrection by silencing the disciples (Acts 4:5f), but he and his council had to concede defeat. It is likely that he was responsible for setting up what were known as 'the booths of the sons of Annas' to sell materials for sacrifice. Christ's violent assault on these stalls and their occupiers (Matthew 21:12-13) would hardly endear him to Annas, whose pockets they helped to line.

ANTIOCHUS IV

Known as Epiphanes. A Greek king of the Seleucid dynasty who ruled Asia Minor and Syria (175-164 BC). Although not mentioned by name in the Bible, his desecration of the temple, setting up an altar to Zeus, and banning the sacrifices to Jehovah, is the theme of several passages in Daniel (e.g. Daniel 8:9-26; 11:21ff). The three and a half years of desecration become a type-picture of crises in the church in the book of Revelation (e.g. Revelation 11:1-13).

ANTIPAS NT
See **Herod**

APOLLOS NT

An Alexandrian Jew who came to live in Ephesus (Acts 18:24). He had been attracted by the message of John the Baptist, and knew something about the life of Jesus, but evidently was not convinced that Jesus was the Messiah of whom John had spoken (18:25). Probably the half-Christians of Acts 19:1-7 had been won by Apollos. After Apollos had been led to Christ, he moved over to Greece (18:27), and became one of the big names in the

Corinthian church (1 Corinthians 3:4-6). This was not of his seeking, and there was no rivalry between him and Paul.

Apollos did not jump at the opportunity of a fresh visit to Corinth in Paul's absence (1 Corinthians 16:12). Paul finally refers to him as undertaking a journey in Titus 3:13. Luther suggested that he was the author of the Epistle to the Hebrews, and his name is as likely as some others that have been put forward.

APPHIA[NT]
It is likely from the wording of Philemon 2 that Apphia was the wife of Philemon and mother of Archippus. Their house formed the meeting place for the local Christians. (See **Philemon**.)

AQUILA[NT]
He and his wife Priscilla were expelled from Rome with other Jews under an edict of the emperor (Acts 18:2). They were already Christians when they settled in Corinth, and found a congenial companion in Paul, a fellow tentmaker (verse 3). They went with Paul when he returned to Asia Minor, but stopped at Ephesus while Paul went on to Palestine (18:19). They were responsible for bringing Apollos to the knowledge of Christ (18:24-28). Aquila and Priscilla were still at Ephesus when Paul wrote 1 Corinthians, and sent their greetings to the Christians they had known (1 Corinthians 16:19). They returned to Rome, and their home became a place of meeting. Paul refers to their having saved his life, though we do not know the occasion (Romans 16:3-5). Aquila has been suggested as author of the Epistle to the Hebrews.

ARAUNAH
The Jebusite owner of the site that David bought for the temple after a vision of the angel of the pestilence (2 Samuel 24:15-25). Although Araunah offered to give the site freely, David insisted on a proper price, first 50 shekels of silver for the central threshing-floor and oxen, so that he could build an altar there

(24:24-25), and later 600 shekels of gold for the whole area big enough for the temple site (1 Chronicles 21:25). In Chronicles, Araunah is called Oman. Either name could be the equivalent of the Hittite *arawanis,* meaning *freeman* or *noble.*

ARCHELAUS[NT]
See **Herod**.

ARCHIPPUS[NT]
Perhaps son of Philemon and Apphia (Philemon 2). The same verse suggests that Archippus had worked with Paul, but he was also commissioned for some special work (Colossians 4:17).

ARETAS[NT]
The Nabataean king, Aretas IV, was father-in-law to Herod Antipas, although Antipas divorced Aretas' daughter in order to marry Herodias (Mark 6:17). Paul records that at a time when Aretas held Damascus, the disciples there evaded the governor and enabled Paul to escape down the walls in a basket (2 Corinthians 11:32-33; Acts 9:23-25).

ARIOCH
An unidentified king who joined Amraphel and others in an invasion of Palestine in Abraham's day (Genesis 14:1). The name Ari-aku is found on Hurrian tablets in various places and at various dates. Arioch's kingdom of Ellasar has been by some identified with Larsa, a Babylonian city between Ur and Erech, but this is far from certain.

Another **Arioch** is captain of Nebuchadnezzar's guard, commissioned to kill Daniel and other wise men (Daniel 2:12-25).

ARISTARCHUS[NT]
A Jew (NB: reference to circumcision in Colossians 4:10-11), a native of Thessalonica (Acts 20:4; 27:2), who as Paul's travelling companion was nearly killed in the Ephesus riot (19:29). He went

with Paul on his dangerous journey to Jerusalem (20:4), and managed to get a place with him on the convict ship, perhaps as his servant (27:2). At Rome he shared Paul's imprisonment (Colossians 4:10; Philemon 24). Only by following through these references can we see what a fine companion he must have been.

ARTAXERXES

Three Persian kings had this name, but probably only Artaxerxes I (464-424 BC) occurs in the Bible. He sent Ezra to report on Jewish affairs, since Judah was part of his empire (Ezra 7). Shortly afterwards he banned attempts to rebuild the walls of Jerusalem (4:7-23), but left it open for a reversal of his decree (verse 21, compare Daniel 6:8), which happened when he allowed Nehemiah to go back as governor and rebuild the walls (Nehemiah 1 and 2).

It is likely that in Ezra 4:6-23 the writer has brought forward two later attempts to harass the Jewish builders so as to link them to the first attempt soon after the return in the reign of Cyrus. The Greek Septuagint version has Artaxerxes in place of Ahasuerus in the story of Esther. This would be Artaxerxes II (404-359 BC). Some think the compiler of Ezra and Nehemiah has confused the kings, and that Ezra came to Jerusalem after Nehemiah in the reign of Artaxerxes II, but this creates more difficulties than it solves.

ASA. *Healer*

King of Judah (c. 911-870 BC). His record in 1 Kings 15:9-24; 2 Chronicles 14-16, show him to be a good man who tried to undo the nasty work of his predecessors. He was under pressure from his grandmother, Maacah, a confirmed idolatress who evidently tried to continue in the influential position of queen mother as she had done under Asa's father (1 Kings 15:2,10). Asa deposed her, and publicly burned her favourite idol (verse 13).

Asa cleared the land of most other idolatrous worship, evidently making a distinction between high places that had the Canaanite images, which he destroyed (2 Chronicles 14:3), and those sanctuaries where Jehovah was worshipped sincerely, although wrongly, since the temple should have been the single centre of worship (1 Kings 15:14).

At a united convention in Jerusalem the Jews, and some who chose to join in from the northern kingdom, held a special service of consecration (2 Chronicles 15:8-18). One of his military exploits was outstanding, when he threw back an invasion of Ethiopians, although hopelessly outnumbered (14:9-15). He was equally successful in destroying some Israelite fortified cities that were threatening him, but first bribed Syria to break her alliance with Israel, and join him in attacking the cities (1 Kings 15:16-22).

Being rebuked by the prophet Hanani for joining with Syria instead of trusting the Lord, as he had done when Ethiopia attacked him, he showed the touchiness that could not take a rebuke, and not only put Hanani in prison but turned on others of his subjects as well (2 Chronicles 16:7-10). Perhaps his self-control was already being affected by an unspecified severe disease in his feet (verse 12). It may be that, as the pain grew harder and harder to bear, his depression made it difficult to pray for healing, especially since he had refused to accept God's rebuke through Hanani. So while the best doctors did what they could, he was never cured (verse 12).

ASAHEL. *One whom God made*
Younger brother of Joab and Abishai. Asahel joined his uncle David in his outlaw days, and became one of the noble band of the Thirty (2 Samuel 23:24). After David became king, he was made one of the regular commanders of the army (1 Chronicles 27:7), but shortly afterwards he met a violent death at the hands of Saul's former general, Abner, who was escaping after a savage tournament between his men and David's.

Asahel was a great runner, and overhauled the self-indulgent Abner. But Abner was more crafty, and as he ran he brought back the butt of his spear so that the impact drove even the blunt end into Asahel's body (2 Samuel 2:12-23). Although Abner acted in self-defence and unwillingly (verses 21-22), he started a vendetta which ended in his own death at the hands of Asahel's brothers. (See **Abner**.)

ASAPH

David, himself a knowledgeable musician and composer, chose Asaph to lead the temple choirs (1 Chronicles 16:4-7). Asaph had previously been chosen by his fellow Levites as one of the musical leaders when David brought the ark of the covenant into Jerusalem (15:16-28). There is an interesting collection of Psalms ascribed to Asaph (Psalms 50; 73-83). Undoubtedly Asaph composed some of them (2 Chronicles 29:30), but it is likely that his successors added to the Asaph collection such a psalm as 79, which describes the ruin of Jerusalem. The sons of Asaph kept their position in the new temple after the exile (e.g. Ezra 3:10; Nehemiah 7:44).

ASENATH

Joseph's wife, daughter of the chief priest at On (Genesis 41:45). Her name may mean *She belongs to Nut* (the sky goddess), but she would naturally follow Joseph in worshipping Jehovah. She became the mother of Manasseh and Ephraim (verses 50-52).

ASHER. *Happy*

Jacob's eighth son, the second by Zilpah, Leah's maid (Genesis 30:9-13). It was a socially recognized practice for a childless wife to let her husband have a child by her maid, and the child would then be one of the family. Leah already had three sons of her own, and was to have three more, but she was determined to come out with more children than Rachel and her maid could produce. Thus Zilpah's two children were very happy events for her, and she called them Good Fortune and Happy. Asher, though ancestor of the tribe that bore his name, was himself a nonentity, so far as the records go.

ASHURBANIPAL. *(The God) Ashur creates a son*
King of Assyria about 670 BC. His name is rendered as Osnappar in Ezra 4:10, where he is quoted as having transported groups of foreigners into Israel. This could have been about 640 BC, after he had captured Susa. Although he is not named, he was the king who took Manasseh prisoner (2 Chronicles 33:10-13).

ATHALIAH. *Jehovah is exalted*
In spite of her name, she is one of the really wicked women of the Bible and is actually named as 'that wicked woman' (2 Chronicles 24:7). She had a bad start, since she was the daughter of Ahab and Jezebel (2 Kings 8:18,26). Doubtless it was regarded as a tactical alliance when she married Jehoram of Judah, but she took after her mother and exerted the same influence on her husband as Jezebel did on Ahab. When her husband died, she dominated her son Ahaziah in the same way (verses 26-27).

The unexpected death of Ahaziah after a single year gave her the chance of becoming the only ruling queen in the history of Israel and Judah. Her grandson Jehoash, heir to the throne, was only a year old, and Athaliah marked him down to be murdered with all other possible claimants to the throne including, presumably, her other sons who are mentioned in 2 Chronicles 24:7. By the good providence of God, who had promised that the Messiah would come of David's line, the baby's aunt smuggled him and his nurse into a room in the temple (2 Kings 11:1-3).

The priests and Levites had no love for Athaliah, whose sons had pillaged the temple (2 Chronicles 24:7), and no one gave away the secret. After six years the high priest organized the Levites and the temple guard to proclaim the young Joash as king. Athaliah rushed to the temple to see what the cheering meant, and was arrested and put to death. After destroying Athaliah's shrine to Baal, the whole of Jerusalem marched Joash to the palace and crowned him king (2 Kings 11; 2 Chronicles 23).

AUGUSTUS[NT]
Although this may read like a proper name in Luke 2:1, it is a

title, *The Honourable,* conferred by the Senate on Gaius Octavius in 31 BC, and borne by his successors. Although Luke transliterates the Latin form in 2:1, he uses the Greek equivalent, *sebastos* (RSV, 'emperor') in Acts 25:21,25. (See **Caesar**.)

AZARIAH. *Jehovah has helped*
Some 28 men in the Old Testament have this name. In particular it was an alternative name for King Uzziah (2 Kings 15:1-7, see **Uzziah**). **It** was also the name of a prophet who persuaded King Asa to destroy his country's idols (2 Chronicles 15). It was the Hebrew name of one of Daniel's three friends, renamed Abed-nego when Nebuchadnezzar had the four of them educated in the language and literature of Babylon (Daniel 1:5-7, see **Abed-nego**).

BAALIS
An otherwise unknown king of Ammon, who instigated the murder of the Jewish governor Gedaliah after the fall of Jerusalem (Jeremiah 40:14). During the exile period most of the small powers tried to grab extra territory for themselves. (See also **Gedaliah, Ishmael**.)

BAASHA. *Boldness*
In recent years we have become accustomed to seeing dictators and presidents seize power by revolution. This also happened several times with the kingship of the northern kingdom. Baasha was the first revolutionary, after only two kings had ruled since the split on the death of Solomon (1 Kings 15:27ff). He assassinated King Nadab, son of Jeroboam I, executed all claimants to the throne and became the strong man who would lead the people against Asa of Judah. Unfortunately for him, Asa paid Benhadad of Syria a substantial sum from the temple to attack Israel, and Baasha had to withdraw and see his new frontier fort at Ramah pulled to pieces by Asa (15:16-22). In exterminating the family of Jeroboam, Baasha fulfilled an earlier prophecy (15:29-30, compare 14:10), but his own behaviour was similar to

that which had brought God's displeasure on the Jeroboam dynasty. Hence, he also received a prophecy of doom on his own dynasty (16:1-4). His date was about 900-877 BC.

BALAAM. Meaning uncertain, but perhaps *Devourer* or *Glutton*
A remarkable man from Pethor, in northern Syria near the Euphrates. He had unusual psychic gifts, and although he willingly allowed God to take them over, he valued the gifts more than the Giver. The true prophets allowed the message to mould their own lives. Balaam kept the two in separate compartments. Thus, when Balak king of Moab offered him a substantial payment to put a curse on Israel, he first accepted God's command not to go, but on being asked a second time by the top men from Moab and Midian, he managed, as he thought, to persuade God to change his mind (Numbers 22:1-20).

On the way he realized his mistake when he was stopped by an angel with a drawn sword. His ass alone at first saw the angel, and turned aside in spite of Balaam's savage attempts to stop her. As she brayed her protests, Balaam, with his psychic capacity for clairvoyance and clairaudience, heard in coherent form what she was trying to communicate (Numbers 22:21-35). Some people, who are not psychic, can well understand what their dog or cat wants to communicate. Some feel strongly that 2 Peter 2:16 shows that the ass actually enunciated words, and this cannot be treated as impossible. The essential thing is that Balaam heard the ass's objection in the form of human speech. Balaam by this time was prepared to let himself be a channel for whatever God chose to say, and so delivered a blessing rather than the curse he had been hired to give (Numbers 23 and 24).

The apparently contradictory translations of Numbers 24:3-4,15-16, indicate either that in trance his outer eyes were closed or that his inner eye was opened, in either case so that he could perceive the message of God. But after acting as a true messenger of God, he decided to give Balak value for his money and so suggested that he could get what he wanted by inviting the Israelite men to the sex orgies that were part and parcel of the high place religions (25:1-5; 31:16).

Balaam was eventually caught by the Israelites, probably on a further visit to the scene of his triumphs, and was put to death (Numbers 31:8). The New Testament shows that Balaam is not simply a figure of past history but always has his counterparts (2 Peter 2:15; Jude 11; Revelation 2:14).

BALAK
The king of Moab who co-operated with Midian in sending for Balaam to curse the invading Israelites (Numbers chapters 22-24; Micah 6:5).

BARABBAS[NT]
Unlike Jesus, Barabbas chose the way of violence to gain his political ends, and was arrested after killing at least one person in a riot (Mark 15:7; Luke 23:19). There was a tradition that one prisoner should be given an amnesty at the Passover, and while Pilate wanted Jesus to be the man, the priests worked on the people to demand Barabbas (Mark 15:6-15).

An interesting addition to the accepted text of Matthew 27:16 gives his name as Jesus Barabbas (RSV margin). Scholars differ over whether this reading is to be accepted, but if it is, we have the remarkable balance between Jesus Christ, the Son of God, and Jesus Barabbas, whose name means *Son of the Father*.

BARACHIAH
See **Zechariah**.

BARAK. *Lightning*
One of the great judges, or leaders, who receives honourable mention in the roll of heroes in Hebrews 11:32. The book of Judges records the moral and spiritual ups and downs of sections of the nation after the settlement in Palestine. Declension always brought subjugation by some foreign power, and this time Jabin of Hazor was the power (Judges 4 and 5). Deborah the prophetess commissioned Barak to gather an Israelite army, and most of

the tribes, though not all, rallied to their support. It seems that a sudden storm bogged down the armoured vehicles (4:13; 5:20-21), and the Israelites won a magnificent victory. There is no record of Barak afterwards. Probably he retired into ordinary life again, having been raised up for this single occasion. (See **Deborah**.)

BAR-JESUS^{NT}. *Son of Joshua*

A Jewish practitioner of magic who was in favour with the proconsul Sergius Paulus on the isle of Cyprus (Acts 13:1-12). His alternative name, Elymas (verse 8), is not an interpretation of Bar-Jesus, but probably means *Wise man,* i.e. wise in magical arts. Hence the RSV of Acts 13:8, 'Elymas the magician (for that is the meaning of his name)' is clearer than the KJV. He resisted the preaching of the gospel by Paul and Barnabas, but his magical arts were not strong enough to deflect God's answer of temporary blindness.

BARNABAS^{NT}

A Levite from Cyprus whose life-style gave him this name in place of his family name of Joseph (Acts 4:36). Luke says that the name means *Son of Encouragement* (the same root as the title Paraclete, Comforter, for the Holy Spirit). Although it is not easy to derive this meaning from the Hebrew or Aramaic, it is obvious that Luke, who knew the apostles well, was aware what they intended by the name. Perhaps *nabas* is linked with an Aramaic work *newakhah,* meaning *pacification.* Barnabas first encouraged the infant church by a generous gift from the sale of land (Acts 4:37).

Next, he introduced Paul to the Jerusalem church when the Christians were still afraid of him after his conversion (Acts 9:27). He was sent to report on the first attempts to bring in Gentiles at Antioch, and was wise enough to see the hand of God here, and to send for Paul to join him in the work. (11:19-26. NB: verse 24 for his character.) He was commissioned by the Holy Spirit to go with Paul on the first missionary journey, and they established a chain of churches with considerable Gentile membership (13 and 14).

Barnabus and Paul had to answer to the council at Jerusalem for admitting Gentiles as equals to Jewish converts, but the council commended them (Acts 15). When Paul asked him to join in another journey, Barnabas would not go unless they took his cousin Mark who had deserted them on the previous journey. It was characteristic of Barnabas to give Mark another chance, but the two leaders parted company over the affair (15:36-41). Barnabas and Mark went to Cyprus (see **Mark**).

Barnabas is criticized in Galatians 2:13, since at Antioch he and Paul mixed freely with the Gentile converts, until under pressure from the anti-Gentile Jewish Christians he joined Peter in segregation for meals. A gentle character may easily do the wrong thing for the sake of apparent peace. He followed Paul in working for his living while preaching the gospel (1 Corinthians 9:6).

BARTHOLOMEW[NT]. *Son of Tolmai*

One of the twelve apostles (Matthew 10:3). Nothing further is recorded about him. The Lord chose the unspectacular as well as those who figure largely in the records. Some think Bartholomew was a second name for Nathanael, since he is linked with Philip in Matthew 10:3, and Philip was Nathanael's close friend (John 1:45). John does not mention Bartholomew, and the other three Gospel writers do not mention Nathanael, but the identification of the two cannot be conclusive on these grounds.

BARTIMAEUS[NT]. *Son of Timaeus*

One of two blind beggars whom Jesus healed on the outskirts of Jericho (Matthew 20:29-34; Mark 10:46-52; Luke 18:35-43). Matthew and Mark say that the cure happened as Jesus was leaving Jericho. Luke says it was as Jesus was entering. Mark is the only writer who names Bartimaeus. Doubtless he became better known among Christ's followers than the other man. If we knew the circumstances, we could bring the accounts together.

Possibilities are:

1. We know that there was an Old Jericho and a New Jericho, the latter built by Herod the Great, and Jesus might enter and leave one before the other.

2. An unnamed blind beggar was healed as Jesus entered Jericho. Since beggars commonly know one another and share out their pitches, the news stimulated Bartimaeus and a friend, perhaps the only other two blind beggars in the town, to use the same appeal as Jesus was leaving on the following day. This seems the more likely.

BARUCH. *Blessed*
It is thanks to Baruch that we have our book of Jeremiah. About 604 BC Jeremiah recalled and dictated the main messages that God had given him over the past 20 years. Baruch was his secretary for this (Jeremiah 36:1-4). Baruch took the scroll and read it first to the people, then to the king, who promptly burnt it column by column. Undaunted, Jeremiah and Baruch made a fresh copy, to which they added further prophecies from time to time (36:5-32). Later, Jeremiah in prison handed over a deed of purchase to Baruch (32:12-16).

Baruch kept his association with the prophet after the destruction of Jerusalem, and was in fact accused by some of the survivors of exerting pressure on Jeremiah to deliver an unpopular prophecy (Jeremiah 43:3). The refugees forced Jeremiah and Baruch to go with them into Egypt (43:6). It would seem from 45:5 that Baruch had to choose between suffering with Jeremiah or taking a government post through his brother's influence (compare for relationship 32:12 and 51:59).

BARZILLAI. *Of iron character*
A delightful aristocrat from Gilead. As an old friend of David, he had no time at the age of eighty for the young rebel, Absalom. He and two other friends brought provisions and other things from their estates for David's tired men (2 Samuel 17:27-29). After the campaign he escorted David as far as the Jordan, but in an old-

fashioned way refused David's offer to come back to court, although he asked David to receive a friend of his in his place (19:31-40).

BATHSHEBA

Possibly granddaughter of Ahithophel if we can link her father, Eliam (2 Samuel 11:3) with the Eliam of 23:34. Although Bathsheba was married to Uriah the Hittite, whose name indicates that he was a convert to Jehovah, David took her during Uriah's absence on a campaign. When a baby was on the way, David tried in vain to father it on Uriah, and then had Uriah killed by what would seem an unfortunate accident (2 Samuel 11). The baby died, but Bathsheba's next child was Solomon, whom God designated as David's successor (2 Samuel 12 and 1 Chronicles 22:9).

Bathsheba is not mentioned again until the end of David's life, when she intervened to stop the coronation of Adonijah in place of her son (1 Kings 1). Later she was unwisely persuaded to ask Solomon to let Adonijah marry David's former nurse, Abishag (2:13-25). A pleasant Jewish tradition is that she composed Proverbs 31:10-31 for Solomon on his first wedding day!

BELSHAZZAR

Son of Nabonidus, king of Babylon. About 556 BC his father, according to Babylonian records, entrusted the kingship to him, while he himself went to Arabia for a number of years. Belshazzar was thus king when Babylon was captured by Cyrus in 539 BC (Daniel 5). The Greek historian Xenophon confirms that the army of Cyrus entered the city by night during a festival, and killed the king. Daniel describes the bravado with which Belshazzar profaned the temple vessels from Jerusalem (5:3-4), followed by the mystery writing on the wall, which could be read as three weights, suggesting the doom words; Numbered, Weighed, Divided (5:25-28).

BENAIAH. *Jehovah has built up*
One of the Thirty while David was an outlaw. Three of Benaiah's exploits are recorded in 2 Samuel 23:20, but the first is a mystery. The RSV leaves the Hebrew noun untranslated; 'He smote two ariels of Moab'. Others translate as personal (e.g. 'champions' NEB). The RSV, by rendering the verb as 'smote', suggests that the ariels were idolatrous objects, and this is probably correct, since on the Moabite Stone (see **Mesha**) a similar word is usually translated 'altar hearth' or 'lion figure'.

When David came to the throne, Benaiah was put over the mercenaries that had been recruited from among the Philistines (2 Samuel 8:18). He was one of three entrusted with the coronation of Solomon when it seemed that Adonijah was about to seize the throne (1 Kings 1:32-40). Later Solomon ordered him to execute Adonijah, Joab and Shimei, and made him commander-in-chief of the army (2:25-46).

BEN-HADAD
Two or three kings of Damascus (Syria) with this name are mentioned in the Bible.
   1. Ben-Hadad I. About 895 BC, King Asa bribed him to attack Israel (1 Kings 15:18-20).
   2. Ben-hadad II. Some think this was still Ben-hadad I. He was defeated by King Ahab (1 Kings 20), but later campaigned against Israel and almost took Samaria (2 Kings 6). He was murdered by Hazael, his general, about 843 BC (8:7-14).
   3. Ben-hadad III, son of Hazael (2 Kings 13:24), was less successful than his father against Israel (13:22-25). Date about 796-770 BC.

BENJAMIN
Since Rachel was the only woman Jacob really loved, one can understand why he was especially devoted to the two sons that he had by her, Joseph and Benjamin. Benjamin was the only one of Jacob's sons born in Canaan, on the way to Bethlehem. His mother died in giving him birth, and in her pain named him

Benoni, *Son of my sorrow*. Jacob, however, changed this depressing name to one expressing strength, *Son of the right hand* (Genesis 35:16-20).

After Joseph's disappearance, his father specially treasured Benjamin, and with the greatest reluctance allowed his brothers to take him to Egypt. Here Joseph, unrecognized by his brothers, planted his silver cup in Benjamin's luggage and had him arrested (Genesis 43 and 44).

After the whole family had settled in Egypt, Benjamin had several children (Genesis 46:21), and was the original ancestor of the small tribe that bore his name. In blessing his sons, Jacob foresaw a fierce future as warriors for Benjamin's descendants. Some specialized in the use of the sling and bow (Judges 20:16; 1 Chronicles 8:40). It is a curious coincidence that so many *Sons-of-the-right-hand* were actually left-handed (Judges 20:16; 3:15). Notable descendants included Saul (1 Samuel 9:1-2) and Paul (Romans 11:1).

BERNICE[NT]
Eldest daughter of Herod Agrippa I, whose marriages and affairs would have furnished unending material for the less savoury press today. When we meet her listening to Paul in Acts 25, she is living in a doubtful relationship with her brother, Agrippa II. It would be good to think that Agrippa's words in verse 28 mark the beginning of conversion, and that this led to his parting with Bernice, who became, in turn, the mistress of two Roman emperors, Vespasian and Titus. For those interested in astronomy, the constellation Berenice's Hair is not named after her, but after an Egyptian queen some 300 years earlier.

BEZALEEL or **Bezalel**. *In God's shadow*
A skilled craftsman in metals, precious stones and wood carving, chosen with Oholiab to work on the tabernacle (Exodus 31:1-11). They had other craftsmen under them (31:6; 36:1). The Spirit of God filled Bezalel so that he could use what were evidently natural and trained gifts in the right way (31:3).

In the Old Testament the Holy Spirit fills people for some specific task, but does not come to indwell all God's people permanently as at Pentecost (e.g. John 7:39; 14:16). Yet we still need Holy Spirit equipment in the use of such gifts as we have by nature or by grace (compare Romans 12:1-8 in the light of 1 Corinthians 12:4-11).

BILDAD
One of Job's three friends, perhaps descended from Abraham's second wife, Keturah, through Shuah (Job 2:11; Genesis 25:1-2). Each of the friends uses a different approach, and Bildad quotes the wisdom of the ancients. In the third round of speeches he can manage only a brief statement. (See Job 8; 18; 25, also **Job, Eliphaz, Zophar**.)

BILHAH
The personal maid of Rachel (Genesis 29:29). When Rachel seemed unable to have children, she followed a custom of the day and let her maid bear two children, Dan and Naphtali, by Jacob (30:1-8). Later Reuben had a casual affair with her, but Genesis 35:22 implies that she was not a willing partner.

BOANERGES[NT]
The nickname given by Jesus to the impetuous disciples, James and John (Mark 3:17). Commentators find difficulty over Mark's statement that the title means *Sons of thunder*; but Mark, who worked closely with Peter, must have known how the other disciples interpreted the name. Perhaps the word is compounded of *bene* (sons of) and the root *ragash* (to be in noisy tumult, e.g. like the crash of thunder). In transliterating an original Aramaic title into Greek, Mark may well have approximated it to two Greek words, *boe* or *boa* (a loud noise) and the root seen in *ergon* (work or deed). For the aptness of the title, see **James, John**.

BOAZ
See **Ruth**.

CAESAR[NT]
The famous Julius Caesar is not mentioned in the Bible, but his name was adopted as a title by his nephew Octavius, and subsequently by all other Roman emperors until the 3rd century AD. Later it passed to Germany as Kaiser, and to Russia as Czar. The following Caesars are mentioned in the New Testament.

1. Augustus (31 BC-AD 14). Emperor when Jesus Christ was born (Luke 2:1).

2. Tiberius (AD 14-37). Emperor during the whole of Christ's ministry (Luke 3:1). His head was on the coin shown to Jesus (Mark 12:16). Naturally the Jews hated being under him, but when it suited them they obtained Jesus' conviction through charging him with rebellion against Caesar (John 19:12-15).

His successor, Caligula, is not mentioned in Scripture.

3. Claudius (AD 41-54) is mentioned in Acts 18:2 as forcing all Jews, including Aquila and Priscilla, to leave Rome. In his days there was a great famine (Acts 11:28).

4. Nero (AD 54-68). Cruel and vindictive, and a persecutor of Christians. Paul appealed to him as the supreme dispenser of justice (Acts 25:11). Although it seems that Paul was acquitted in Rome on the first occasion, he was later arrested again, and according to tradition the martyrdom of Peter and Paul occurred in Nero's reign.

CAIAPHAS[NT]
Joseph Caiaphas was appointed high priest by the Romans in AD 18, and deposed by them in AD 36. Son in law of Annas, the previous high priest (John 18:13). The two of them worked hand in glove, and Annas, as high priest emeritus, still was the big man in the eyes of the Jews (Luke 3:2, John 18:12-24, Acts 4:6).

The crafty suggestion of Caiaphas to sacrifice Jesus to save the whole nation (i.e. from rebellion and consequent destruction by Rome) became an unconscious prophecy of the atonement

(John 11:49-52). He took the lead in the trial of Jesus, and he and his fellow priests made sure of obtaining the death penalty by a gross perversion of justice (Matthew 26:57, etc.). After the resurrection, Caiaphas did his best to recoup his failure by silencing the witness of the Christians (Acts 4:6, and probably 5:17,21,27; 7:1; 9:1).

CAIN His name suggests the Hebrew word *qanah, get* (Genesis 4:1).
Whatever language his parents spoke, an equivalent play on words was probably there. The first son of Adam and Eve. Jealousy drove him to murder his brother Abel when his own offering was not accepted by God. One cannot say what was wrong with his offering, but the implication of Genesis 4:7 is that the failure lay in his personal conduct, whether or not there is the further thought that atonement through animal sacrifice had already been revealed to Adam and Eve when God made garments of skins for them (Genesis 3:21).

Cain began by being an agriculturalist, and archaeology shows that there was no settled agriculture until the New Stone Age after about 9000 BC. Later he built a city, and discoveries (e.g. by Professor James Mellaart) have found at least one Stone Age city, Catal Huyuk, on the highlands of Anatolia. Cain's fear of being killed by others raises the question of whether there were pre-Adamic men still living (see **Adam**), or whether he foresaw a quick spread of the human race through further children to Adam and Eve. Similarly his wife (Genesis 4:17) might have been of pre-Adamic race, or Cain might have married one of his sisters (Genesis 5:4). This would not have been incest, since there would have been no other way of launching the race other than by family intermarriage.

CALEB
Since names were given either to commemorate something in the present or some hope for the future, it is difficult to see why a child was given a name which means *Dog,* since dogs were

despised scavengers. But perhaps his father Jephunneh was a shepherd, and valued his dogs for their usefulness in controlling the flock (compare Job 30:1, although even here they are spoken of as inferior animals). Caleb certainly appears as a good watchdog.

As a Kenizzite (Numbers 32:12), Caleb was descended from Esau (Genesis 36:11), but his family were integrated into Judah, perhaps after famine conditions in Palestine had brought them, like Israel and his family, into Egypt. Many countries today are familiar with the naturalized foreigner who is able to identify completely with his new nationality after a generation. Caleb was so well integrated that he was chosen as Judah's representative to spy out the land of Canaan (Numbers 13:6), and he and Joshua were the only two members of the group who believed that God could enable them to overcome the powerful Canaanites.

He almost lost his life at the hands of his compatriots (Numbers 14:4-10), but God secured that he and Joshua were the only two adults to survive the following forty years in the wilderness (14:28-38). Consequently, he was able to speak to Joshua as man to man after the conquest, and after declaring that God had kept him as strong at eighty-five as at forty, asked to be given an area of territory round Hebron that the spies had found to be one of the toughest regions (Joshua 14:6-15). This was not yet a soft option, since the area was still occupied by three well-known Canaanite leaders, but Caleb and his nephew Othniel made short work of them (15:13-17).

Othniel seemed an eligible husband for Caleb's daughter, Achsah. As a dowry he gave Achsah a piece of land, and in words that have been spiritualized in countless convention addresses, she asked for, and received, further land that included springs of water (Joshua 15:17-19; Judges 1:11-15).

Two less important characters also bear the name of Caleb in the genealogical list in 1 Chronicles 2:18,42.

CANAAN
See **Ham**

CANDACE[NT]
According to Pliny this was the title of the queens of Ethiopia, corresponding to the title Pharaoh. In Acts 8:26-39 her powerful treasurer was converted on the way home from a visit to Jerusalem through Philip's help in interpreting the Scriptures. The Ethiopian church tradition is likely to be correct in claiming the converted treasurer as the first evangelist in the country.

CARPUS[NT]
Apparently Paul's host at Troas. He stored Paul's cloak, and probably some of his books, since Paul would have needed to reduce his luggage on his way to his final imprisonment in Rome (2 Timothy 4:13). Tradition makes him one of the Seventy (Luke 10), and consequently he is honoured with a Saint's Day in the Roman and Greek churches, October 13 and May 26 respectively.

CHEDOR-LAOMER
An unidentified king of Elam who dominated Palestine for some thirteen years (Genesis 14:4). When his subjects rebelled, Chedor-laomer enlisted the help of other kings and successfully invaded the country. On their way home they were unexpectedly routed by Abraham with a scratch force, and had to lose their prisoners, including Lot (Genesis 14).

CHILEAB
See **Abigail**.

CHLOE[NT]. *Verdant*
A lady in Corinth who was an early victim of those who split the church in support of some individual and his teaching (1 Corinthians 1:11-12). The church that met in her house had supposedly not seen some needed truth that others found in Paul, some in Apollos, some in Peter! This was not zeal for

spiritual truth but a carry-over of a fallen human pride (3:4-9).

CHRIST[NT]
Not the surname of Jesus, as some suppose! Christ, or the Christ, is the Greek form of Messiah, the Anointed One – the long-promised Saviour. (See **Jesus**.)

CHUZA[NT]
Herod's steward, so doubtless an influential man. It is encouraging to find that a top man in a court of iniquity allowed his wife, Joanna, to join other women in ministering to Jesus at some cost to themselves and, we presume, consequently to Chuza himself (Luke 8:3).

CLAUDIA[NT]
See **Pudens**.

CLAUDIUS[NT]
See **Caesar**.

CLAUDIUS LYSIAS[NT]
Commander of the Roman garrison in Jerusalem when Paul was arrested by the Jews (Acts 21). Unlike Pontius Pilate, he risked unpopularity by rescuing Paul and seeing that he had a fair trial as a Roman citizen. He smuggled Paul out of the city, forestalling an ambush, and sent him for trial before Felix the Roman governor in Caesarea (23:16-30). It was a dramatic occasion when he and Paul compared their qualifications as Roman citizens. Lysias had paid a fortune for his citizenship, whereas Paul was born in a city whose inhabitants were Romans by birth (22:27-28).

CLEMENT[NT]
One of Paul's fellow workers (Philippians 4:3). Some Christian writers (e.g. Origen) identified him with the Clement who had the oversight of the church at Rome at the end of the century, but

the name was common, and there is no other evidence for the link.

CLEOPAS[NT]
One of the two disciples whom Jesus met on the way to Emmaus on the afternoon of his resurrection day. The other disciple, unnamed, may have been his wife. The fact that they did not recognize Jesus was not due to any substantial change in his appearance, but to the clouding of their faculties (Luke 24:16,31). This would be somewhat similar to an effect of hypnotism, as happened to the Syrian army when God struck them with a blindness, which was clearly an inner, not an outer, experience (2 Kings 6:18). If Cleopas had recognized Jesus immediately, the pair would have missed the opportunity of recognizing him first in the Scriptures, as we have to do (Luke 24:25-27).

CLOPAS[NT] (KJV, **Cleophas**)
Not usually identified with the Cleopas of the Emmaus walk. Mentioned only in John 19:25, where one of the women at the cross is Mary the wife of Clopas. This Mary may be the one described in Mark 15:40 as the mother of James the younger. Mark 3:18 names one of the Twelve as James the son of Alphaeus, and Alphaeus and Cleopas, or Clopas, could be variant renderings of a Hebrew name, *khalphai*. (For further complications see **James, Mary**.)

CONIAH
See **Jehoiachin**.

CORNELIUS[NT]
With Paul, he shares the honour of having the story of his conversion told three times (Acts 10; 11:1-18; 15:7-14). Its importance lies in its being the occasion of the Gentile Pentecost, placing Jewish and Gentile believers in identical positions (Acts 15:8-9). Cornelius was a centurion in charge of an auxiliary cohort in Caesarea. Like some other seriously-minded Romans,

he was disillusioned with pagan idolatry, and had found in Judaism the most satisfying faith as yet (10:2). God sent an angel to tell him to send for Peter, and Peter preached to him and his household, telling them the Gospel of Christ.

We may note that neither God nor angels preach the Gospel of redemption directly, but the task of preaching is ours. The admission of the Gentiles was such a revolutionary step that God did not let it rest upon Peter's opinion, but demonstrated their full acceptance by pouring out the Holy Spirit, attested by tongues, even before they had been baptized (Acts 10:44-48). We note from the story that while God accepts the sincerity of Gentile seekers, they still need the Gospel of Jesus Christ.

CRISPUS[NT]

The man responsible for supervising the services in the synagogue at Corinth. Paul was lodging next door, and doubtless private conversations with Crispus, as well as public preaching, led to the startling conversion of such an influential man (Acts 18:7-8). He was one of the very few converts baptized by Paul himself (1 Corinthians 1:14).

CUSHAN-RISHATHAIM

An unidentified king who dominated northern Israel for eight years. Othniel, Caleb's younger brother, broke his hold (Judges 3:7-10).

CYRUS

One of the world's great generals. He began about 559 BC as king of Anshan, a city in Elam. He soon annexed Persia, and by 550 BC had conquered Media, followed by Lydia, and on to Babylon which he entered in 539, thus replacing the great Babylonian empire by the Persian. Unlike many conquerors he was a merciful man and took steps to release the many foreigners who had been interned in Babylonia.

Records show that in addressing the Babylonians he acknowledged the good hand of their god, Marduk, in giving him victory; and in his decree allowing the Jews to return and build their temple, he acknowledged Jehovah as the god who had given him the kingdoms of the earth (Ezra 1:2-4). His formal edict, stating the limits of the grant that he was prepared to give for the temple, is less flamboyant and purely businesslike (6:2-5). Other nations had their idols returned to them. Since the Jews had no idols, they were given what remained of the temple treasures (1:7-11). Cyrus was finally killed in battle in 530 BC.

Cyrus is named in a prophecy ascribed to Isaiah some 200 years earlier (Isaiah 44:28; 45:1). Those who do not believe that God would give such a detailed prediction regard this section of Isaiah as written at about the time when Cyrus captured Babylon. Recent investigations and experiments, however, have established the reality of precognition under certain conditions, even to the extent of giving a name beforehand.

That strange man, Nostradamus, who died in 1566, foresaw the French Revolution of 1789 (his book exists to prove it), and declared correctly that the Comte de Narbonne would be traitor to the king, and also produced in the same verse the name of Saulce as a seller of oil. A man named Sauce turned out to be mayor of Varennes, a grocer and chandler, who arrested Louis XVI on his attempted flight. If such prediction is possible to man (we do not know how), it is certainly possible to God in order to assure his people that he had long before planned the ending to their exile in Babylon. (See **Isaiah**.)

DAN

One of Jacob's sons by Bilhah, Rachel's maid (see **Bilhah**). His name, connected with the Hebrew word *judge,* was given by Rachel as a claim that God had compensated her for her own childlessness. Dan plays no part in the Genesis story, but was the ancestor of the tribe that bears his name (Genesis 30:6). The tribe first settled in the south, but Philistine pressure forced it to move north (Joshua 19:40-48).

J Stafford Wright

DANIEL. *God is my judge*
The hero of the book that bears his name. He claims to be the author of the section that records the visions (Daniel 7-12), since this section is largely in the first person singular (NB: also Daniel 12:4), and traditionally he also recorded the narratives of chapters 1-6. Some suppose that the fulfilled details in the visions show that they are not real predictions but are written after the events, but Jesus Christ referred to Daniel as a prophet who foresaw the future (Matthew 24:15). (See also comments on **Cyrus**.)

Daniel was taken among hostages to Babylon after Nebuchadnezzar had broken the power of Egypt at the battle of Carchemish in 605 BC. He and three others were picked out for their ability and given a three-year training. Daniel was renamed Belteshazzar, which we can roughly translate as Lifeguard. In spite of, or perhaps because of, demanding a simple diet, the four friends came out top of all the prisoners (Daniel 1). They were enrolled among the king's wise men, but when a crisis came and the king demanded the interpretation of a dream*. Daniel was the only wise man who, under God's guidance, was able both to tell the king of his dream and give the interpretation (Daniel 2). He interpreted another dream in chapter 4. (See **Nebuchadnezzar**.)

After Nebuchadnezzar's death, Daniel evidently slipped into obscurity, but he emerged again when the last king, Belshazzar, was terrified by mysterious writing that suddenly appeared on the wall where he was feasting. The ex-queen reminded Belshazzar of Daniel, and Daniel interpreted the four words on the wall (Daniel 5). (See **Belshazzar**.)

Soon after the fall of Babylon it is likely that Daniel was taken to Media by Darius (see **Darius**), and although a favourite of the king, he fell foul of a crafty law which banned all prayer for thirty

---

* The KJV implies that the king has forgotten the dream. 'The thing is gone from me.' Most translations, both old and new, generally translate this as it being the king's word or command, to interpret the dream, that has gone out to the wise men.

days. When Daniel prayed, as he always did, his enemies demanded that the king should carry out the penalty of having him lowered into the den of royal lions. The king did his best to save him, but could not go back on the edict that he had signed. He was, however, sufficiently impressed by Daniel's faith to hope that God might have preserved his life, and after a worse night than Daniel evidently was experiencing, he hurried to the lions' den and found Daniel fit and well (Daniel 6).

The remainder of the book records visions of the future that Daniel had on various occasions. These showed him that the final persecution of the Jews before the coming of the Messiah would be under the Grecian empire. The persecutor was, in fact, Antiochus Epiphanes about 170-164 BC (Daniel 8). The Messiah would come under the next empire, Rome, and would make an end of the Jewish sacrifices by himself being cut off in death. Subsequently Rome would destroy Jerusalem (Daniel 9:24-27). Daniel also looked on to God's final judgment (chapter 12).

The Daniel of Ezekiel 14:14; 28:3, renowned for his righteousness and his wisdom, may be our Daniel, but his association with the figures of old, Noah and Job, suggest that he may be the righteous king of this name who is mentioned in a Canaanite story.

DARIUS I

King of Persia, 521-486 BC. After conquering Babylon, Cyrus allowed the Jews to return and rebuild the temple in 538 BC. By 520 the work had come to a standstill, but a revival under Haggai and Zechariah led to an appeal to Darius to produce the original decree of Cyrus. Darius found it in the archives, and confirmed it himself in answer to the obstructive measures of the enemies of the Jews (Ezra 5 and 6).

DARIUS II. (423-408 BC) or III (336-331 BC)

Simply called 'Darius the Persian' (Nehemiah 12:22). The priestly lists here, beginning from the return from exile, are said to be recorded until the reign of Darius. None of the names of the high priests here need be later than Darius II, but there was a second Jaddua who met Alexander the Great shortly before he overthrew Darius III.

DARIUS THE MEDE

In Daniel 5:31 Darius the Mede is said to have 'received the kingdom' at the age of 62 after the fall of Babylon. No such name is known in secular history, and there is considerable discussion about his identification. We know that Cyrus was the Medo-Persian king who conquered Babylon, and he also is mentioned in Daniel 1:21; 6:28; 10:1. Hence some identify Darius with Cyrus, who was about 62, and who in one Babylonian document is called King of the Medes. If this is correct, we must translate legitimately in Daniel 6:28, 'Daniel prospered during the reign of Darius, even the reign of Cyrus the Persian.' There is a similar use of 'and = even' in 1 Chronicles 5:26; 'the spirit of Pul king of Assyria, even the spirit of Tilgath-pilneser king of Assyria'; we know from inscriptions that a single Assyrian king bore these two names.

Others identify this Darius with Gubaru, whom Cyrus appointed governor of Babylon with considerable powers. Others suggest Cyaxares, the uncle of Cyrus and king of Media. The Jewish historian, Josephus, says that Darius 'who had another name among the Greeks', took Daniel to Media, and certainly in Daniel 10:4 Daniel is by the Tigris, a branch of which rose in Media, and not by the Euphrates which flowed through Babylon. The reference in Daniel 6:28 would then be to concurrent reigns. Whoever he was, this Darius is the king who had the highest opinion of Daniel, but who was tricked into casting him into the den of lions (Daniel 6). At the end of the chapter he publicly confessed his faith that Daniel's God was the living God (Daniel 25-27).

DATHAN. *Fount*
Brother of Abiram, who joined in a demonstration against Moses and Aaron (Numbers 16). (See **Abiram**.)

DAVID. Meaning uncertain. Suggested *Beloved,* or *Leader*
Important in himself, and as the royal ancestor of the Messiah, Jesus Christ. His great-grandparents were Ruth and Boaz (Ruth 4:17), and he himself was the youngest of Jesse's eight sons (1 Samuel 16:10-11). He was a fine shepherd, and risked his life for his father's flock (1 Samuel 17:34-37, compare John 10:11-15).

When Saul failed as king in his obedience to God, Samuel was sent by God to Bethlehem where he anointed David secretly as the future king. God opened up the way for his introduction to court (such as it was in Saul's days) when Saul was under intense depression through a bad spirit that God allowed to obtain a hold on him when Saul rejected the control of the Spirit of God. David, already known as a top musician, was summoned to play to Saul, and since in those days singing normally accompanied playing, David's psalms restored Saul to health again temporarily (1 Samuel 16:14-23). Robert Browning's poem *Saul* is particularly fine in this connection; the longer version is the better of the two that he wrote.

David returned home when he was not wanted, but in the Philistine war he was the contact man with his brothers who were serving in Saul's army (1 Samuel 17:12-18). This was how he heard Goliath's challenge, and went out and slew him after knocking him out with his well-used sling. Saul had declared that anyone who killed Goliath would have his father's house made free, presumably from taxes, so Saul asks the name of David's father, not as is sometimes thought from superficial reading of 17:55-58, the name of David, whom he already knew (17:25). The successful champion was also promised Saul's daughter in marriage, and after some jealous attempts to get rid of David who was taking Saul's place in the affections of the people, Saul gave him his daughter Michal (1 Samuel 18). (See **Michal**)

David's success as commander against the Philistines brought Saul's jealousy to a head, and he made several attempts to kill him in spite of the protection of Michal and Saul's son, Jonathan (1 Samuel 19 to 21). Eventually David became an outlaw, and after a narrow escape at the court of Achish of Gath (see **Achish**) he made provision for his father and mother to stay with the king of Moab to escape reprisals, gathering a Robin Hood band of supporters, some of whom formed the nucleus of his commanders when he came to the throne (1 Samuel 21:10–22:5). David was joined by the new high priest, Abiathar, an important acquisition to his cause (22:20-23). This did not stop Saul hunting him up and down the countryside (chapters 23, 24, 26), though when David and his men were able to settle, they acted as protectors of honest men and their possessions, which led to David's marriage to Abigail (chapter 25.). (See **Abigail**).

Eventually David escaped to Gath once more, this time with a considerable force of men whom he professed to put at the service of Achish against Israel. They were stationed at Ziklag, but raided other towns instead of towns of Judah (1 Samuel 27). When the final battle against Saul was looming up, David narrowly escaped being called in on the Philistine side (chapter 30). After the battle, David executed an Amalekite who had imagined David would reward him if he claimed, falsely as it happened, to have killed Saul (1 Samuel 31:3-5; 2 Samuel 1:8-10). David's lament for Saul and Jonathan is one of the masterpieces of literature (2 Samuel 1:17-27).

David left Gath and established himself at Hebron as king of Judah, while Saul's son Ishbosheth ruled over the northern tribes. (See **Ishbosheth**, **Abner**.) After seven and a half years Ishbosheth was murdered, and David became king of all Israel (2 Samuel 2 to 5). He carried out successful campaigns against the Philistines (5:17-25; 8:1), Moab, Zobah, Syria and Edom (8:2-14), but his important success for later history was the capture of Jerusalem from the Jebusites (5:6-10). He made this his new capital, as being a city which had not previously been held by his own tribe of Judah or by any of the northern tribes.

As a further factor in uniting his kingdom, David brought back the ark of the covenant which had been stored for some years at Kiriath-jearim (also called Baale-judah) some ten miles west of Jerusalem (2 Samuel 6:1-19). He thus centralized the worship of Jehovah, but was not allowed by God to build a temple (chapter 7), although he made preparations for his son to build it (2 Samuel 7; 1 Chronicles 28-29). One reason was that God wished his temple, a material picture of the living church, to be built by a man of peace (1 Chronicles 28:3, compare Ephesians 2:14-22).

David's domestic life was far from happy, partly owing to his attempts at eastern greatness through collecting a spectacular harem (2 Samuel 5:13). This led to sex troubles between half-brothers and -sisters (2 Samuel 13), murder, and subsequent rebellion against David. Polygamy was no help for David's own sex life, and he found another man's wife so attractive that he committed adultery with her, and virtually murdered her husband (2 Samuel 11 and 12). This woman, Bathsheba, became the mother of Solomon after her first baby died and she had been legitimately married to David, and strange though it seems to us, Solomon inherited the throne and the promises. After all, he was not to blame for what his father and mother had done. (See **Bathsheba**).

David showed singular lack of wisdom in dealing with his son Absalom after Absalom had killed his brother and gone into voluntary exile. David first would not recall him, and then when he allowed him to return he refused to communicate with him (2 Samuel 13 and 14). It almost seems as though Absalom was right in claiming that his father was no longer competent to rule, and so stirring up a rebellion with himself at the head. David's whole attitude in chapter 15 suggests indecision. In the subsequent battle he scarcely knew what he wanted, and needed a sharp rebuke from Joab when he withdrew in unrestrained grief for the death of Absalom (chapters 18 and 19). His extraordinary appointment of Absalom's general, Amasa, as commander over the head of Joab (20:4) was an act of senility.

The Bible records his final act of folly in numbering the people, presumably as an act of pride (2 Samuel 24). God certainly treated it as sin, and this is a passage which shows, as we know from sad experience, that a bad leader can bring disaster on a whole nation. In the end David retrieved some good from the pestilence that destroyed many of those he had proudly numbered, and bought the site for the future temple, first paying 50 shekels of silver for a small area for an altar, and then later increasing the price to 600 shekels of gold to secure the whole future temple area for a worthy sum. This is probably the interpretation of the two figures in 2 Samuel 24:25 and 1 Chronicles 21:25.

When David finally took to his bed with a young female nurse to look after him (1 Kings 1:1-4), he was nearly outwitted by his spoilt son Adonijah who tried to seize the throne, but Bathsheba reminded him of God's wish for Solomon to be king, and David rallied enough to ensure that this happened (1 Kings 1). But David's last hours were clouded by his charge to Solomon, not only to be faithful to God, but to put Joab to death, and also Shimei who had once cursed him and to whom he had promised pardon (1 Kings 2:1-9, compare 2 Samuel 19:23).

Like some other leaders, David found comfort in music and song. Since almost everyone accepts the lament for Saul and Jonathan (2 Samuel 1:17ff) as a genuine song of David, it would be perverse to refuse to recognize many of the Psalms as by him, especially as his musical reputation is accepted as a well-known fact as early as the time of Amos (6:5), and Jesus Christ himself bases an argument on his authorship of Psalm 110 Luke (20:42).

The heading of a psalm as *A Psalm of David* need mean no more than that it comes from a hymn book with a good nucleus of Davidic psalms, but it is always worth while thinking seriously whether any such psalm fits the life and character of David. Psalm 51, ascribed to David's repentance after his adultery with Bathsheba and his virtual murder of her husband (e.g. verse 14), rings absolutely true, and helps us to understand why David remained in the line of God's promised blessing (2 Samuel 23:1-7). David's musical interest led him to organize the choirs for the future temple (1 Chronicles 25).

It is remarkable how many prophecies declare that the Messiah would come from the line of David. Jesus Christ is the only founder of a world religion whose coming was foretold (e.g. Isaiah 9:6-7; 11:1ff; Jeremiah 33:15; Ezekiel 37:24-25; Hosea 3:5; Amos 9:11; Micah 5:2; Psalm 89:35-37).

DEBORAH

Her name, meaning *Bee,* suggests a busy little body who carried a sting on occasions. Since worker bees are females, her husband Lappidoth, like a drone, plays no part in the exciting events recorded in Judges 4:4-16. Deborah, who calls herself 'a mother in Israel' (5:5), held a clinic under a palm tree in the hill country of Ephraim (4:5). As a prophetess (4:4) she would receive direct guidance from God in giving her advice on problems.

The northern areas were dominated by Jabin of Hazor, with the powerful Sisera as his general (Judges 4:1-3). Deborah in the name of Jehovah summoned Barak as the deliverer, and commissioned him to raise an army from the Israelite tribes. With ten thousand troops he routed Sisera, helped by a sudden storm which bogged down the enemy chariots. Deborah's song of victory (5:1-31) is one of the classics of literature, though it needs careful rehearsal before being read aloud in a church service.

DELILAH

One of Samson's mistresses who put an end to his effectiveness as a judge (Judges 16). As a Philistine she had pressure put on her by Philistine chiefs to discover the secret of her lover's strength. Although she gave herself away several times, she eventually loved and nagged him into telling her the truth instead of teasing her (16:16). Her horror at seeing Samson savagely blinded was doubtless more than compensated for by the substantial bribe she had earned (16:5).

DEMAS[NT]

One of Paul's fellow-workers (Colossians 4:14; Philemon 24) who in the end chose to pursue his own interests in Thessalonica rather than remain with Paul in Rome (2 Timothy 4:10).

DEMETRIUS[NT]
A silversmith of Ephesus, a city that was an extensive employer of craftsmen to make mini-shrines containing models of the statue of Artemis, the great goddess of the city. He recognized a threat in Paul's preaching, and by appealing to self-interest raised a riot against him and other Christians. In the end the town clerk called his bluff (Acts 19:23-41).

DINAH. *Judgment*
Jacob's only daughter, Leah being her mother (Genesis 30:21). On Jacob's return to Canaan she was raped by Shechem, the eldest son of the prince of a town, which was probably Shechem. Shechem then did the honourable thing, and asked for her hand in marriage. Jacob was willing, but by tricking all the men of the town into accepting circumcision, Simeon and Levi attacked and killed them when they were physically incapacitated, and plundered the town. Jacob was bitterly angry, and years later recalled the incident in his prophecy of the future of his sons and their descendants (Genesis 34; 49:5-7).

DIONYSIUS[NT]
A member of the Athenian 'parliament' that met on or near the Areopagus. Dionysius was one of the converts won through Paul's preaching (Acts 17:34). In the 5th century a book purporting to be by him set the tone for much of the mystical theology in the Christian church, emphasising what has become known as the *via negativa* as the method of approach to the transcendent God.

DIOTREPHES[NT]
A man whose natural desire to be the top dog was disguised as zeal for the truth. He managed the church in his own way, raked up imaginary scandals against the apostle John, and excommunicated members who invited any visiting preachers of whom he did not approve (3 John 9-10).

DOEG
Saul's head cattle man. Although an Edomite by birth he was evidently a convert to Jehovah, for in 1 Samuel 21:7 he is at the sanctuary at Nob, 'detained before the Lord'. He was either seeking cleansing for some sin, or he was under a vow. He saw how Ahimelech the high priest assisted David, and reported him to Saul (22:6-19). As readers of the Bible, we tend to see David through holy eyes, but to Doeg, David was only a troublesome outlaw who annoyed Doeg's employer. We cannot blame him for answering Saul's challenge that far too many people secretly favoured David (22:7-8). But we certainly can blame him for executing Ahimelech and 85 priests, when all Saul's servants refused (22:11-19).

DORCAS[NT]
Also called Tabitha. The only woman actually called a disciple (Acts 9:36-43), she was a fine practical Christian living in Joppa. When she died, her friends sent for Peter, and he was led to restore her to life using a quiet method similar to that which Jesus had used with a little girl (Mark 5:40-43).

DRUSILLA[NT]
Youngest daughter of Herod Agrippa I. Married first to King Azizus of Emesa. Felix the Roman procurator fell in love with her, and used a magician to persuade her to leave her husband. Felix and Drusilla heard Paul's defence after his arrest (Acts 24:24-26), and perhaps some of the conviction that Felix felt on hearing Paul preaching about 'justice and self-control and future judgment' was occasioned by another man's wife sitting beside him. Drusilla's brother and sister, Herod Agrippa II and Bernice, had a similar unpleasant opportunity to hear Paul preach (25:23ff). (See **Bernice**.)

EBED-MELECH. *Servant of the king*
An immigrant from Africa, a Cushite, who showed more pity for Jeremiah than did the prophet's own countrymen (Jeremiah

38:7ff). Jeremiah's enemies had left him to die at the bottom of a half-drained pit. Ebed-melech obtained permission from the king to bring him out, and had the sense to bring some old clothes for the prophet to put under the ropes as he was hauled out. His kindness, and probable unpopularity with Jeremiah's enemies, were rewarded by God promise of safety when Jerusalem was destroyed (39:15-18).

EBER. *One who passes over*
He has no more than a mention in the genealogical table in Genesis 11:16-17, but recent discoveries at Ebla show that a man of this name was king of an ancient empire in northern Syria. Eber gave his name to the Hebrews. From the Biblical standpoint the most important branch of the Hebrew stock came through Abraham (Genesis 14:13). It is often thought, though not yet proved, that the peoples known as *habiru* who appear in Mesopotamian and Egyptian documents, are of Hebrew origin, although joined by non-Semitic peoples also.

EGLON
An exceptionally fat king of Moab (Judges 3:17). In Bible times fatness was regarded as a desirable state (e.g. Job 15:27; Psalm 73:7; Jeremiah 5:28). Eglon dominated southern Israel for 18 years, establishing himself at Jericho, but was assassinated by Ehud as he was trying to cool off in his summer house.

EHUD. *Union*
Like some other Benjamites he was left-handed (Judges 3:15, compare 20:16), and he made use of this when he went to assassinate Eglon. He carried his sword on what would normally be the wrong side, and unexpectedly whipped it out with his left hand. After his pretended audience with Eglon, he was able to evade the guards and escape before the murder was detected. He at once rallied an Israelite force and drove the Moabites out of Israelite territory.

ELAH. *Terebinth*
King of Israel who, after a two year reign, was assassinated by one of his generals, Zimri, while blind drunk (1 Kings 16:8-10).

ELDAD. *God has loved*
One of seventy responsible men selected to assist Moses in controlling the people (Numbers 11:10-30). He and another, Medad, did not join the others for their commissioning at the tabernacle. They may have felt unworthy. When the other 68 received the Spirit of God to equip them, and began to prophesy under the power of the Spirit, Eldad and Medad received the same gift in the camp. Joshua wished to rebuke them, but Moses hailed them as displaying what he wished would be a foretaste of the gift of the Spirit for all God's people everywhere, in the camp of daily life as well as in the holiness of the tabernacle.

ELEAZAR. *God is helper*
Third son of Aaron, who took the place of the eldest when his brothers Nadab and Abihu died (Numbers 3:1-4) (see **Ahibu**). During Aaron's lifetime he was given the special oversight of the Levites who assisted in the sanctuary (3:32), and also was personally responsible for the purificatory ritual of the Red Heifer (19:1-10). He had the task of beating out the censers of the rebels into a covering for the altar (16:36-40).

Eleazar saw his father die on Mount Hor, after Moses had transferred the high priestly vestments to him. Thereafter he acted as high priest during the rest of the wilderness wanderings, and one of the last acts of Moses before his death was to link Eleazar and Joshua as joint leaders of the nation (Numbers 27:12-23). The two were given the responsibility for dividing up the land among the tribes (Numbers 34:16; Joshua 14:1). Eleazar died shortly after Joshua, and was succeeded by his son Phinehas (Joshua 24:33).

ELHANAN
In 2 Samuel 21:19 he is said to have killed Goliath, whereas in 1

Chronicles 20:5 he killed the brother of Goliath. It is far fetched to suggest that Elhanan was David's original name, but not far fetched to hold that there is a copyist's error in 2 Samuel 21:19, since specialists in Hebrew and Hebraic studies agree that there are three other errors in the verse, as compared with 1 Chronicles 20:5. The copyist was probably sleepy at the end of a hard day's writing. Many English translations, including the KJV, add the words *brother of*, usually with a footnote or some other indication of this addition.

ELI. *Jehovah is high*
His genealogy is not given, but a complicated comparison shows that Eli was descended from Aaron's youngest son, Ithamar. Thus in 1 Chronicles 24:3,6, Ahimelech is the son of Abiathar, and is of the line of Ithamar, while in 1 Kings 2:27 Abiathar is descended from Eli (see **Ahimelech**). Eli is evidently high priest with the ark of the covenant in Shiloh (1 Samuel 1), but we are not told how the line came to be changed from Eleazar and Phinehas to the secondary line of Ithamar. It reverted to the Eleazar line with Zadok (1 Chronicles 6:1-15).

The ark was housed at Shiloh in a permanent building, whether or not the tabernacle was pitched there (1 Samuel 3:15). Eli appears as a rather weak man who could not control his sons (2:12-25), although he was quick to deal with a woman whom he thought to be drunk (1:13-16). But he was warm-hearted enough to rectify his mistake (1:17-18), and was rewarded by having Samuel to assist him in the temple work.

It was to Samuel that the Lord revealed the coming doom on Eli's line. Shortly afterwards there was an invasion by the Philistines, and Eli's sons carried the ark into battle. But the ark was no magic charm, and the battle ended with its capture by the Philistines and the death of Eli's two sons. Eli, now nearly blind and at the great age of 98, heard the news of the defeat and of the death of his sons, but on the additional report of the capture of the ark he collapsed and died, overwhelmed by his failure in the sacred trust that had been his as high priest (1 Samuel 4:12-22).

ELIAB. *God is Father*
David's eldest brother (1 Samuel 16:6-7). He did not take kindly to having to give place to David when Samuel came to anoint the future king, and he played the part of the heavy elder brother in scolding David when he arrived in time to hear Goliath's challenge (17:28-29).

ELIAKIM. *God sets up*
Steward of the royal household, who was one of three negotiators with Sennacherib's general at the siege of Jerusalem (2 Kings 18:18). An interesting prophecy in Isaiah 22:15-25 discloses that his predecessor was a foreigner, Shebna. Unfortunately Eliakim was seen by Isaiah as one who would abuse his position by appointing his relatives to lucrative offices; but he would be disgraced and his dependants would fall with him. How different from Christ (1 Samuel 22, compare Revelation 3:7) who never fails (1 Samuel 24 and 25) and who carries his brethren securely. (See **Jehoiakim** for another man born with this name.)

ELIASHIB. *God restores*
When Ezra returned to Jerusalem in 458 BC, Eliashib is mentioned, though not as high priest (Ezra 10:6); but on the death of his father Joiakim he had become high priest by the time Nehemiah returned in 445 BC (Nehemiah 3:1,20-21). This chapter shows him taking a practical part in rebuilding the city wall. Later he took advantage of Nehemiah's absence to turn out one of the large temple storerooms and give it as a bedsit to Tobiah, one of Nehemiah's chief opponents (13:4-9). His grandson married the daughter of Sanballat, Nehemiah's other chief opponent (13:28-29), so he evidently wanted to keep in with both sides.

ELIEZER. *God is my help*
1. Abraham's steward, a native of Damascus (Genesis 15:2). Before the birth of Ishmael and Isaac, Abraham followed a regular custom of the day and adopted Eliezer as his heir (15:2).

It was recognized that any son born subsequently would take precedence over the adopted heir. Although he is not named in 24:2, it is likely that Eliezer was the one chosen to go and find a bride for Isaac, and he does this without any trace of bitterness or jealousy.

2. The second son of Moses and Zipporah (Exodus 18:4), about whom we know nothing except that his descendants were in charge of the treasuries of David for the use of the temple (1 Chronicles 26:24-28). Zipporah's refusal to have him circumcised nearly cost Moses his life (Exodus 4:24-26). (See **Moses, Zipporah**.)

ELIHU. *My God is He*

An enthusiastic young man who joined the crowd listening to the fascinating debate between Job and his friends. He describes how he literally nearly burst with rage when the three friends gave up the argument (Job 32:1-5,18-20). He must have become more and more irritated when Job simply ignored him, although in fact he made a useful contribution to the discussion, especially by speaking of suffering as discipline (e.g. 33:19-28). Indeed, Elihu's closing words in 36:24–37:24 to some extent anticipate God's own answer, based on the wonders of his created order. But like the three friends, he also believes that Job is guilty of some secret sin. However, God does not rebuke him as he does the others (42:7), since 38:2 most likely refers to Job, to whom verse 3 is clearly addressed (compare 42:3).

ELIJAH

He certainly lived up to his name, *Jehovah is God*. The Greek form of his name, *Elias*, appears in the New Testament. Elijah and Moses, as representing the Law and the Prophets, were seen and heard at the transfiguration (Mark 9:2-8). It would seem that, whereas prophets had been raised up sporadically before Elijah, God now began to speak through a line of prophets using the 'still small voice' (1 Kings 19:12). There is some doubt about the location of his native place, Tishbe, but Elijah evidently had his headquarters in Gilead (Kings 17:1), and his ministry was only to the northern kingdom.

His main clash was with Ahab and Jezebel, his Phoenician wife, who was doing her best to suppress all the leading followers of Jehovah (1 Kings 18:13), filling the court with her own prophets of Melkart Baal, the official god of Tyre and Sidon. In the name of Jehovah, Elijah decreed a three-year drought (17:1), and he himself retreated first east of Jordan, and then into Baal's own territory (chapter 17). On Mount Carmel he challenged the prophets of Baal to call down fire from heaven on the altar of sacrifice, a fair challenge since Baal was the god of lightning and storm.

When they failed, Elijah soaked the sacrifice with water from a spring which to this day has never been known to dry up, and called on God to act. Fire fell from a cloudless sky and burnt up the sacrifice. The miracle brought shouts of loyalty to Jehovah from the people, and Elijah called for the execution of the prophets of Baal (1 Kings 18:1-40). He then prayed for rain, and when a small cloud appeared on the horizon, he ran triumphantly ahead of King Ahab to Jezreel (1 Kings 18:41-46, compare James 5:17-18).

Jezebel had not been present, but now she threatened to execute Elijah. The prophet collapsed like a pricked balloon and escaped into the desert, where an angel diagnosed some of his depression as due to lack of food and provided him with a simple meal (1 Kings 19:1-8). Elijah then travelled to Horeb where Moses had received the law. Here he was shown that, whereas the giving of the law had been accompanied by the violence of storm, earthquake and fire (Exodus 19:16; 24:17), the new prophetic revelation would come by a still small voice (1 Kings 19:11,12). Elijah regarded himself as the only witness left in the land, but God assured him that there were at least seven thousand others — a thought for weary ministers who think there is not a single converted person in their congregation, and forget the 'dimly burning wick' of Isaiah 42:3.

Elijah was commissioned to anoint Elisha as his successor

and Hazael as the future king of Syria (1 Kings 19:15-21). He clashed with Ahab and Jezebel again when Jezebel arranged the murder of Naboth, and he foretold the ignominious death of both king and queen (21:1-29). When Ahab's son Ahaziah consulted the god of Ekron about his recovery from an accident, Elijah intercepted the messengers and told them that the accident would prove fatal. Finally, Elijah knew that his time had come, and crossed the Jordan with Elisha. Suddenly there appeared a chariot of fire which separated the two men, and simultaneously a whirlwind lifted Elijah out of sight.

Just as God set his seal on the new movement through Moses by miracles, so he chose to launch the new prophetic movement, and later the Messianic age, by miracles. Thus Elijah was fed by ravens, though this need not be miraculous, since crows are easily tamed (1 Kings 17:1-7). The widow's cruse and meal jar were continually supplied (17:8-16). Her son was restored to life (17:17-24). Fire fell from a cloudless sky (18:1-40). Fire again fell and destroyed two companies of men who came to arrest Elijah. This would not have happened if they had treated the prophet with proper reverence as the man of God which they knew him to be, as did the third group (2 Kings 1:9-16). We cannot tell what happened to Elijah when he was caught up in the whirlwind, which the Bible does not identify with the chariot of fire, but there is no reason to hold that he did not die.

In Malachi 4:5-6 there is a prophecy that Elijah would return before the final judgment. On the basis of Matthew 17:11-13, some have supposed that John the Baptist was a reincarnation of Elijah, but Luke 1:17 explains that John would resemble Elijah in his mission, not that he was Elijah reborn.

Joseph Smith, the founder of Mormonism, did not realize that *Elias* is merely the Greek form of Elijah (Mark 9:12 KJV), and twice over in his 'inspired' work, *Doctrine and Covenants,* makes them out to be two separate individuals (sections 27 and 110).

ELIMELECH
See **Naomi**

ELIPHAZ. Perhaps *God is gold*
From Teman in Edom. One of Job's three friends who came to comfort him and stayed to argue with him in his suffering. Each friend held that Job's suffering meant that he had committed some great sin, for which God was punishing him, but each had a different approach. Eliphaz was one who had had a deep spiritual experience, with a vision and a word from God (Job 4:12-21). But he was lacking in understanding, in interpretation of the ways of God, and in sympathy for human suffering as he saw it in Job.

ELISABETH[NT]
See **Elizabeth**

ELISHA. *God is salvation*
In Greek *Eliseus*, as in KJV Luke 4:27. A wealthy farmer from the Jordan Valley (1 Kings 19:19), called to be Elijah's successor by investiture with Elijah's cloak (19:16-21), but first learning through acting as Elijah's servant (1 Kings 19:21; 2 Kings 3:11). When he knew that Elijah would shortly be taken from him, he asked for the double portion of his master's spirit, that is, the recognition and equipment of himself as the heir (2 Kings 2:9, compare Deuteronomy 21:17). Elijah's cloak fell from him as he was caught up, and Elisha took it as the mark of his authority, and used it to part the waters of Jordan as Elijah had recently done (2 Kings 2:8,14).

Unlike Elijah, he fostered prophetic communities, and under God worked three miracles on their behalf (2 Kings 4:38-44; 6:1-7). There is no reason to think that these 'sons of the prophets' were in any way inferior to the prophets whose writings are recorded in Scripture. Elisha was used in other ways also. He reluctantly helped Jehoram and Jehoshaphat in their campaign against Moab (see **Mesha**). Here he asked for a minstrel before the prophetic message came. It is often thought that the music was of an exciting type to work him into an ecstasy, but it is more likely that a single minstrel would play gentle music, perhaps with psalm accompaniment, to quieten him after his outburst with the kings (3:13-15). Like Elijah, he brought a dead child back to life (4:1-37). He was instrumental in curing Naaman of leprosy (5:1-27). (See **Naaman, Gehazi**).

When Syria again declared war on Israel, Elisha was made aware of Syria's secret plans (2 Kings 6:8-12) and the Syrian army besieged Dothan in order to arrest him. But Elisha was protected by an invisible army. In answer to his prayer, God sent blindness on the Syrian army, and Elisha led them into the middle of Israelite territory before letting them go. Obviously the Syrians did not lose their eyesight, or they would not have been able to march away, but the Hebrew word occurs elsewhere only in a similar context of the men of Sodom (Genesis 19:11). It is clearly the equivalent of the completely suggestive state brought about by hypnotism (2 Kings 6:11-23). Later Ben-hadad of Syria reduced Samaria to a state of starvation (2 Kings 6:24-31), but Elisha foretold when relief would come, and the Syrians unexpectedly withdrew in panic (2 Kings 7:1-20).

Eventually Elisha carried out the commission that Elijah had been given to anoint Hazael as king of Syria (1 Kings 19:15; 2 Kings 8:7-15). Benhadad was ill and sent his general, Hazael, to ask Elisha whether he would recover. Elisha perceived that Hazael had it in mind to murder his master, and fixed him with his eyes until Hazael knew that his guilty secret was out. The Lord had shown Elisha that Hazael would be king, but he certainly did not inspire the murder, and indeed the king's illness by itself would not have been fatal (2 Kings 8:10). The further commission to Elijah to anoint Jehu to be king of Israel (1 Kings 19:16) was carried out by an actual anointing through one of the sons of the prophets (2 Kings 9). (See **Jehu**).

In his final illness, Elisha tried to encourage King Joash to claim victory over Syria (2 Kings 13:14-19). After his death his body worked a strange miracle and restored a young man to life (13:20-21). Judging by the reigns in which he lived, he was probably nearly ninety at the time of his death.

ELIZABETH^{NT} spelt **Elisabeth** in some translations.
Mother of John the Baptist and wife of Zechariah. Luke carefully distinguishes the unexpectedness — almost a miracle — of herself and her husband having a child at an advanced age, from the unique miracle of the virgin birth (Luke 1). Elizabeth concealed her pregnancy as long as possible, probably through embarrassment, but at six months she was visited by her kinswoman Mary, and in the presence of the newly conceived Son of God felt sudden, violent movements of her unborn baby. Under the guidance of the Holy Spirit, Elizabeth spoke triumphantly of the incredible blessing that Mary had received in being chosen as the mother of 'my Lord' (Luke 1:39-45).

ELKANAH. *God has possessed*
Father of Samuel. His genealogy in 1 Chronicles 6:33ff shows that he was a Levite stationed in Ephraim (1 Samuel 1:1). Of his two wives, Hannah was childless, although he was more fond of her than of Peninnah and her children. He went up annually to worship at the central shrine at Shiloh, and on one of these occasions Hannah received the promise of a son, Samuel.

ELYMAS^{NT}
See **Bar-Jesus**.

ENOCH. Perhaps *Consecrated*
A strange figure about whom little is known, except that he was a man who lived in close touch with God, and in the end 'he was not, for God took him' (Genesis 5:21-23), which is usually taken to mean that he was like those Christians who will be living when Christ returns, and who will be instantly caught up and changed (1 Thessalonians 4:17). He was a man of deep faith in God (Hebrews 11:5). During the last 200 years before Christ several books were produced which were ascribed to Enoch, on the ground that his unique experience enabled him to reveal

heavenly secrets. The opening of the first book contains the prophecy ascribed to Enoch in Jude 14. This is a general statement about the Second Coming and the judgment, and these truths could well have been shown to Enoch himself. This does not mean that the whole book of Enoch is inspired, but only that the writers set an authentic traditional word at the beginning, and then amplified it in their own way.

EPAPHRAS[NT]
A citizen of Colossae, who brought news of the church to Paul (Colossians 1:7; 4:12). Later he shared Paul's imprisonment, either as his servant, or more probably under arrest also (Philemon 23). His name is a shortened form of **Epaphroditus**.

EPAPHRODITUS[NT]
Although a few have identified him with Epaphras, this is unlikely. He probably was a native of Philippi, and brought this church's gift to Paul in prison (Philippians 2:25-29). He suffered a breakdown in health through his exertions in Christ's service, and Paul uses a gambling metaphor of him, saying that he staked his life for the work of Christ (literal Greek of Philippians 2:29f; RSV has 'risking'). The passage implies that he was Paul's postman for this letter to the Philippians.

EPHRAIM. *Double fruit*
Second son of Joseph and Asenath (Genesis 41:52), but given seniority over his elder brother Manasseh in his grandfather's blessing (Genesis 48:8-20). In fact the tribe of Ephraim became so powerful that it is often used as equivalent to the northern kingdom of Israel (e.g. Isaiah 7:2; Hosea 5:3, etc.).

ESAR-HADDON
Son of Sennacherib, king of Assyria, 681-669 BC (2 Kings 19:37). He was an energetic and successful campaigner, but the only other allusion to him in the Old Testament is in Ezra 4:2, where some of the mixed race of Samaritans say that they were settled

in the country by Esar-haddon (compare 2 Kings 17:24-28, a passage which is not dated).

ESAU. *Hairy*
Jacob's twin, the elder of the two (Genesis 25:25-26). Before their birth, God declared that he had chosen the younger as the head of the promised line (25:23), a promise that Paul quotes as an example of the free undeserved choice of God (Romans 9:10-12). In fact, Esau himself showed his unfitness as being an 'irreligious person' (Hebrews 12:16-17) who valued his senior birthright so little that he sold it to Jacob for a plate of lentils (Genesis 25:29-34). Naturally, he hoped to get it back when his father came to bless the two sons, but he could hardly complain when Jacob took steps to make sure he obtained what Esau had already sold, even though one cannot commend Jacob's deceit (Genesis 27).

Esau had already shown his lack of concern for the promised line by marrying two Canaanite wives who did not get on well with his parents (Genesis 26:34-35), but later he tried to make amends by marrying one of the daughters of Ishmael (28:9). Indeed, after this he appears in a better light and is surprisingly generous to Jacob when the latter returned from Paddan-aram (Genesis 32 and 33).

He settled in Edom, and his descendants subdued the original inhabitants (Genesis 36:9-43). There was continual friction between Edom and Israel, but ultimately in 109 BC John Hyrcanus conquered the country and absorbed the Edomites into Judah. In fact, the Herods were Idumeans, or Edomites.

ESTHER
Her Jewish name was Hadassah, or Myrtle (Esther 2:7). Her Persian name may be linked to the word *stara,* or star. Perhaps it was a nickname given her by her Persian playmates. If Hadassah had lived today, her friends might have called her Dusty, as sounding somewhat the same in English. She was brought up by her cousin Mordecai (2:7, see **Mordecai**), and was chosen to be

the chief wife of King Ahasuerus, or Xerxes (Esther 2). (See **Ahasuerus**). She risked her life by appealing to the king against an attempt by the prime minister Haman to massacre all the Jews (chapters 3-7). Haman was hanged. Mordecai succeeded him, and he and Esther were able to avert the massacre, and even allowed the Jews to kill their assailants (chapters 8 and 9).

There is no indication that Esther had a child, and she probably died or dropped out of favour soon after the book closes about 473 BC. There is a tendency to treat the book as unhistorical, but it can easily be fitted into the existing records of Xerxes' reign, as is shown under **Mordecai** and **Vashti**. The Apocrypha contains later Greek additions to the book of Esther. These introduce the name of God, which is absent from the Hebrew version. (For a possible reason, see **Mordecai**.)

ETHAN. *Enduring*
A wise man, called an Ezrahite, probably the equivalent of Zerahite, i.e. descended from Judah's son, Zerah (Genesis 38:30; Numbers 26:20). He was not as wise as Solomon (1 Kings 4:31). He may have composed Psalm 89.

EUNICE[NT]
Mother of Timothy (2 Timothy 1:5), a Jewess who had married a Greek (Acts 16:1). She and her mother had brought up Timothy with a fine knowledge of the Scriptures (2 Timothy 1:5), but had not been able to persuade her husband to allow him to be circumcised (Acts 16:3).

EUODIA[NT]
She and another woman, Syntyche, worked well with Paul at Philippi, but fell out with one another after Paul had left (Philippians 4:2-3).

EUTYCHUS[NT]
His name, *lucky,* is an apt one for the young man who literally dropped off during Paul's sermon at Troas and fell out of the

window. His good fortune lay in Paul's restoring him to life (Acts 20:7-12).

EVE
Wife of Adam, the first modern man (see **Adam**). In Eden she was tempted by Satan, who used the form of a serpent, to eat the fruit of the tree of the knowledge of good and evil, and she then persuaded her husband to eat also (Genesis 3:1-6). The tree was evidently regarded in a sacramental sense, and to eat of it indicated that Adam and Eve wished to decide matters of right and wrong with their own finite understanding rather than to accept the guidance of God.

This misuse of their freedom brought physical death and a barrier between themselves and God which meant spiritual death also. Eve's punishment of pain in child-bearing was tempered by the first promise, gradually augmented throughout the Old Testament, that a woman should be the mother of a child who would crush Satan after himself suffering Satan's poisonous bite (Genesis 3:8-16).

The story of the creation of Eve from one of Adam's ribs is commonly taken as symbolic. Woman is taken from man's rib to be beside him, not above him or kept under him. But modern biology suggests that the account may contain literal truth. Living animal cells have been removed and cloned into replicas of the creature from which they came. All that was needed for Eve was that God should remove a body cell, or more probably a sperm cell, from Adam, and build it into a woman, taking away the Y chromosome that is the determinant of maleness.

We are not tied to the translation, *rib*. The Hebrew word, *tsela,* is used of *side chambers* of the temple (1 Kings 6:5), of the *boards* that lined the temple (6:15), and of the *sides* of the ark of the covenant (Exodus 25:12). Today we can understand that the word could certainly describe the enclosed cell, and we can interpret the forming of Eve in a way that was impossible to previous generations, although the picture of the rib conveyed the essential fact.

EVIL-MERODACH

His name is not as wicked as it sounds, but is the Hebrew rendering of the Babylonian, Amel-Marduk, man of Marduk, the Babylonian god. He reigned two years (562-560 BC), and is the king who released King Jehoiachin from prison, and received him into court circles (2 Kings 25:27-30).

EZEKIEL. *God strengthens*

As a young man, Ezekiel was taken to Babylon with King Jehoiachin in 597 BC, and there is no indication that he ever returned to his native land, except in a prophetic vision. His father was a priest. He joined a Jewish settlement by a large canal on the east of the Euphrates (Ezekiel 1:1-3). His call to be a prophet was linked to a striking vision of the glory of God (Ezekiel 1:4-28), and he was given a written scroll to eat, symbolizing that his words were to be God-given (Ezekiel 2 and 3).

In chapters 1-24 he foretells the coming doom of Jerusalem, which was not yet destroyed. So that he could see for himself the atrocious wickedness and godlessness, he was transported by God's Spirit to Jerusalem, and after being shown scenes of evil, he saw the glory of God departing from the temple (chapters 8-11). By symbolic signs, parables and straight preaching, he prepared the exiles around him for the coming doom. The sudden death of his wife led him to draw the lesson that the fall of Jerusalem would mean the loss of all delights for the inhabitants (Ezekiel 24:15-27). At various times Ezekiel was led to speak of the future of other nations, and this collection of prophecies is bound together in chapters 25-32.

Before the news of the fall of Jerusalem came through in 587 BC, Ezekiel had a period of silence (Ezekiel 33:21-22), but from this time onwards he began to speak of the return from exile with a cleansed and renewed community. His promise of the water and the Spirit in 36:25-27 may well have been in Christ's mind as He spoke to Nicodemus (John 3:5). The return would be like a resurrection of dry bones (Ezekiel 37:1-14).

The people in the northern kingdom of Israel, many of whom, though certainly not all, had gone into captivity in 721 BC, would once more be reunited with Judah (Ezekiel 37:15-23), as happened with those who had remained true to God (Ezra 6:21). But since this prophecy is connected with the coming of 'my servant David' (37:24-28) it has a full fulfilment in the breaking down of all national barriers in Jesus Christ (Acts 1:8) and the forming of the one 'Israel of God' (Galatians 6:16).

In Ezekiel 38 and 39, Ezekiel sees a great invasion of the land by Gog and Magog, which is defeated by the intervention of God in an earthquake. This may well be the setting of Armageddon before the Second Coming of Christ, but Revelation 20:7-9 refers to it, or to a repetition of it, as coming at the end of the Millennium. There are differing interpretations of the millennial reign of Christ, which cannot be explored here.

Finally, Ezekiel was given a very detailed vision of a new temple, together with plans for the division of the Promised Land. This temple is unlike the one which was built after the return from exile, and unlike Herod's temple. Some think that it will yet be built, but a literal interpretation would involve the reintroduction of animal sacrifices (Ezekiel 43:18-27) which, according to the epistle to the Hebrews were done away through the sacrifice of Christ on the cross (e.g. Hebrews 8). Hence, it is likely that Ezekiel was shown a symbolic temple which expressed the glory of God and the separation of himself and his servants from the sort of contamination that had spoilt the old temple. When God is enthroned, the water of life flows out (Ezekiel 47:1-12, compare John 7:38-39; Revelation 22:1-2). Since Ezekiel was a priest, this type of prophetic message was especially suitable for him.

EZRA. *Help*
It would seem that Ezra held a post in Persia equivalent to Secretary of State for Jewish Affairs. Persian kings were usually concerned to have harmonious religious relationships in their empire. Artaxerxes sent Ezra to Jerusalem in 458 BC to examine

and, if necessary, enforce the proper forms of Judaism (Ezra 7). A fresh group of exiles returned with him to join those who had resettled in Judah some eighty years before, and they brought a large amount of silver and gold presented by the Persian king and other members of the court, as well as by Jews and Israelites who still chose to stay in Persia (Ezra 8). He was confronted by the problem of mixed marriages with non-Jewish peoples, a thing which had done so much harm in pre-exilic days, and he formed a panel of enquiry to deal with this, and demand the divorce of the pagan wives (Ezekiel 9 and 10).

Almost certainly Ezra returned to report to the king, and we do not hear any more of him until after Nehemiah had been appointed governor in 444 BC, and had built the city walls. Then Ezra, as priest and scribe, was called to read the law of Moses to the people as the basis of a fresh covenant (Nehemiah 8-10). When the city walls were dedicated, Nehemiah led one procession while Ezra led the other (Nehemiah 12:36,38). Some hold that the historian made a mistake and that Ezra came in the reign of Artaxerxes II in 398 BC, long after Nehemiah, but this creates more problems than it solves.

The Greek rendering of Ezra's name is Esdras. In the Apocrypha, 1 Esdras is a Greek translation of the history from Josiah to Ezra's reading of the law, though with some chronological mix-ups, and with an addition of a Persian story of the three guardsmen who took part in a competition to argue for the strongest power on earth. The first suggests wine, the second the king, but Zerubbabel, the winner, proves that woman is strong but truth is stronger. The popular quotation, 'Great is truth and it shall prevail' comes from the Latin Vulgate's version of the competition. 2 Esdras seems to be a Christian amplification of a Jewish apocalyptic work.

FELIX[NT].

Marcus Antoninus Felix was procurator of Judea from about AD 52 until about 59. The Roman historian Tacitus says that Felix was a savage and lustful man who wielded the powers of a king while having the disposition of a slave. He crushed a rebellion initiated by a pretended Messiah from Egypt, although the leader himself escaped, and Paul was mistaken for him when he was arrested in the temple (Acts 21:38). Felix persuaded Drusilla, daughter of Herod Agrippa I, to leave her first husband and marry him, and the two of them summoned Paul to plead his case in front of them (Acts 24:24-27).

Felix already had some knowledge of 'the Way', i.e. the truths of Christianity (24:22), but Paul's straight talking about 'justice, self-control and future judgment' alarmed him, although the mood quickly passed. His further interviews with Paul had the ulterior motive of a possible bribe (24:26). When Felix was recalled by Nero, there was the threat of proceedings being taken against him by the Jews. This would account for the statement, 'Desiring to do the Jews a favour, Felix left Paul in prison' (24:27).

FESTUS^{NT}.

Nothing substantial is known about Porcius Festus, who succeeded Felix as procurator of Judea about AD 59, except that the Jewish historian Josephus says that he was a sensible and just man. He died after two years in office. Festus showed the same sort of indecision over Paul and the Jewish demands as Pilate showed over Jesus (Acts 25:1-12), and in the end exasperated Paul into appealing to the emperor. Before sending Paul to Rome, Felix took the opportunity of hearing Paul's defence in open court before King Agrippa, brother of Felix's wife Drusilla. (See **Herod**, **Bernice**.) Once again Paul's words, as with Felix, impressed Agrippa (26:28), but bewildered Festus (26:24).

GAAL. *Loathing*

After Abimelech had set himself up as king (Judges 9), Gaal and his relatives staged a revolution, making Shechem, already a discontented town, their headquarters. Zebul the governor of Shechem acted for Abimelech, who came and routed Gaal's forces. The governor refused to allow Gaal to retreat into the town, but on the following day his supporters once more attacked Abimelech, and were again defeated and Shechem destroyed. Nothing is said about Gaal's fate.

GAD. *Good fortune*
1. The first of two sons born to Leah's maid, Zilpah (see **Asher** for discussion.) Ancestor of the tribe of Gad.

2. One of David's seers. It is probable that God provided at least one court prophet for every king of Judah. David was advised by Nathan also. Gad was already with David in his outlaw days (1 Samuel 22:5). He was evidently musical, since he helped David in planning the singing in the temple (2 Chronicles 29:25). He was God's messenger to David after David's boastful numbering of the people (2 Samuel 24:11), and after the subsequent plague he told David to build an altar on the site of the future temple (24:18). (See **Araunah**). Like other court prophets, Gad wrote down records of contemporary events (1 Chronicles 29:29), probably giving God's interpretation of them in the manner of the later written prophets. It is likely that these records were available for the compilers of Kings and Chronicles. It may be significant that the Jews speak of Joshua, Judges, Samuel and Kings as 'The Former Prophets', and apply the term 'The Latter Prophets' to the prophets who gave their name to their books.

GAIUS[NT]
A common name. One from Macedonia was arrested at Ephesus as a companion of Paul (Acts 19:29). It is sensible to interpret 20:4 of the same man by following an alternative manuscript reading, *Douberios* instead of *Derbaios,* i.e. from Doberus, a Macedonian town.

Another Gaius entertained Paul at Corinth (Romans 16:23) and was baptized by him (1 Corinthians 1:14).

A third Gaius was a sound and effective church leader to whom John wrote 3 John.

GAMALIEL^{NT}. *God's reward*

Grandson of the famous rabbi Hillel, and himself the first to be given the even more august title of Rabban (i.e. 'our teacher' instead of 'my teacher'). With his death it was said 'the glory of the Law ceased'. Paul was one of Gamaliel's pupils, and thus learnt all that Judaism had to give before he became a Christian (Acts 22:3; Philippians 3:5-6). When the apostles were tried before the Sanhedrin, Gamaliel asked for a private session, and advised their release on probation. If the new movement was not of God, it would fail; if it was of God, he must not be opposed (Acts 5:33-40).

GASHMU

In the Hebrew of Nehemiah 6:6, the equivalent of **Geshem**.

GEDALIAH. *Jehovah is great*

Grandson of the helpful **Shaphan**. Appointed governor of Judah by Nebuchadnezzar after the fall of Jerusalem in 587 BC (Jeremiah 40). His headquarters were at Mizpah, where Jeremiah joined him. Unfortunately, the king of Ammon prompted Ishmael, a possible claimant to the throne, to murder Gedaliah, producing anarchy and panic (40:13–41:18). (See **Ishmael, Johanan**.)

GEHAZI

The rather earthy servant of Elisha. We assume that he is the servant who needed the heavenly vision of the angelic forces around Dothan (2 Kings 6:15ff). He is definitely named as suggesting to Elisha that the childless Shunammite woman should be rewarded with the gift of a son (4:11-17). Later, when the child died, Elisha sent Gehazi ahead to place the prophet's staff across the child's face, but without effect. Elisha himself was used to restore the son to life (4:18-37).

After Naaman had been healed of leprosy, Gehazi obtained a substantial reward for himself under false pretences. For this he himself was struck down with leprosy, but was able to continue as Elisha's servant, since this leprosy, or perhaps some severe skin disease, turned his whole body white, and according to the law of Leviticus 13:12-13 this rendered the victim 'clean' (2 Kings 5). Gehazi appears once more, telling King Jehoram of how the Shunammite's son was restored (8:1-6).

GESHEM
Included among the leading opponents of Nehemiah in Nehemiah 2:19; 6:1-2; 6:6. Two contemporary inscriptions lead to the conclusion that although Nehemiah simply calls him 'the Arab', he was ruler of Kedar to the east of Palestine. He tried to decoy Nehemiah out of Jerusalem for a conference in one of the villages, but Nehemiah suspected treachery and refused. Geshem and others were annoyed that the Israelite territory, which had been overrun by various peoples after the destruction of Jerusalem, was being reoccupied under Persian authority.

GIDEON. *Smiter*
Three lively chapters in Judges 6-8 recount how Gideon delivered Israel from Midianite domination. God called him through an angel (6:11-24), and the same night spoke to him prophetically, telling him to destroy his father's shrine dedicated to Baal and his consort, and build a fresh altar to Jehovah. For this, his fellow-townsmen tried to kill him, but his father saved him by using the same type of argument as Gamaliel did (Judges 6:25-32, compare Acts 5:38). Hence he received the nickname, Jerubbaal, *Baal contends,* or *contender with Baal.*

After two tests which defied scientific probability (Judges 6:36-40), Gideon gathered an army from the northern tribes, but was given a test for selecting an army of 300 only. Under a trial at a river, most of the thirsty men crouched down and plunged their faces into the water. But 300 scooped up water and lapped it up from their hands. This showed that they were alert for any surprise attack. Gideon provided them with clay pitchers with smouldering torches inside. In a night attack on the Midianite army, the men broke their pitchers, and the inrush of air made the torches flare up, while the troops also blew loudly on trumpets. The Midianites in panic fought among themselves in the darkness, and then retired in disorder. A fresh body of Ephraimites killed two of the kings of Midian, Oreb and Zeeb, and Gideon killed the two remaining kings, Zebah and Zalmunna (7:1–8:21). More or less any lord of a town could be styled king.

Gideon then had a strange spiritual lapse. After refusing an offer of kingship, he invited gifts of golden earrings that had been taken from the enemy, and made an ephod out of them, which he placed in his own town of Ophrah for people to worship (Judges 8:22-27). Normally an ephod was a priestly robe, but here it may have been a shell of beaten gold that would stand up like the form of a man (see **Micah**). Gideon had many wives and seventy sons, of whom the most important was Abimelech, who took the kingship.

GOG.
See **Magog**

GOLIATH
It seems that there was a family in Gath whose genetic structure produced men much taller than the average (2 Samuel 21:18-22). Goliath was the most famous, in view of his duel with David. Reckoning the cubit as about eighteen inches, Goliath was a little over nine feet tall (1 Samuel 17:4). David knocked him unconscious with a sling stone in his forehead, and then beheaded him with the giant's own sword.

Later David secured the sword for himself, with the words 'There is none like it' (21:8-9). For the statement in 2 Samuel 21:19 that Elhanan killed Goliath, see **Elhanan**.

GOMER
The wife of Hosea, whose behaviour caused Hosea much distress, while at the same time giving him some realization of God's feelings when his bride, Israel, was unfaithful to him. There is a difference among commentators as to the actual course of events

in Hosea 1 and 3. One reasonable interpretation is that Hosea was told to marry a woman who was a prostitute, perhaps from one of the high places where sex rites were carried on (1:2-3). The marriage was an unhappy one, and Hosea did not even know whether he was the father of his two sons and one daughter, and they are called 'children of harlotry' (1:2). God gave them the names of Jezreel *(God scatters),* Lo-ruhamah *(Unpitied),* and Lo-ammi *(Not my people)* symbolizing God's reaction to his unfaithful people.

From chapter 3 it seems that Gomer left Hosea, and he lost sight of her until he found her on sale as a slave in the market. He bought her back, and this time he kept her in seclusion, away from all her lovers. This fits the application to Israel as it is worked out in Hosea 2 and 3:4-5. Eventually the children's names are to be reversed. Jezreel, instead of meaning that God scatters in judgment, now means God scatters the seed, and the negative is removed from the other two children.

HABAKKUK. *Embrace*
The date of his book is not known, but the reference to the coming of the Chaldeans (Habakkuk 1:6) suggests that he was a contemporary of Jeremiah, some time after 630 BC. Habakkuk, like Jeremiah and Ezekiel, is conscious of the breakdown of just law (1:2-4). The nation must suffer, and the Babylonians will be God's instruments (1:5-11). Yet the Babylonians themselves are wicked; how then can the righteous God use them (1:12-17)?

Habakkuk waits for God's answer, which will surely come to those who live by faithful trust in him (Habakkuk 2:1-4). The Babylonians and their leaders will all be put down for their evil deeds, and it seems probable that Habakkuk is including some of his own people in his list of crimes (2:5-19). From the positive side, God will one day be acknowledged in all his glory (2:14,20). In the last chapter, Habakkuk produces a magnificent psalm (see notes in 3:1,19) of the coming of the glory of the Lord (verses 1-16), and of quiet confidence during the waiting time (verses 17-19).

HADADEZER or **Hadarezer**. *Hadad is my helper*
King of Zobah, north of Damascus. Defeated by David, who then brought back the gold shields of the king's personal bodyguard (2 Samuel 8:3-12). Later Hadadezer rallied the Syrians to attack David, but was again defeated (10:15-19).

HAGAR. *Flight* (compare Mohammed's *hegira*)
Sarah's personal maid, an Egyptian girl probably picked up when Abraham was in Egypt (Genesis 16:1). When Sarah was beyond hope of a child, she followed the practice of the day and let Abraham have a son by Hagar (16:2-3). After Hagar knew she was pregnant, her superior manner so exasperated Sarah that she made Abraham drive her out. In the desert an angel told her to return and mend her ways, and promised that her son would be the ancestor of countless generations (16:4-14). She returned, and a son, Ishmael, was born (16:15).

Some fourteen years later, when Sarah herself had become a mother, there was an unpleasant scene at the party which was held to celebrate the weaning of Isaac. We cannot say for certain who was to blame. The Hebrew text seems to put the blame on Ishmael, who was superciliously mocking (Genesis 21:9) or laughing at Isaac (NEB). He now knew that his chances of being the heir had gone for ever, and he over-reacted. But the word for *mocking* can also be translated *playing,* and this is followed by the RSV and the JB, with additional words from the Septuagint, 'playing with her son Isaac', in which case it was Sarah who was jealous. Those who take this latter translation suppose that there is some confusion in the Hebrew over the ages of the children, and that Ishmael was still a child himself, instead of being fifteen or sixteen. (16:16; 17:24-25).

Whatever the cause, Sarah demanded that Abraham should turn Hagar and Ishmael out of the house. This was contrary to the custom of the day. If a slave wife behaved cheekily before a child was born, she could be turned out as Hagar had been previously; but after a child was born, proper provision had to be made for that child. God relieved the tension in Abraham's mind by assuring him that Ishmael, like Isaac, would be the ancestor of a great nation (compare Genesis 16:10).

So Hagar once more went out into the wilderness, and although some modern versions say that she carried Ishmael on her shoulder, the KJV and the RV give the literal Hebrew, which implies that Abraham gave Hagar bread and a skin of water to carry on her shoulder, and gave her Ishmael to take with her. Hagar was a tough little person, and her resistance under desert conditions proved a little stronger than Ishmael's, and he collapsed first. Once again God intervened, and directed Hagar to a well that she had not noticed, and she and her son were saved. When they found somewhere to settle, Hagar continued to live with him, and chose him an Egyptian wife (Genesis 21:8-21). (See **Ishmael**)

HAGGAI. *Festal*
The first contingent of Jews returned from exile in 538 BC. They began to rebuild the temple, but became discouraged by the opposition of the peoples around them (Ezra 1-4). In 520 BC Haggai and Zechariah started to preach for revival, and in four years the temple was completed in spite of further opposition (Ezra 5 and 6). Some of Haggai's and Zechariah's prophecies are incorporated in the books that bear their names. Haggai shows the depression that had led to concentration on personal survival, and in some quarters to luxury building, while the temple still lay in ruins (Haggai 1:1-6). Haggai is not afraid to disclose that the prevailing drought was God's recall to sanity (1:9-11). The response was immediate, and work began on the temple again (1:12-14).

At first everything looked so small compared with Solomon's temple, but Haggai assured the builders that God's Spirit was with them, and that this temple would be adorned with treasures from other nations from whom God would, as it were, shake them out (Haggai 2:1-9, compare Ezra 5:8-12). Meanwhile the ruined temple was contaminating the whole nation (Haggai 2:10-14), but from now onwards the land and its produce would gradually become fruitful (2:15-19).

Finally, the secular leader Zerubbabel is promised security during a coming revolutionary period, and the signet ring which was torn off God's finger in Jeremiah 22:24 is now replaced (Haggai 2:20-23). We may wonder why Haggai and Zechariah waited until 520 BC before rebuking the builders, but either they returned with a small party of exiles in 520 BC, or more probably they were babies at the time of the original return, and were called to be prophets in their late teens.

HAM

One of Noah's sons, of whom we know nothing except that he told his brothers that his father was lying naked in his tent in a drunken stupor (Genesis 9:20-22). Obviously we are intended to gather something deeper from the story, and probably Ham's detailed description to his brothers showed a nasty mind. But the story is complicated by the fact that Noah cursed Ham's son, Canaan, and not Ham himself (9:24-25). It may be that Noah foresaw that Canaanite religion would be bound up with sex, such as Ham may have joked about. (See **Japheth, Shem**.)

On the other hand, some point out that in Genesis 9:24 Ham is referred to as Noah's youngest son, instead of being named in the second place as elsewhere. The Hebrew is literally, 'his son, the little one'. Son is sometimes the equivalent of grandson, and hence the reference in verse 24 could be to Noah's grandson, Canaan. If so, we must suppose that the full story would have indicated some involvement with Canaan as well as with Ham. We are given a list of Ham's descendants (10:6-20). As peoples spread, there was naturally intermingling between them, and the lists here indicate the prime lines of descent.

HAMAN. Perhaps named after a god named *Human*
The Grand Vizier of the Persian king, Xerxes. The Hebrew text calls him an Agagite (Esther 3:1), in which case he may have been descended from King Agag whom Saul spared (1 Samuel 15). The Septuagint here has the unknown adjective *bougaios,* and in

Esther 9:24 calls him a Macedonian. Mordecai, the Jew, refused to bow to him when he passed. Haman determined to have his revenge on all Jews, and obtained the king's permission on the ground that the Jews were a seditious people. Being superstitious, he cast lots to find a lucky day to fix for the massacre of all Jews in the empire, and was given the thirteenth day of the month Adar (Esther 3). But Mordecai and Esther worked behind the scenes, and when Haman seemed to have reached the heights of favour with the king and Queen Esther he was denounced by Esther as a traitor, and his plea for mercy at the queen's divan was interpreted by the king as an assault upon her. Haman was hurriedly arrested and hanged on the gallows that he had conveniently prepared for Mordecai (chapters 5-7). (See **Esther, Mordecai**.)

HANAMEL. *Gift of God*
Jeremiah's cousin who persuaded him to buy a piece of land which belonged to the family at Anathoth, at a time when the bottom had fallen out of the market owing to the Babylonian invasion and occupation of the country round Jerusalem. But Jeremiah had already been told by God of his cousin's impending visit, and gladly bought the land as a mark of confidence in God's word that after the destruction of the city by the Babylonians and after the exile the new generation would return and reoccupy the land (Jeremiah 32).

HANANI. *Gracious*
Brother of Nehemiah, who had already returned to Jerusalem, and who had brought news to Nehemiah in Persia of the fresh devastation of the city (Nehemiah 1:3). After Nehemiah had returned and rebuilt the walls, he appointed Hanani to have charge of Jerusalem (7:2). We do not know whether he was still in charge when Nehemiah returned to report to the Persian king, but if so he must have turned a blind eye to the infiltration by Nehemiah's enemies (13:4-9). Perhaps Nehemiah does not name him at this point in his memoirs so as not to let the family down.

HANANIAH. *Jehovah is gracious*
A seer who imagined that he was receiving messages from God, but who merely produced the wishes of his own unconscious mind. After Jehoiachin's captivity in 597 BC, he declared as the word of God that Babylon would fall in two years, and the king and the captured treasures would all be returned. He then turned on Jeremiah, who had been told by God to wear a wooden yoke as a sign that the Babylonian domination would last for a long time. He tore it roughly from the old man's neck, so that Jeremiah had to retire to his house.

Some time afterwards, he received a message for Hananiah that God would substitute an unbreakable iron yoke of Babylonian domination. As for Hananiah, God would take away his life before the end of the year, and in fact he died within two months (Jeremiah 28). Some false prophets gave themselves over to bad spirit inspiration, e.g. the prophets of Baal (1 Kings 18:19). Others like Hananiah claimed to be inspired by the God of Israel, but were opened up only to their own inner world of desires (e.g. Jeremiah 23:26).

HANNAH. *Favour, grace*
One of the two wives of Elkanah (1 Samuel 1). The other wife, Peninnah, had several children, and used to make fun of the childless Hannah. On one of the annual visits to Shiloh, Hannah prayed more fervently than ever, promising that if the Lord sent her a son she would hand him over to the service of the Lord as a Nazirite (1 Samuel 1:11; Numbers 6:5). The high priest Eli thought she was drunk, since her lips moved silently in their expression of heart prayer. When he knew the truth he blessed her, and Hannah accepted God's answer to her prayer and went happily away.

In due course, Samuel was born to her, and as soon as he was weaned — which could be any time from two to five years old — she took him back to Shiloh and left him with Eli. Probably Eli's daughters-in-law looked after him. We have Hannah's poem of gratitude in 1 Samuel 2, with a close resemblance to Mary's

Magnificat (Luke 1:46-55). Both poems acclaim the Lord for his strange reversal of human standards. Hannah saw her son once a year at least, and brought him a new coat each year to keep pace with his growth. Having given Samuel to the Lord she was rewarded with five more children (1 Samuel 2:18-21).

HARHUR
Curiously enough there are several men, whose names begin with H, who like Harhur (Ezra 2.51) returned from exile as leaders among the Nethinim. This note can cover all, by saying that *Nethinim* means *Given ones,* and describes those whom David appointed to assist the Levites (8:20). RSV translates as *temple servants*.

HAZAEL. *God sees*
A trusted high official at the court of Benhadad of Syria. When Benhadad was taken ill, he sent Hazael to Elisha to ask whether he would recover (2 Kings 8:7-15). Elisha replied that it was not a fatal illness, but he was able to read Hazael's thoughts and knew that he was plotting to murder his master. It was God's will that Hazael should come to the throne to join Elisha and Jehu in stamping out Baal worship (1 Kings 19:15-18), but God did not plan this murder.

Once on the throne, Hazael became a menace to both the northern and the southern kingdoms, and doubtless his threats helped to turn people back from Baal to the true God, as happened so frequently in Judges. Some of Hazael's campaigns are recorded in 2 Kings 8:28-29; 10:32; 12:17-18; 13:3,22. His name occurs in Assyrian inscriptions where he is described as 'son of nobody', but in his latter days another inscription shows that he bore the title of *Lord*. His reign may probably be dated 843-796 BC.

HELI[NT]
Appears in the genealogical table of Christ's ancestry in Luke 3:23. Joseph is here said to be 'the son of Heli', whereas in

Matthew 1:16 Joseph's father is Jacob. (See **Joseph**)

HEMAN
A Levite descended from Kohath, who was one of the chief musicians with Asaph under David and Solomon (e.g. 1 Chronicles 6:33; 2 Chronicles 5:12). Their descendants kept up the musical tradition (2 Chronicles 35:15; Psalm 88 title).

HEROD[NT]
Of Idumean, or Edomite, stock, Edom having been absorbed into Israel. The name was borne by the line of kings, of whom the following are mentioned in the New Testament.

1. Herod the Great (40-4 BC). Julius Caesar appointed his father Antipater as procurator of Judea. Both before and after succeeding to the throne, Herod showed himself an effective general against brigands and invading Parthians, and earned the title 'King of the Jews' from the Roman senate. In 19 BC he began to rebuild the temple in magnificent style, and in fact additions were still being made to it 46 years later (John 2:20). He also rebuilt Samaria. Without going into details, Herod's policy was the fatal one of trying to please everyone, being kind and brutal by turns according to the party he wished to placate. Before he died in 4 BC, he was breaking down physically and mentally, and his massacre of the babies of Bethlehem (Matthew 2:16) was typical of his fear of personal attack, and of his unpredictable cruelties.

2. Archelaus. Mentioned only in Matthew 2:22 as the successor of Herod the Great. Herod the Great divided his kingdom in his will, and Archelaus, his eldest son by Malthace, a Samaritan wife, had Judea and Perea. It has been said of him that he inherited his father's vices without his ability. His cruelty produced revolutions in Jerusalem, and his reputation caused Joseph and Mary to go to the quiet town of Nazareth on their return from Egypt (Matthew 2:22). His race to Rome to get Caesar to confirm him as king is said to be referred to in Christ's parable in Luke 19:12, especially as Christ and his disciples would just have seen the palace that Archelaus built in Jericho. In AD 6 Jewish pressure secured his banishment to France, i.e. Gaul.

3. Antipas. Called Herod the Tetrarch. Herod's younger son by Malthace, who received Galilee and Perea. This is the Herod of the Gospels. He divorced his first wife, daughter of the Nabatean King Aretas IV, and married his niece Herodias, the wife of his half-brother Philip (not Philip the Tetrarch) whom he met on a visit to Rome. He was rebuked for this by John the Baptist, and this led to John's imprisonment and execution (Mark 6:16-29). He was in general an able man, but Jesus censured his unwholesome craftiness when he described him as 'that fox' (Luke 13:32). Pilate gave him the privilege of examining Jesus during his trial (Luke 23:6-16), and Pilate's action reconciled a quarrel between the two leaders, even though Herod was disappointed at not seeing any miracle done by the prisoner. Eventually he was denounced for treason by his nephew, Agrippa, and was exiled in AD 39.

4. Philip. Son of Herod the Great's fifth wife, Cleopatra of Jerusalem (unrelated to the Hasmonean Dynasty). In the division of the kingdom he received Iturea and Trachonitis (Luke 3:1) and adjoining territory. He was a sensible and beneficent ruler. He rebuilt Caesarea Philippi (Matthew 16:13). He married Salome, who asked for John the Baptist's head (Mark 6:22-28). But see **Salome**. He died in AD 33.

5. Agrippa I. Mentioned only in Acts 12. Grandson of Herod the Great and brother of Herodias. He was brought up in Rome, and eventually was made king of Philip's tetrarchy in AD 37, and after denouncing his uncle Antipas, Galilee and Perea were added to his kingdom, with Judea and Samaria in AD 41. Josephus, the Jewish historian, regarded him with admiration, since he ingratiated himself with the Jews. This ties up with his persecution of the Christians (Acts 12:1-3). He died suddenly with a severe intestinal complaint after being hailed as a god by the people he was addressing. Josephus (Antiquities xix.8.2) gives a longer account of his death. This was in AD 44.

6. Agrippa II. Son of Agrippa I. He did his best to prevent the final conflict between Rome and Judah, which resulted in the destruction of Jerusalem, but in the war he supported Rome. He died about AD 100. In the New Testament he appears only in Acts 25 and 26, when he and his much married sister Bernice gave Paul an informal trial, and either jestingly or seriously declared that Paul was almost making a Christian of him. (See **Bernice**.)

HERODIAS[NT]
Granddaughter of Herod the Great and sister of Agrippa I. Married her uncle Philip (not the Tetrarch), and by him had a daughter, Salome. Her other uncle, Antipas, took her away and married her. When Antipas was exiled she chose to go with him.

HEZEKIAH. *Jehovah has strengthened*
One of the better kings of Judah (2 Kings 18 to 20). The date of his reign is uncertain, since the fall of Samaria in 722 BC is said to be in the sixth year of his reign, whereas the invasion of Sennacherib in 701 BC is in his fourteenth year (18:9-10,13). It occasionally happens that apparent confusion over such dates is due to a king reigning jointly with his father before becoming sole monarch on his father's death. Probably Hezekiah began a joint reign with his father Ahaz in 729 BC, and became sole monarch about 716 BC.

Hezekiah was a thoroughgoing reformer, and destroyed the idolatrous high places (2 Kings 18:1-6). Finally he arranged a magnificent Passover celebration in Jerusalem, to which he invited those members of the northern kingdom who had not been taken into captivity (2 Chronicles 29-31). The Bible and Assyrian records show that Hezekiah clashed with Sennacherib, king of Assyria. Sennacherib himself records an invasion in 701 BC to put down a rebellion in which Hezekiah was the ringleader, and although he does not claim to have captured Jerusalem, he records the heavy tribute that Hezekiah had to pay.

Scholars have connected this with the records of Jerusalem's deliverance in 2 Kings 18 and 19. But it is simpler to see three invasions here. That of 701 BC tallies with 18:13-16. At a later date Sennacherib's envoys failed to obtain any further response from Hezekiah and they returned to Sennacherib empty handed (18:17–19:8). A third invasion was crushed by a sudden plague that struck down the Assyrian army (19:9-37). Assyrian records are scanty for the last part of Sennacherib's reign, but the reference to Tirhakah as king of Ethiopia and the immediate sequel of Sennacherib's murder (19:9,36-37) suggest that the events belong to the last years of Hezekiah and Sennacherib (say, 688 BC). (See **Sennacherib**.)

There are two further personal incidents. Hezekiah was struck down with an illness that God told him would be fatal (2 Kings 20:1), but in answer to prayer he was granted a further fifteen years of life. (See also 2 Chronicles 32:24). As a sign to the desperately sick man, the sun's shadow on the step sundial of the palace suddenly moved backwards. Some have supposed a movement of the earth's axis, but a more moderate explanation would be that a hole in the clouds allowed the sun, temporarily hidden at the side, to beam through strongly enough to cast a retrospective shadow. The miracle lay in its happening at the time when a sign was needed.

The other event was a visit from the emissaries of Merodach-baladan, king of Babylon (2 Kings 20:12-19). Hezekiah proudly displayed all his treasures, only to be told by Isaiah that one day all these things would be taken as spoil to Babylon, together with Hezekiah's own descendants. This is not said as a criticism of Hezekiah's action, unless this is intended by 2 Chronicles 32:31, but is given as a prophecy of the future, and the king is grateful that he has been allowed to bring peace to his people during his own reign. (See also **Isaiah**.)

Visitors to Jerusalem can still walk through the tunnel that Hezekiah made to bring water into Jerusalem, a remarkable piece of engineering (2 Kings 20:20; 2 Chronicles 32:30).

HIEL

When Joshua destroyed Jericho, he put a curse on the man who should rebuild it (Joshua 6:26). A man from Bethel, Hiel, undertook the rebuilding during the idolatrous reign of Ahab (1 Kings 16:34), and according to Joshua's words he lost his firstborn son at the foundation ceremony and his youngest at the final setting up of the gates. In view of the idolatry of the time, his children may have been sacrificed as foundation and topping-off sacrifices.

HILKIAH. *Jehovah's portion*
The high priest in the reign of Josiah who found the lost book of the Law when he was renovating the temple (2 Kings 22). King Manasseh had done his best to obliterate true worship, and doubtless this was the only copy of the Pentateuch remaining. Either it had been hidden by a loyal priest, who had then been put to death before he could reveal the hiding place, or this copy had been buried in the foundations by Solomon as part of the consecration of the temple. (See **Josiah**). It is not usually thought that this Hilkiah was the father of Jeremiah (Jeremiah 1:1), but it is by no means impossible, and it would account for the action of Hilkiah in consulting the prophetess Huldah about the judgments in the book (2 Kings 22:14), rather than keeping it as a family affair.

HIRAM
By a coincidence, two men of this name had dealings with Solomon.

1. Hiram, king of Tyre, first sent cedar wood and builders for David's palace (2 Samuel 5:11), and had a high personal regard for him (1 Kings 5:1). He tried to keep up the same relationship with Solomon, and negotiated a deal to supply timber for the temple (5:2-12). There was a slight coolness later when apparently Solomon sold Hiram some rather inferior towns in the north (9:10-14). But this did not prevent the two nations joining in trading by sea, in which the Phoenicians were perhaps the greatest experts in the ancient world (10:11,12,22).

2. The other Hiram was a highly skilled craftsman, son of a Tyrian craftsman and a widow of the tribe of Naphtali (1 Kings 7:13-14). This chapter shows that he was responsible for all the metal work in the temple. It is significant that a man of Gentile origin should contribute to the temple, as Gentiles now contribute to the new spiritual temple (Ephesians 2:11-22).

HOBAB. *Beloved*
There is some doubt as to his identity. In Judges 4:11 he is the father-in-law of Moses. In Numbers 10:29 he is either Moses' father-in-law or the son of Moses' father-in-law, Reuel. Since Reuel was certainly Moses' father-in-law (Exodus 2:18), it is likely that the Hebrew word, usually translated father-in-law, has a wider use in Judges 4:11 of other relatives by marriage. If so, Hobab was Moses' brother-in-law. He was invited to accompany the Israelites, and at first refused, but on being urged to come because of his knowledge of the territory, the implication is that he agreed, although the text leaves this open (Numbers 10:29-32).

HOPHNI. Perhaps *Strong* (see also **Phinehas 2**)
One of Eli's two sons (1 Samuel 1:3), who were self-indulgent and immoral priests (2:12-17, 22-25). The point of verses 13-16 is that they insisted on helping themselves to parts of the sacrificial animal that should have belonged to the worshipper himself, and to other parts that should have been offered to God.

HOSEA. *Salvation*
Hosea and Amos were the two prophets called to speak primarily to the northern kingdom of Israel in the second half of the 8th century BC. Whereas Amos was a 'foreign missionary' from Judah, Hosea was a native of the north; e.g. he refers to the king of Israel as 'our king' (Hosea 7:5). God's inspiration takes account of the natural disposition of the prophets and writers, so that they are not simply God's dictation machines. Amos was a stern prophet of judgment. Hosea was a more emotional man,

whose marriage experiences enabled him to feel something of the grief of God for his unfaithful people. For the message that came to him through his unhappy marriage, see **Gomer**.

Hosea chapters 1 to 3 run consecutively, relating Hosea's marriage story and applying it to Israel, unfaithful, exiled and restored. Thereafter the book is difficult to analyse, since much of it is largely composed of short messages speaking of the rottenness of priests, secular leaders and the people generally. All the time one senses the love of God, longing for his people to return. Sometimes return seems imminent (5:15–6:3), but next moment all hope has evaporated like morning mist (6:4-5). The people were unable to see that inner life means more to God than a multiplicity of sacrifices (6:6), and that trust in God, which naturally means repentance, is worth more than foreign alliances which leave one morally static (7:8-13).

Yet in a sense it had always been so, and Hosea takes up the gloomy side of Israel's history (chapters 10-12). In chapter 13 it seems that all is lost, and in verse 14 God calls on the plagues of death and destruction to fall on the nation. Paul reverses the meaning in 1 Corinthians 15:55, knowing that destruction was not to be God's last word for those who listened to him, and this in fact is what Hosea describes in his final beautiful chapter, rejoicing in true repentance, faith and turning humbly and happily to God.

HOSHEA. *Salvation*
The last king of the northern kingdom of Israel (2 Kings 17:6). As a vassal of Assyria, he attempted a rebellion under promise of help from Egypt. Shalmaneser V of Assyria began, and Sargon completed, the destruction of Samaria (721 BC), when many Israelites, though certainly not all (see **Hezekiah**, **Josiah**), were deported to the east (17:3-6).

HULDAH
It is an interesting speculation why she was given her name, which means *Weasel*. Had she a sharp nose or a long body when

she was born? She married Shallum, a court official, and became a well-known prophetess in Josiah's reign (2 Kings 22:14-20). When the book of the law was found (see **Hilkiah**), she was consulted as to whether the judgments which the nation's sins had deserved would match the warnings written there. God showed her that eventually they would, but Josiah's reformation would delay them. We conclude that if subsequent kings were as good as Josiah, the judgments would have continued to be held back.

HUR. *Noble*
For our encouragement, God includes some less flamboyant characters alongside the top men such as Moses, Aaron and Joshua. Hur occurs twice only, in each occasion as a quiet and useful man. With Aaron he supported the tired arms of Moses as they were uplifted in prayer during the battle against Amalek, and doubtless joined him in prayer (Exodus 17:8-13). When Moses went up into the mountain to receive the Law, Hur and Aaron were put in charge of the people below (24:14). Since Aaron alone was blamed for the golden calf, he evidently overruled Hur.

HUSHAI
One of the Archite clan who occupied Ataroth on the borders of Ephraim (Joshua 16:2,7). The Fifth Columnist of 2 Samuel 15:32–17:16. As David's friend (15:37) he was sent to counter the wise counsels of Ahithophel, and to act as David's spy on Absalom's movements.

HYMENAEUS[NT]
A man who had joined Alexander in a moral lapse (1 Timothy 1:19-20), and Philetus in an error of doctrine (2 Timothy 2:17-18), this being that there is no such thing as a future bodily resurrection. The same error is common today, among Christians as well as spiritualists. In the intermediate state human beings lack an essential part of their being. When Christ returns we shall

again be given the capacity to gather what we need to express ourselves in bodies similar to Christ's risen body. (See **Alexander**.)

IBZAN. *Perhaps, Splendid*
A minor judge from Bethlehem, who brought off a successful marriage deal for his thirty sons and thirty daughters (Judges 12:8-10).

ICHABOD. *Where has the glory gone?*
An example of how the Hebrews often chose highly significant names for their children. Ichabod was born to the unnamed wife of Phinehas when the news came that the ark of the covenant had been captured by the Philistines and Phinehas was dead. It is striking that his mother was even more concerned for the lost glory of God than for her husband (1 Samuel 4:19-22). Ichabod's repeated unfaithfulness to her (2:22) had perhaps cost him her love.

IDDO. *Timely*
Out of eight who bear this name, we may note the seer who produced an account of the struggles between Jeroboam and the kings of Judah (2 Chronicles 9:29; 12:15; 13:22). It seems to have been a regular thing for court prophets to act as historians, usually interpreting God's approval or disapproval of motivated events.

IRA. *Watcher*
Two with this name were among David's mighty men (2 Samuel 23:26,38), but it is puzzling to find one of them called 'David's priest' (20:26). Probably the king had certain religious duties which might be termed priestly, but did not include those temple services which belonged to the Levitical priests (e.g. 2 Chronicles 26:16-21). These duties would include blessing the people and actually killing sacrifices on behalf of the nation (2 Samuel 6:13,18; 1 Kings 8:55). The king was certainly responsible for

overseeing what went on in the temple, and it could be that Ira was David's liaison officer between the court and the services in the tabernacle, when the temple was not yet built. He may also have been a kind of private chaplain for David's household.

ISAAC. *One laughs*

His name always reminded Abraham and Sarah of the incredulous laughter with which they both reacted to God's promise of a baby in their old age (Genesis 17:17; 18:12-15), a very human reaction to God's gracious promises, but Sarah gave a turn to the name as a sign that all who heard the news would join in her happiness (21:6). With scientists today producing and withholding conception through their knowledge of hormones, one need not be surprised if God, who knows more about body chemicals than any scientist, could bring about the miracle of conception and of birth even in extreme old age.

Isaac is a far less flamboyant character than his father and his twin sons Jacob and Esau, especially Jacob, but we have several interesting incidents of his life. The first was when Abraham was told by God to offer him in sacrifice (Genesis 22). Since God had promised that Abraham's race would descend through Isaac (21:12) and Isaac was not yet married, Abraham could only conclude that God would work a miracle of resurrection if he obeyed to the end. This statement in Hebrews 11:17-18 is the only one that makes sense. In fact, once Abraham had demonstrated outwardly the faith that he had inwardly (James 2:21-24), God provided a ram as a substitute. (See **Abraham**).

We do not know Isaac's age at this time, but he was old enough to carry the wood for the fire, and even if he was still small he would have been active enough to have struggled away from his old father. Thus, Christians have seen him as a picture of Jesus Christ going willingly to the sacrifice of the cross.

Another well-known incident is Isaac's blessing of his sons (Genesis 27). Although in fact death was not as close as he suspected, he had the good sense to make his will in good time. In ancient times this was usually done verbally. Although God had said that the second son, Jacob, would have the place of the elder (Genesis 25:23; Romans 9:10-13), and Esau had already sold his birthright to Jacob (Genesis 25:29-34), Isaac still wished to name Esau as heir of the promises. Whatever legitimate means God would have used to bring the blessing to Jacob, Jacob and his mother cheated blind Isaac into giving the firstborn blessing to the second son.

The story of the finding of a bride for Isaac is more the story of Rebekah (Genesis 24) but the closing verses show the anxious bridegroom taking a walk in the evening in the direction from which his new bride would come. Later he moved for a time to Gerar because of a famine, but foolishly followed the example of his father and tried to pass Rebekah off as his sister (26:1-11). (See **Abimelech**). He became so successful as an agriculturalist, cattle breeder and well-digger, that the Philistines politely suggested that he should move on and leave their natural resources alone (26:17-33).

Towards the very end of Isaac's life, Jacob came back to him, and his two sons both met again at his funeral (Genesis 35:27-29).

ISAIAH. *Jehovah is salvation*
One of the great prophets of Judah and a contemporary of Micah, Isaiah being a prophet who moved in court circles, while Micah was a man of the people. Isaiah's date was from about 760 to some time after 700 BC (Isaiah 1:1). He was called to be a prophet in the year of Uzziah's death in 740 BC (6:1). He was married, with at least two sons (7:3; 8:3), both with significant names (see **Shear-jashub, Maher-shalal-hash-baz**).

We know little about Isaiah's life. He had a confrontation with Ahaz when the king was calling on Assyria for help (Isaiah 7), and encouraged Hezekiah to resist Sennacherib when he invaded the land (chapters 36 and 37).

His book begins with five chapters that expose the social evils of his day. His call in chapter 6 has probably formed the subject of more Christian addresses than any other single passage in the

Old Testament. As against Jehovah's Witnesses, John 12:39-41 says that Isaiah's vision of Jehovah (Isaiah 6:5) was a vision of Jesus Christ, while Jehovah's Witnesses deny that Jesus Christ is ever referred to as Jehovah. Chapters 7-12 centre in the Messiah, who will overthrow the wrongs of society. When he comes, the line of David will be at a low ebb (e.g. 11:1).

The next block of chapters is largely concerned with foreign nations (chapters 13 to 23), and this is followed by the theme of the Day of the Lord, with its blessings and judgments (chapters 24 to 27). The sins of Israel and Judah come up again in 28-35, but the coming exile will be followed by a redemptive return. The historical chapters 36 to 39 describe the defeat of the Assyrians (see **Sennacherib**), and end with the prophecy that in the end Judah will be taken captive to Babylon.

The second part of the book, chapters 40 to 66, follow naturally after the prediction of the captivity in Babylon, since they are written from the point of view of the people awaiting deliverance there, and then returning to Jerusalem. The difference of atmosphere, however, has led to the view that these chapters are by at least one different author, and probably two. Some suppose that they came from a circle of Isaiah's disciples, who, as it were, formed an Isaiah Society for the study of his prophecies, and who continued as a group into the period of the exile. But Isaiah may well have been taken forward in time to the captivity, just as Jeremiah 'experienced' an invasion that had not yet happened (Jeremiah 4). Certainly he is taken further still when, as a climax to what he sees of Jesus Christ, as the suffering servant, he stands at the foot of the cross in Isaiah 53.

In point of time Isaiah sees that Christ has died bearing our sins, but the resurrection, though anticipated, has not yet taken place (Isaiah 53:10). Because of the place that the suffering Messiah holds in these chapters (42:1-9; 49:1-7; 50:4-9; 52:13–53:12; 61:1-3) the redemption from Babylon has an even fuller significance in the light of our redemption from the exile of sin. It is significant that in these chapters we have repeated claims that God can predict the future (e.g. 41:21-29; 42:9;

44:7,25-26; 45:21; 46:10-11; 48:3-8, 14-16), and in view of this one looks for some startling proof, such as the naming of Cyrus (44:28; 45:1), and the life and death of Jesus Christ.

Isaiah could well have written these chapters so that the people in exile would know that God had planned their punishment with a view to their purging and redemption. It is perfectly possible that these chapters were the testimony and teaching that Isaiah's disciples had to bind up, so that they could be opened as the exile neared its end (Isaiah 8:16-17).

A late Jewish book, with Christian additions, *The Martyrdom and Ascension of Isaiah,* describes how Isaiah fled from Manasseh when he was murdering those who resisted him, but was betrayed by a false prophet and martyred by being sawn asunder (compare Hebrews 11:37). (See **Manasseh**).

ISHBI-BENOB
One of the Philistine giants (see **Goliath**), who nearly killed David during a campaign after he had become king (2 Samuel 21:15-17).

ISHBOSHETH. *Man of shame*
An interesting example of how one may sometimes have to change a word to avoid creating later misunderstanding. Ishbosheth, the son of Saul, was originally named Eshbaal (1 Chronicles 8:33). Since *baal* was actually a neutral word, meaning *lord* or *master,* it could be applied to Jehovah (Hosea 2:16), and doubtless Saul intended to honour God by naming his son The Lord's man. Later the term *baal* became almost a monopoly of the Canaanite lord, and was used as a proper name, just as *Messiah* and *Christ,* both meaning 'Anointed', have ended up as a proper name in popular usage. The ordinary reader at a later date would surely hold it against Saul that he had called his son *Baal's man.* Thus a copyist substituted the contemptuous name applied to Baal in his day, namely *Bosheth,* 'shameful' or 'disgusting'.

Ishbosheth came under Abner's thumb on the death of Saul.

Abner made him king of the northern tribes (2 Samuel 2:8-10), but retained power for himself. When Ishbosheth had a confrontation with Abner over one of Saul's women, Abner opened negotiations to hand the kingdom over to David (3:7-11), but was assassinated by David's men during the negotiations (3:17-30). Ishbosheth lost heart, but almost immediately he himself was murdered by two traitors who thought they would get a handsome reward by taking his head to David. They had misjudged their man, and David had both of them executed for deliberately murdering a good man in his bed (4:5-12).

ISHMAEL. *God hears*
1. Abraham's eldest son. For his birth and early days, see **Hagar**. He grew up in the Sinai peninsula, and was an expert with the bow. He married an Egyptian girl (Genesis 21:20-21), and had a number of sons, who settled all over the Middle East (25:12-18). One of his daughters married Esau (36:3). He met his half-brother Isaac again when both of them came to their father's funeral (25:9). Obviously Ishmael collected a clan of followers, who took his name, since as early as the time of Jacob we read of Ishmaelite traders (37:25).

It seems that this clan was largely drawn from the Midianites (Genesis 37:28), and in Judges 8:24 those Midianites who were linked to Ishmaelites were noted for their gold ear-rings. Muslims claim descent from Ishmael. The New Testament distinguishes between the line of promise through Isaac, into which promise Gentiles as well as Jews may enter, and the Ishmael line of the Sinai peninsula, representing the purely natural descent, when Abraham stepped aside from the promise in order to obtain an heir (Galatians 3:10-14; 4:21-31).

2. Another Ishmael, a distant member of the royal family, was instigated by the king of Ammon to murder the governor, Gedaliah (Jeremiah 41). (See **Johanan**, **Gedaliah**.)

ISRAEL
(See **Jacob**.)

ISSACHAR. *Payment for services rendered*
The fifth of six sons which Leah bore to Jacob. In the mad rivalry to provide him with children, Leah had lent her handmaid to Jacob, and she regarded Issachar as her reward for her loan (Genesis 30:18). Issachar's descendants settled in the Jezreel area (Joshua 19:17-23).

ITHIEL. *God is*
One of three friends who enjoyed discussing proverbs (Proverbs 30:1). Some translators have spoilt a beautiful friendship by slightly emending the Hebrew, and leaving the speaker on his own, lamenting 'I am weary, O God, I am weary and worn out' (NEB). (See **Ucal** and **Agur**.)

ITTAI. Perhaps, *He is with me*
A soldier from Gath who became one of David's generals (2 Samuel 15:19-22; 18:2). The ordinary reader does not realize that David had a force of Philistine mercenaries who owed their loyalty only to him. They were the Cherethites and Pelethites, and they naturally remained loyal to David during Absalom's rebellion (15:18). Probably Ittai was not their commander (20:23), but he was in David's retinue as a free agent with his own group of men (15:22). Uriah the Hittite had a similar status, being an officer in the Israelite army.

JA-AZANIAH. *Jehovah hears*
When Ezekiel is taken in vision to Jerusalem, he sees Ja-azaniah among 70 men who are engaged in some occult ceremony which included the invocation of animals or perhaps of animal deities such as the Egyptians worshipped (Ezekiel 8:7-12). This Ja-azaniah is 'the son of Shaphan', presumably the faithful assistant of King Josiah (2 Kings 22). If so, he is a sad example of the strange fact that not all children of godly parents maintain the faith in which they are brought up. His three brothers appear to have followed in their father's footsteps, Ahikam shielded Jeremiah (Jeremiah 26:24), Elasah carried a letter from

Jeremiah to the exiles (29:3), and Gemariah tried to stop King Jehoiakim from destroying Jeremiah's scroll of prophecies (36:10,25).

Ezekiel also sees another leader with this name among 25 others who 'devise iniquity and who give wicked counsel' (Ezekiel 11:1-3). The proper translation and meaning of the slogan in verse 3 has taxed commentators, but verse 9 suggests that the general sense is that the rubbish has gone into exile with Jehoiachin (and Ezekiel), while we sit snugly in our protective saucepan as the tasty morsels. We may then follow the margin for the first sentence, and translate 'Is not the time near to build houses?' i.e. we can settle down comfortably. Although this second man is the son of Azzur, it is surprising to find two apostate leaders with the same name, and it could be that Azzur was yet another son of Shaphan, making Ja-azaniah Shaphan's grandson. Certainly Azzur fathered another failure in Jeremiah's opponent, Hananiah (Jeremiah 28:1).

JABAL
Son of Lamech and Adah (Genesis 4:20). Just as Abel began sheep breeding, so Jabal began breeding cattle. Archaeological findings indicate that domestication began probably in the Middle East after about 9000 BC, and that sheep preceded cattle.

JABIN. *Discerner*
A king of Hazor who rallied neighbouring kings against Joshua, only to suffer defeat and death (Joshua 11:1-15). Since the Israelite force could not immediately settle down in the conquered territories, Hazor was rebuilt by the Canaanites, and a second Jabin dominated the northern Israelites for a time after the settlement (Judges 4:2). His general, Sisera, was evidently more influential than Jabin himself, and Jabin is not referred to after the victory of Barak and Deborah.

JACOB (later named Israel).
Twin brother of Esau, born second and grasping Esau's heel

(Genesis 25:26). Hence his name is connected with the Hebrew word for heel *(aqueb),* and in 27:36 it is interpreted as Supplanter, an English word which, by a curious coincidence is derived from the Latin *Sub (under)* and *planta (sole of the foot),* with the sense of tripping someone up, i.e. to get an advantage over him. The connection with grasping the heel is similar, though not quite identical. For his early life see **Esau, Isaac**. In taking the blessing of the firstborn, he took what already belonged to him (25:23,29-34), though this does not justify the trick he played on his father Isaac at the instigation of his mother. Division in the family through favouritism comes out in the reference in 27:5-6 to 'his son Esau' and 'her son Jacob'. The result of Jacob's trickery was exile for many years. He was in danger of his life from Esau, and his mother was afraid that he would follow Esau's example and marry Canaanite women, with whom she had already clashed as mother-in-law (26:34-35; 27:46).

Jacob therefore went to the old family home in Paddan-aram to find a cousin as his wife (Genesis 28:1-5). On the way he had a startling dream at Bethel. He saw a ladder set up from earth to heaven. The Hebrew word does not occur elsewhere, and it is hard to picture angels climbing up and down the rungs of a builder's ladder. Hence the ladder is likely to have been a flight of steps, like the rock slabs that rise up the hillside at Bethel.

The two-way movement of the angels showed that earth was not entirely cut off from heaven, and the vision of God at the head of the stairway confirmed this, as he reaffirmed the promise made to Abraham and Isaac, and assured Jacob that he would be with him and bring him safely back into the Promised Land. On waking, Jacob realized that on earth one could find the house of God and the gate of heaven, and he set up the stone that had been his pillow to mark the place where he would one day set up an altar to Jehovah. Jacob is sometimes accused of bargaining with God at the conclusion of this chapter 28, but in fact he is simply rehearsing and accepting the promises that God has made. The 'if' is not bargaining, but has the same significance as in Romans 8:31. In John 1:51 Christ gives a final interpretation of the vision, with himself as the ladder between earth and heaven.

Uncle Laban welcomed Jacob to the old home in Paddan-aram, but for the next few years uncle and nephew played a crafty game, like two chess players, each trying to outwit the other. Laban had two daughters. Leah the elder was not a good-looker; NEB calls her 'dull-eyed', and JB says, 'there was no sparkle in her eyes' (Genesis 29:17). It would be difficult to arrange a match for her, but Laban managed to trick Jacob into marrying her by the same sort of scheme as Jacob himself had used to get the blessing of Isaac. Having married her off, Laban was willing to let his nephew marry the daughter that he really loved, namely Rachel, a week later (29:15-29). Then followed a mad competition between the two girls to provide their husband with sons, and Jacob was exasperated to find that at first Rachel could not give him a child. When eventually she gave birth to Joseph, and much later to Benjamin, these became his favourites (29:31-30:24).

Jacob had earned his keep by looking after Laban's sheep, goats and cattle, for an agreed seven years followed by a further seven (Genesis 29:20,27). He did so well that Laban did not want to part with him when Jacob asked to leave. So Jacob made his next move in the game. He agreed with Laban that he should have all the mottled lambs and kids that would be born during the next seasons.

Laban at once countered by moving all the mottled rams, ewes, billies and nannies, into a separate flock in charge of his sons, leaving Jacob with the white ones (Genesis 30:25-36). Jacob had a strange theory of genetics, but in practice a mixed flock naturally produced a proportion of mottled lambs and kids, which Jacob then used for selective breeding, so that he secured a large flock of strong animals for himself (30:37-43).

Now Laban and his sons, who must have been young boys when Jacob first arrived, realized that they must deal with Jacob, but before they could do anything drastic Jacob persuaded Leah and Rachel that their father had given all three of them a raw deal, and they were happy to return with him to Canaan. So, as checkmate, Jacob moved off with all his possessions while Laban was away shearing the sheep that he had so carefully moved to be well away from Jacob's flock (31:17-21). All that Laban could do was to chase Jacob, but was stopped by God from harming him. The only thing left was to make a treaty of non-interference (31:22-55). (See also **Rachel**).

After a further vision of angels, Jacob humiliated himself before Esau, who in fact received him without malice (Genesis 32 and 33). But before the meeting, Jacob had the strange experience of wrestling with God at a ford over Jabbok (32:22-32). Such an experience is so difficult for us to imagine that it is hard to interpret it properly. How does Jacob's statement that he had seen God face to face square with John 1:18 that no man has ever seen God? John refers to what we may call God in his essential Being, but since the verse says that the Son has made him known it is likely that already in the Old Testament the appearances of the Angel of the Lord, who speaks as God himself (e.g. Genesis 21:17-18; Exodus 3:2-6, etc.) were pre-incarnation appearances of the Second Person of the Trinity, as was the 'Man' at Jabbok. They were not redemptive appearances, since for this a full incarnation was necessary.

The significance of the wrestling may be, as with Abraham's willingness to sacrifice Isaac, a test of Jacob's persistence in acting on the promises of God against all appearances. God had promised to bring Jacob safely back to Canaan; now it seemed that Jacob was in danger of his life from Esau or from God himself. Jacob, however, insisted on 'defying' God to stop him, since God had already promised to bring him through. He won the victory, but learned the further lesson of his own humanness when God quietly put his thigh out of joint. The incident has been magnificently spiritualized in Wesley's hymn, 'Come, O thou Traveller unknown'.

After the violence involving his daughter at Shechem (see **Dinah**), Jacob returned to Bethel and built an altar there. This was a rededication of his life, and he made it an occasion of dedication for all his family and household. Some of them had brought little idols and charms from Paddan-aram, and they handed them over to be buried for ever (Genesis 35:1-4). On the occasion of the wrestling, Jacob had been renamed Israel, or Striver with God, and now God attached this to a renewal of the Abrahamic promise, once more at Bethel (35:9-15). At some time afterwards, Jacob's beloved wife Rachel died giving birth to Benjamin (35:16-21), although she was still alive when Joseph had his dreams (37:10).

The next part of Jacob's life is chiefly taken up with the story of **Joseph**. He finally went down to Egypt and settled there, after a touching interview with Joseph and also with Pharaoh (Genesis 46:1 to 47:12). Before he died he gave a particular blessing to Joseph's two sons, Manasseh and Ephraim, although strangely enough he deliberately, as Isaac had done unwittingly, put the younger over the elder (chapter 48). Finally, he blessed all his sons, foretelling the future of their descendants often in the light of their own past and present (chapter 49). (For his prophecy of the Messiah, see **Judah**.) On his death, Jacob was taken to the family burial cave near Mamre after being embalmed and presumably mummified according to Egyptian custom (chapter 50).

Jacob is commemorated in the blue flower, *Polemonium caeruleum*, known as Jacob's Ladder. Also by the Jacob Sheep, which you may see in a wildlife park or occasionally in the country. It is a patchy creature, and has four horns.

JADDUA. *Known*
A high priest whose name occurs in the list in Nehemiah 12:11,22. He is linked with 'Darius the Persian', probably Darius II (423-404 BC), but there was a Jaddua who, according to Josephus, met Alexander the Great during his campaign against Darius III in 334 BC.

JAEL
Wife of Heber the Kenite, a clan originally settled with Judah,

though Heber had moved north (Judges 4:11,17). After his defeat, Sisera took refuge in Jael's tent since Jabin and Heber were friends. She received him kindly, but murdered him as he slept (4:17-22). Some have seen this as a means of protecting her good name, since Sisera had come into the tent where only her husband or women friends should come. But Deborah's estimate in 5:24-27 is more likely to be right. Unlike cursed Meroz, who held back from coming in on the Lord's side, Jael did not allow victory to be snatched from Israel by letting Sisera escape and collect another army. She acted in the only way that seemed open to her. Some perverse critics find a difference between the story of the murder in 4:21 and 5:26-27, as though the latter makes Jael smash Sisera's head while he is drinking. The picture is of course poetical of his lying dead at her feet. One does not knock a man down by driving a tent peg into his head with a mallet. NB: The tent peg is mentioned in 5:26.

JAIR. *He enlightens*
A judge from Gilead (Judges 10:3-5). It is pleasant to know that God has a sense of the trivial. Here was a ruler, and all that God tells us of him is that he had thirty sons who rode on thirty asses and had thirty cities! (Compare **Ibzan.**)

JAIRUS[NT]. *He enlightens*
The head of a synagogue, who had the responsibility of arranging and taking part in the services. He came to Jesus and begged him to heal his daughter. On the way to his house he received news that his daughter was dead, but he continued to trust Jesus, and when they reached the house, Jesus restored the child to life (Mark 5:21-43). Matthew compresses the story, and begins with Jairus's expression of faith even when he knew that his daughter was dead (Matthew 9:18-25).

JAMES[NT]
The strange English rendering, from about the 12th century of the New Testament *Iakobos,* i.e. Jacob, following a late Latin

J Stafford Wright

variant, Iacomus. In the British Isles the Gaelic New Testament *(Seumas)* and the Irish *(Seamus)* keep the M, but Welsh comes nearer the original with Iago. The French preferred Jacques, whence our Jack. Four men bear this name in the New Testament.

1. Son of Zebedee, and brother of John (Matthew 4:21). By some intricate comparisons we find that their mother may have been Salome and that she may have been the sister of the Virgin Mary (see **Salome**). This would make them cousins of Jesus, and would give special point to her request, backed by her sons, that in his Kingdom Jesus would keep the power in the family (Matthew 20:20-24; Mark 10:35-40). James and John are closely linked in the Gospels. They were called together from their fishing (Matthew 4:21-22), enrolled among the Twelve (Matthew 10:1-2), privileged to be with Jesus when he raised Jairus's daughter (Mark 5:37) and at his transfiguration (Mark 9:2) and in Gethsemane (Mark 14:33). For their nickname, see **Boanerges**, Sons of Thunder (Mark 3:17), a character which came out when they wanted to call down fire from heaven on villagers who had refused them hospitality (Luke 9:51-56). At an early date James was martyred by Herod (Acts 12:2, compare Mark 10:39), and God did not save him from death as he saved Peter (Acts 12:3-17).

2. The son of Alphaeus. Mentioned only in the list of the Twelve (Matthew 10:3, etc.). See **Clopas** for the suggestion that Alphaeus and Clopas are different renderings of the same name, and that this James may be the same as the next.

3. Known as James the Less, the Little, or the Younger (Mark 15:40), but nothing is known of anything that he did.

4. The brother of Jesus (Matthew 13:55). Although Roman Catholics commonly believe that this James was the son of Joseph by a former marriage, this stems from some of the early Fathers who thought it derogatory to the Virgin Mary to suppose that she had further children in the normal way. Matthew 1:25, however, implies that she did. Obviously James was not impressed with the claims of his elder brother (compare Mark

3:21 with the sequel in verses 31-35; also John 7:3-5). His conversion probably took place about the time of the crucifixion, and he was one of those to whom the Lord appeared individually after his resurrection (1 Corinthians 15:7).

James and his brothers joined the disciples after the ascension (Acts 1:14). His close relationship with the Lord perhaps accounted for his place as leader of the church in Jerusalem, where he presided at the Council in Acts 15. He first met Paul soon after the latter's conversion (Galatians 1:19), and later took part with him in serious discussions concerning the relationship of converted Jews and converted Gentiles. They reached the conclusion that Paul and Barnabas were specially equipped by God to concentrate on the Gentiles, while James, Peter and John could best work among the Jews (Galatians 2:7-10).

His appreciation of Jewish customs came out when he asked Paul to help four men to discharge their obligations to a vow, which would involve going with them into the temple (Acts 21:17-26). We must remember that there was a transition period during which converted Jews were gradually disentangling themselves from the Judaism in which they had been brought up, whereas converted Gentiles had no such scruples.

Paul, as a converted Jew ministering to Gentiles, was attacked from both sides. James as a Jewish Christian did not go out of his way to antagonize his Jewish compatriots, and early Christian writers say that he was known as The Just, and respected for the uprightness of his life. Josephus describes how eventually he was stoned at the instigation of the high priest Ananus, who decided to have a clean-up of heretics in the interval between the death of Festus and the arrival of the new governor in AD 61.

There is no reason to doubt the early identification of this James with the writer of the epistle of James. This letter has the atmosphere of one with a Jewish background, yet it is clearly Christian, with the Lord Jesus described as 'The Lord of glory' or even, translated literally, 'Our Lord Jesus Christ, the glory', i.e. perhaps a reference to the Shekinah glory which manifested the presence of God in the tabernacle and temple (James 2:1). After presenting God as the source of all goodness and strength (James 1), James turns to practical human goodness in chapter 2.

It has sometimes been supposed that in 2:14-26 James is contradicting Paul's teaching of justification by faith. Careful reading shows that he speaks of works as demonstrating to others the true inward faith, which they cannot see as a thing in itself. Note the emphasis on 'you see' in verses 22,24. In chapter 3 James describes the wisdom of self-control, or rather God-control, while in chapter 4 he takes the quarrelsome to task.

Chapter 5 chastises the fraudulent rich in the manner of the prophets, concluding with a call to patience in the hands of the Lord, and advice about prayer and healing. Probably the healing here is a corporate act where no individual in the local church has a gift of healing. In James 5:20 the sins that are covered are those of the convert, and it would be contrary to the whole of Scripture to interpret it of the merit accumulated by the soul-winner himself.

JANNES and Jambres
Names of two of Pharaoh's magicians who resisted Moses, in the same way as some of Paul's contemporaries resisted the truth (2 Timothy 3:8). The names occur in some Jewish writings; and the pagan writers, Pliny the Elder and Apuleius, include Jannes and Moses in a list of magicians.

JAPHETH. *One who extends*
One of Noah's three sons, whose descendants moved into the Mediterranean area and south eastern Europe (Genesis 10:2-5). The promise that he would extend into the territory of Shem and Canaan (9:26) may refer to Palestine coming under Greek control after Alexander the Great, or be an allusion to Gentiles inheriting the Abrahamic promise alongside of the Jews, and together conquering Canaanite paganism with the gospel. (See **Javan, Shem, Ham.**)

JAREB

In the KJV a proper name applied to the king of Assyria in Hosea 5:13; 10:6. Modern translations generally give this as a title, The Great King. The reference in Hosea in probably to Menahem's appeal to Assyria (2 Kings 15:19).

JASHAR. *Upright*

The references to the book of Jashar in Joshua 10:13 and 2 Samuel 1:18 are not to an individual of this name. The book is probably a collection of poems associated with some of the upright heroes of Israel (see **Joshua**). A fictitious book centred round an individual with this name was written and published in 1751, by a certain Jacob Hive, and was reprinted by the Rosicrucians in 1934.

JAVAN

Son of Japheth (Genesis 10:2,4). His name later became synonymous with Greece, and is so translated in Daniel 8:21; Zechariah 9:13.

JECONIAH

This name is used four times in Jeremiah (e.g. Jeremiah 24:1) and three times elsewhere of the king more commonly known as **Jehoiachin**.

JEDUTHUN. *Praise*

A leading musician, linked with Asaph and Heman, who with his descendants led the worship of God (e.g. 1 Chronicles 25:1-7). The titles of Psalms 39, 62, 77 suggest that he was the composer of the tunes to which they were sung.

JEHOAHAZ. *Jehovah has grasped*

Two kings bore this name.

1. Son of Jehu. Reigned over the northern kingdom 815-800 BC. Although his father had professed to strike a blow for Jehovah against Baal when he came to the throne, Jehoahaz turned back to earlier forms of idolatry. Consequently he brought the nation into hard times through repeated invasions by Syria, which were averted only when Jehoahaz turned to God in repentance (2 Kings 13:1-9).

2. On the death of the good king, Josiah, in 608 BC, popular choice put his youngest son on the throne, rather than the next in succession, Jehoiakim (1 Chronicles 3:15). Sadly enough, Pharaoh defeated Josiah, and deposed Jehoahaz after only three months, putting Jehoiakim in his place. Doubtless Jehoahaz was not sufficiently pro-Egyptian. He was taken to Egypt and died there (2 Kings 23:30-34). In 1 Chronicles 3:15 and Jeremiah 22:11 he is called by his pre-coronation name of Shallum *(Recompense)*. Jeremiah foretold that he would not return from Egypt.

JEHOASH
See **Joash**.

JEHOHANAN
See **Johanan**

JEHOIACHIN. *Jehovah establishes*
Son of Jehoiakim, taken captive to Babylon in 597 BC (2 Kings 24:8-16). A number of influential men were taken with him, including Ezekiel. He was kept in prison for thirty-seven years, and a tablet discovered in recent times records the prison rations for himself and his sons. Eventually he was released and treated honourably by King Evil-merodach (2 Kings 25:27-30). Jeremiah refers to him under what could be his pre-coronation name of Jeconiah, shortened in three places to Coniah, probably with a similar meaning to Jehoiachin (see **Jeconiah**). Jeremiah sees him and his fellow exiles as good figs in comparison with those who were left in Jerusalem, described as inedible figs (Jeremiah 24).

In contrast to the prophet Hananiah, Jeremiah declared that Jehoiachin would not return from Babylon (Jeremiah 28, see

Hananiah), and he wrote to the exiles telling them to settle down, since the Babylonian domination, which began in 605 BC, (25:1,11) would last for seventy years before deliverance came (chapter 29).

There is a similar prophecy of no-return in Jeremiah 22:24-30. We know from Scripture (1 Chronicles 3:17) and archaeology that Jehoiachin was not 'childless' (verse 30, RSV). Hence we may understand the word as meaning that it is as though he were childless, since none of his children would come to the throne. Or we could translate with the NEB 'stripped of all honour'. Zerubbabel, the leader at the time of the return (see **Zerubbabel**) was Jehoiachin's grandson, but he never became king. Since Jesus Christ was a descendant both through Mary (Luke 3:27) and legally through Joseph (Matthew 1:12; for this interpretation of the genealogies, see **Joseph**), the reference must be to normal kingship, and not to the Messianic rule spoken of in Jeremiah 23:5-6 (compare Ezekiel 21:27).

JEHOIADA. *Jehovah knows*

Of six with this name the most important is the high priest who saved Joash, the single surviving member of the line of David, when queen Athaliah massacred the heirs to the throne (2 Kings 11; 2 Chronicles 22:10ff). He had married the daughter of the late king, and she smuggled the royal baby into the temple where he was kept safely for six years. At the end of that time he armed the temple guard of Levites, and crowned Joash king.

When Athaliah burst in with cries of 'Treason', she was seized, taken out of the temple, and executed (see **Athaliah**). Jehoiada acted as regent at first and kept Joash on the right lines (2 Kings 12:2), but when the young king grew up and of his own accord told the high priest to repair the temple, Jehoiada dragged his feet and had to be rebuked (2 Kings 12:4-16). He died at a great age, and was buried in the royal tombs, with a fine epitaph: 'He had done good in Israel, and toward God and his house' (2 Chronicles 24:15-16).

JEHOIAKIM. *Jehovah sets up*
A bad son of a good father, King Josiah. When his father was killed by Pharaoh Neco at Megiddo in 609 BC, the people chose his more popular younger brother Jehoahaz as king. Unfortunately he was not Pharaoh's choice, and after a three-month reign Jehoahaz was taken to Egypt, and Jehoiakim (his name now changed from his birth name of Eliakim), was appointed as Pharaoh's vassal (2 Kings 23:31-37). In 605 BC Palestine came under the control of Babylon (24:1), and Nebuchadnezzar took prisoners and hostages back with him, including Daniel.

Later, Jehoiakim rebelled, and Nebuchadnezzar sent a mixed army to attack Jerusalem (2 Kings 24:1-5). It is not entirely clear how Jehoiakim died, but a comparison of the accounts suggests that he was captured in a skirmish outside the city, but before being taken to Babylon he was killed, either deliberately or by accident, and his body thrown out to rot (2 Chronicles 36:6; Jeremiah 22:18-19; 36:30).

Apart from the unpopularity he incurred through raising a capital levy to pay what Egypt demanded (2 Kings 23:35), we learn more about Jehoiakim from Jeremiah. He does not seem to have dipped too deeply into his own pockets, but built a fine house for himself without paying any wages to his employees (Jeremiah 22:13-15), and was known to be open to bribes and engaged in profitable rackets, including 'persuasion' and even murder (Jeremiah 22:15-17; 2 Kings 24:4). He had no time for prophets who spoke against him and the court clique. He went so far as to get an extradition order for Uriah the prophet who had taken refuge in Egypt, and promptly executed him (Jeremiah 26:20-23).

He would like to have executed Jeremiah, but could not catch him (Jeremiah 36:26, compare 26:24). He was not the last to suppose that by getting rid of the Bible he could ignore what the Bible says, so he cut up and burnt the scroll of prophecies that Jeremiah sent to him at the command of God (Jeremiah 36).

JEHONADAB
See **Jonadab**

JEHORAM. Sometimes **Joram.** *Jehovah is exalted*
Two kings bear this name.

1. Second son of Ahab and Jezebel, who succeeded his brother Ahaziah as king of Israel (853-840 BC). He made some attempt to put down the worship of Melkart Baal (2 Kings 3:1-3), in spite of the fact that his mother was still alive all through his reign. For his abortive invasion of Moab, see **Mesha**. Since some of the stories of Elisha (2 Kings 4-6) are not dated by any specific king, we do not know how many took place in Jehoram's reign.

He was severely wounded in a campaign against Syria (2 Kings 8:28-29), and while convalescing with his mother in Jezreel he was assassinated by general Jehu, who flung his body into Naboth's vineyard and left his mother Jezebel's body in the streets to be eaten by the dogs (9:14-37).

2. King of Judah and brother-in-law of the above through his marriage with Ahab's daughter (2 Kings 8:16-18). He reigned 850-843 BC. He began his reign with an action typical of Jezebel, probably prompted by his wife, and murdered all his younger brothers and their possible supporters (2 Chronicles 21:2-4).

Jehoram's reign was marked by the revolt of Edom, which had been forced to pay large sums of money to Judah, and curiously enough by the Jewish city of Libnah declaring its independence (2 Chronicles 21:10). Since this is specifically linked with Jehoram's defection from the true God, one wonders how far the declaration of independence was made through the influence of loyal priests, since Libnah was assigned to the priests by Joshua (Joshua 21:13).

Elijah, who otherwise concentrated on the northern kingdom, sent Jehoram a letter condemning him for following the ideals of Ahab and Jezebel (2 Chronicles 21:11-15). He died of an unpleasant disease, after seeing all his family, except his youngest son, taken into exile and probably killed. He had become so unpopular that he was buried without the usual ceremony of burning aromatic spices at the funeral (2 Chronicles 21:19; Jeremiah 34:5).

JEHOSHAPHAT. *Jehovah is judge*
King of Judah, 871-845 BC. His reign is outlined briefly in 1 Kings 22:41-50, after a vivid description of his narrow escape when he joined Ahab against Syria. There is a further anecdote of a joint expedition against Moab in 2 Kings 3 (see **Mesha**). From the 1 Kings' summary we gather that he suppressed the homosexual practices in the temple, but did not remove the high places (1 Kings 22:43-46).

There is a fuller account of his reign in 2 Chronicles 17-20. It may sound contradictory to read in 17:6 that he *did* remove the high places. We can distinguish between two types of high places. There were some where the local baals were worshipped; these were also marked by wooden pillars, Asherim, which denoted the female elements (NB: 17:6). Jehoshaphat removed these. But there were other high places where Jehovah was honoured, although these were illegal in Judah once the temple was built as the single centre of worship (Deuteronomy 12:1-14). Probably places like Gibeon remained (1 Kings 3:4).

He sent out travelling preachers (2 Chronicles 17:7-9; 19:4), fortified and rearmed the nation, with the result that surrounding countries kept peace with him (17:10-19), appointed just judges (19:5-11), and humbled himself before God in prayer when, faced by a concerted attack by Moab, Ammon and Edom, the opposing armies turned on one another (20:1-30). He was, however, unsuccessful in his merchant navy. He took Ahaziah of Israel as partner in a ship-building project at Ezion-geber, near the modern Elath, but the ships were wrecked before they could leave port (20:35-37). Ahaziah then proposed a further joint expedition, but Jehoshaphat, having been censured by a prophet, refused (1 Kings 22:48-50; 2 Chronicles 20:37).

JEHOSHEBA or **Jehoshabeath**. *Jehovah on oath*
Sister of King Ahaziah and wife of the high priest Jehoiada. She

smuggled baby Joash into the temple when her mother, Athaliah, murdered all the rest of the possible claimants to the throne (2 Kings 11:1-3; 2 Chronicles 22:10-12).

JEHU. *Jehovah is He,* i.e., as we might say, *Jehovah is the One* Presumably, King Jehu (842-815 BC) was given his name by parents who made a stand against idolatry, and superficially he lived up to it. Chosen by God to wipe out the worship of Tyrian Baal, which had been introduced by Jezebel (1 Kings 19:16; 2 Kings 9:1-10), he began as a member of Ahab's bodyguard (2 Kings 9:25-26), and ended as the assassin of Joram, Ahab's son, and incidentally, of Ahaziah, king of Judah, and Jezebel (9:14-37).

Like many other revolutionaries, Jehu was utterly ruthless. He secured the murder of all other heirs to the throne of Israel and also of some relatives of Ahaziah (2 Kings 10:1-14). Then by a trick, pretending to be a fervent supporter of Baal, he arranged a service in honour of Baal, and promptly murdered all the worshippers who joined him, afterwards destroying the place of worship (10:15-28). He showed himself to be on God's side in wiping out the curse of Baalism, and was promised four generations on the throne, during which he and his descendants presumably might prove their genuineness (10:30). But one and all showed that they had no principle of obedience to the true God, and supported other forms of idolatry (10:29,31). Thus the blood that he shed in the revolution returned on the head of his descendants (Hosea 1:4).

Jehu was defeated by the Syrians (2 Kings 10:32-33), and on the so-called Black Obelisk he is depicted in the act of submission to Shal-maneser III of Assyria.

Another Jehu, more worthy of the name, was a prophet who spoke doom to King Baasha (1 Kings 16:1-4) and warning to Jehoshaphat (2 Chronicles 19:1-3), and also contributed to the annals of history (20:34).

JEPHTHAH. *Opener* or *Opened*
Jephthah's father had an affair with a prostitute, but acknowledged her baby as his son. Jephthah's brothers, born legitimately, were less tolerant and turned him out of the Gilead area (Judges 11:1-3). He gained a reputation as a kind of Robin Hood, and when the Israelites were in trouble with the Ammonites, they turned to him and his scratch army for help (11:3-11). Jephthah first tried unsuccessfully to negotiate with Ammon, arguing in terms they would understand that they should be content with the territory that their god had given them (11:12-28). Then he went into battle and routed the enemy (11:29-33)

Once the battle was won, some of the tribe of Ephraim grumbled that they had not been called in to help, and threatened Jephthah's life and property. If they wanted a fight, Jephthah was ready to oblige, and after the battle his men rounded up the Ephraimite fugitives as they tried to cross the fords of Jordan. If they passed themselves off as legitimate travellers, they were made to say the word *Shibboleth*, (*flooded stream*). Ephraimites could not pronounce the *Sh* combination, and so they were detected.

Jephthah is chiefly remembered for the sacrifice of his daughter after vowing before battle to offer to God the first living creature that met him on his return home (Judges 11:29-40). It is quite likely that a rough countryman was sufficiently ignorant of God's requirements as to feel bound to offer his daughter in sacrifice. Careful reading of the conclusion of the chapter suggests that he might, in fact, have fulfilled his vow by dedicating his daughter to perpetual virginity, corresponding to sending her into a nunnery. To be childless was a tragedy for him and for her. The fulfilment of the vow would then be in the sentence, 'She knew no man' (KJV) or 'She died a virgin' (NEB) (11:39). If so, her more fortunate friends used to visit her each year on the anniversary of her dedication (11:40).

JEREMIAH. *Jehovah exalts*
Since prophets are not God's typewriters or keyboards, which

would mean that their writings would all be identical in style, it is fair to say that God chose individuals whose background would enable them to open up more readily to the type of message that he wished to give. Jeremiah was a lonely man, and so was specially suited to understand a message of individualism, although he was certainly ready to grasp national needs. Son of a priest, born at Anathoth, a few miles north east of Jerusalem, Jeremiah was called to be a prophet in 626 BC, under Josiah, and continued through the reigns of Jehoahaz, Jehoiakim, Jehoiachin and Zedekiah, until after the fall of Jerusalem in 587 BC, when he was taken to Egypt. (Jeremiah 1:1-3)

A prophet is regarded as different from ordinary followers of God in that he receives a true communication from God. Thus Ezekiel is given a visionary scroll to eat (Ezekiel 2:8–3:3), and Jeremiah at his call has God's words put into his mouth (Jeremiah 1:9), which will bring about negative destruction or positive restoration (1:11). Jeremiah later learns that there is a conditional element in some of God's pronouncements (18:7-12).

Some of his chapters are dated, but they are not all in chronological order. It was not until 604 BC that Jeremiah was told to write down his prophecies to date, and he dictated them to Baruch (Jeremiah 36:1-2). There is no real problem over faulty memory, since hypnotism shows that memories are stored, and Jeremiah would have the prompting of the Spirit to recover them. King Jehoiachin systematically destroyed the scroll of prophecies, column by column, but the prophet rewrote them and kept the scroll open for further additions (chapter 36). Probably chapters 1 to 20 formed the main block of these writings, and since Baruch remained with Jeremiah, he presumably recorded most of the book.

The book shows how soon religion and morality declined after the death of the good king Josiah. Many of the later chapters are dated in the reigns of Jehoiakim and Zedekiah, when God's judgment was about to fall. When Zedekiah broke his treaty with Babylon, Jeremiah took the risk of being branded as a traitor by urging submission to the invading armies of

Nebuchadnezzar as the only hope of salvation. For this he was imprisoned (Jeremiah 32-34; 37-38).

Nebuchadnezzar obviously heard of his stand, and gave orders that he should be free to go where he wished when Jerusalem fell (Jeremiah 39:11-14). He chose to remain with the people who had rejected his message, but they rejected it once more when he advised them not to go as refugees to Egypt. In rejecting Jeremiah they rejected God, and turned back to the worship of the Queen of Heaven (chapters 42 to 44). Jeremiah was taken with them to Egypt, where presumably he died. A strange tradition makes him come to Ireland with one of the royal princesses (43:6) who became a remote ancestress of the British monarchy.

From time to time Jeremiah spoke about foreign nations, as part of his commission at his call (1:10). In our Bibles these prophecies are grouped together in chapters 46 to 51, but in the Greek Septuagint they are placed after 25:13 for obvious reasons.

Jeremiah's personal 'confessions' are noteworthy. These are found in Jeremiah 11:18–12:6, where he is cheered up (!) by being told that more severe trials are in store; 15:10-21, where he is warned against compromise; 17:14-18, where he is mocked because his words have not been fulfilled; 18:18-23, where he directs his prayer against priests, wise men and false prophets, who refused the word of God; and 20:7-18, where in the stocks he recalls the power of God's words within him, and curses the day of his birth because of the sorrow his ministry had brought him, sorrow for the nation (8:18–9:1) as well as for himself personally. Yet he was given some happy messages also, especially in chapters 30 and 31 (NB: 31:26), including the coming of the Messiah (23:5-6; 33:14-17) and the New covenant (Jeremiah 31:31-34, compare 1 Corinthians 11:25; Hebrews 8:8-13). (See also **Baruch, Jehoiakim, Ebed-melech**.)

JEROBOAM. *The people increases*
1. Jeroboam I. The man who split the kingdom after the death of Solomon, and reigned c. 922-901 BC. Son of Nebat of the tribe of

Ephraim, he was put in charge of certain building operations for which Ephraimites were responsible (1 Kings 11:26-28). One day the prophet Ahijah told him, tearing up a new coat for a powerful object lesson, that Solomon's kingdom had become rotten through Solomon's idolatry, and that God saw fit to divide it.

Jeroboam would become king of ten tribes (1 Kings 11:29-39). Someone told Solomon of what had happened at what should have been a private interview (11:29), and Jeroboam escaped to Egypt (11:29-40). On the death of Solomon he returned, and was made king by the northern tribes who refused to serve Solomon's son, Rehoboam (12:1-24). Unfortunately, Jeroboam did not follow Ahaziah's warning about idolatry (11:37-38), and made two golden calves, which he set up in the north and south of the country, to be centres of worship which would stop his people going up to the temple in Jerusalem (12:25-33). These calves at Dan and Bethel became centres of rampant idolatry, in which Jeroboam took part, although he suffered a temporary paralysis as a warning (12:33–13:34).

When his son was taken ill later, he sent his wife in disguise to Ahijah, the prophet who had first foretold that he would be king, but she returned with the grim message that the baby would die and have a merciful release from the horrors that would fall on the idolatrous house of Jeroboam (1 Kings 14:1-17). Jereboam was long known as the one 'who made Israel to sin' (1 Kings 22:52; 2 Kings 3:3; 10:29,31; 14:24; 15:28; 17:22), a sad epithet for one who was promised so much, but a reminder that God's promises are not unconditional guarantees (Jeremiah 18:7-10).

2. Jeroboam II. King of Israel c. 793-753 BC. Although a disobedient king, he was used to restore some lost Israelite territory, encouraged by the prophet Jonah (2 Kings 14:23-29). The rotten state of the nation, socially and religiously, emerges in Amos. At Bethel, Amos pronounced doom on the nation and on the house of Jeroboam (Amos 7:1-9), and was falsely reported to the king as having said that Jeroboam himself would die by the sword (Amos 7:11). In fact, Jeroboam died in the normal course, but his son was assassinated and the dynasty came to an end, as Amos had said (2 Kings 15:8-12).

JESSE. Perhaps, *Wealthy*
Grandson of Boaz and Ruth (Ruth 4:17), and father of David (1 Samuel 16). When David was being hunted by Saul, he moved his parents from Bethlehem and put them in the care of the king of Moab until things became safer (22:3-4). Saul habitually referred to David contemptuously as 'the son of Jesse' (20:27,30-31; 22:7,13), and this title clung to him (2 Samuel 20:1; 1 Kings 12:16), so that even David himself used it (2 Samuel 23:1, compare Psalm 72:20). Isaiah foretells that Jesse will be the ancestor of the new David, the Messiah (Isaiah 11:1,10), and curiously enough Christian art has depicted the ancestors of Jesus Christ from Jesse, rather than simply David. There is a fine Jesse window in Dorchester Abbey, Oxfordshire, England, and the remains of a carved Jesse Tree in Abergavenny Priory Church in Wales.

JESUS[NT]
The Greek form of Joshua, which has puzzled some readers of the KJV in Hebrews 4:8, where the Greek is translated as Jesus. In a book of the present type, one cannot present a condensation of the life, ministry and person of Jesus Christ, the Messiah.

JETHRO. *Excellence*
This is probably the title, corresponding to *Excellency,* of Reuel, the father-in-law of Moses. He is called Reuel twice only (Exodus 2:18; Numbers 10:29, where KJV strangely transliterates the same Hebrew letters as Raguel). He was a priest of Midian (Exodus 2:16; 18:1), and Moses married his daughter and looked after his flocks while an exile from Egypt (2:16-22). When Israel came out of Egypt, Jethro met them, and acknowledged the greatness of Jehovah (18:1-12).

Jethro's words in verse 11 have been taken either as the joy of one who was himself a priest of Jehovah, or as the words of a new convert. Next morning he was appalled to see the enormous queue at Moses' consulting room, and recommended him to share the load with other wise men before he had a breakdown, but added wisely, 'if God so commands you' (Exodus 18:13-27). Jethro is venerated by the Druze, an Arab splinter group from official Islam, living mainly in Syria and Lebanon. (See also **Hobab**.)

JEZEBEL. Meaning unknown
An utterly ruthless woman, who had the opportunity of having her own way in almost everything. Daughter of Ethbaal, king of Sidon, she married Ahab of Israel and proceeded to kill such old-fashioned conscience as he had (1 Kings 16:29-33; 21:25). Although she allowed Ahab to give their three sons names that incorporated Jehovah (Ahaziah, Jehoram, Athaliah), this was a mere screen for her wholehearted attempt to obliterate the worship of Jehovah in favour of the Tyrian form of Melkart Baal. She systematically hunted down the loyal prophets (18:4,13) and packed the court with nearly a thousand prophets of Baal and his consort (18:19).

False prophets were charismatics who had their inspiration either from an evil spirit or from some self-induced trance. (See **Micaiah**). Those who still used the name of Jehovah, but who had no heart for what Jehovah meant them to say, produced transcendental surges from their own subconscious (Jeremiah 23:16-32). Prophets of Baal, on the other hand, deliberately opened up to their god, and so to inspiration from Satan and the rebellious spirit world. In Jezebel's day we can picture the true prophets travelling round like the Methodist preachers of old, while the prophets of Baal were promoting what would win the queen's pleasure. Hence the ordinary people were bewildered, and went 'limping with two different opinions' (1 Kings 18:21).

The one man who stood between Jezebel and total victory was Elijah. His victory on Carmel was a personal defeat for herself. Elijah had executed her prophets as a sign, in terms that Israel could understand, that Baalism must bow to Jehovah, and that it could be, and must be, obliterated (1 Kings 18:20-40). Jezebel's prophets were expendable; she could easily collect more. But one Elijah was worth a thousand prophets, and she determined to kill him (19:1-3).

After a temporary disappearance, Elijah turned up again at the moment when she had persuaded her conscientious husband to let her deal with **Naboth**. Ahab still had the Israelite belief that a man had the right to his own property. Jezebel thought differently, and had Naboth eliminated. But Elijah met Ahab as he was looking round his new property, and gave him a blistering description of the future fate of himself and his wife (1 Kings 21:1-24).

Jezebel outlived Ahab, and may have been the power behind the throne during the reign of her two sons, Ahaziah and Jehoram. On the other hand, she may have withdrawn into herself, taken lovers, and dabbled in the occult to try to obtain what Baal had denied her (2 Kings 9:22). She died horribly with a bitter taunt on her lips, and a last attempt at glamour, for which she is commemorated in the epithet 'A Painted Jezebel' (9:30-37). A replica of Jezebel appeared at Thyatira (Revelation 2:20-23).

JOAB. *Jehovah is Father*
One of David's three nephews (Joab, Abishai, Asahel) through his sister Zeruiah (1 Chronicles 2:16). Joab, the ruthless realist, was the complete foil to David. Indeed, the events of 2 Samuel show him as the saviour of the throne of David, though sometimes by dubious means. He saw through the schemes of Abner, when David was ready to accept his promise to make him king in place of Ishbosheth, whom Abner professed to serve (2 Samuel 3:24-25).

Joab was unsuccessful in his first attempt on Abner's life, but when Abner killed Joab's brother Asahel, Joab had a vendetta on his hands as well as support for David and the nation (2 Samuel 2:8-31), and on the next occasion when Abner came to negotiate, Joab and Abishai killed him (3:20-34). David's words, 'the sons of Zeruiah are too hard for me', continued to be true.

Yet Joab was utterly loyal to David. He was made supreme commander after leading a raiding party up a water shaft and thus capturing the citadel of Jerusalem (1 Chronicles 11:4-9; 2 Samuel 5:6-8). He led a campaign against Ammon (2 Samuel 11:1), and did not hesitate to obey David's command to bring about the death of Uriah (11:6-25). An unusual trait in a successful general comes out in his generous call to David to come personally to take the Ammonite capital of Rabbah, when Joab had broken its resistance (12:28).

David's emotional life nearly ruined him when Absalom fled to Geshur after killing his half-brother Amnon. David longed to have him back, but would not make a move until Joab tricked him into doing so. Even then David would not meet him, until Absalom forced Joab to act as an intermediary (2 Samuel 14).

When Absalom rebelled and took over Jerusalem, Joab was one of the three commanders in the battle that followed. He had no time for further leniency on the part of David, and himself saw to it that Absalom was killed when he fell into his hands (2 Samuel 18). Again he saw that everything might yet be lost through David's excessive grief, but though he brought David to his senses he lost the position of commander-in-chief through David's extraordinary appointment of Amasa, another of David's nephews through his other sister. He had been Absalom's general (19:13). Amasa proved to be incompetent when Sheba led a second revolt and Joab took his revenge, stabbing him to death, after which he again tacitly assumed command with Abishai, and cleverly brought the campaign to a bloodless conclusion (2 Samuel 20).

As a practical general he knew that the army was adequate to deal with all emergencies, and hence resisted David's orders to take a census of the people, although in the end he allowed himself to be overruled (2 Samuel 24). His end was tragic. When David was on the point of death, Joab decided to back Adonijah as his successor, but Bathsheba and Nathan roused David sufficiently to have Solomon crowned (1 Kings 1).

All David's latent hostility towards Joab, built up during a lifetime, welled up when he was hardly competent to know what he was doing, and he charged Solomon to mark him down to die (1 Kings 2:5-6). When Solomon executed Adonijah and Abiathar, Joab ran for sanctuary to the temple, but on Solomon's orders he was murdered as he clung to the horns at the corner of the altar (2:28-35). He was a remarkable character, and might well be made the hero of an historical novel.

JOANNA[NT]
Wife of Herod's steward (see **Chuza**), who having been healed by Jesus joined other women in helping him and his disciples in material ways (Luke 8:2-3). She was one of the women who came to the tomb of Jesus on the resurrection morning (24:10). If, as some think, two small groups of women came to the tomb – one from Bethany and the other from Jerusalem – Joanna, coming from Herod's household, would have been in the second group.

JOASH. *Jehovah has given*
Three of the eight who bore this name should be noted.
    1. Father of Gideon. A cynic who had a private altar to Baal, and defended his son when he pulled it down, passing the buck to Baal to deal with the insult (Judges 6:25-32).
    2. King of Judah, c. 840-800 BC. Also called Jehoash. When his grandmother Athaliah seized the throne and tried to massacre all other claimants, baby Joash was smuggled into the temple where he remained for six years before Jehoiada the high priest proclaimed him king (2 Kings 11). (See **Athaliah**, **Jehoiada**). Jehoiada guided him as regent, though he slipped up himself over seeing to the temple repairs (12:1-16). Joash was unsuccessful in battle, and had to buy off Hazael from attacking Jerusalem (12:17-18). After the death of Jehoiada there was a reaction among the leaders, and Joash followed them into the old idolatries. Jehoiada's son, Zechariah, had the spirit of prophecy, and spoke strongly against the new movement, but under the degrading influence of the Canaanite religion Joash had him

stoned in the temple court. Yet he had probably played with him as a baby (2 Chronicles 24:17-22). Shortly afterwards, Joash met his own disastrous end. A Syrian attack on Jerusalem left him wounded, and his servants turned on him and killed him (2 Kings 24:23-26).

3. To complicate matters for the reader, Joash (Jehoash) became king of Israel shortly before the death of his namesake in Judah (2 Kings 13:10). When Elisha was on his death-bed, he gave Joash a sign of victory over Syria, telling him to strike the ground with a bundle of arrows. When Joash struck three times only, Elisha saw that he had not the will to follow through his victories, and foretold that he would win no more than three campaigns – which happened a few years later (13:14-25). He gave a cheeky answer to Amaziah of Judah, who challenged him to battle (14:8-10) but was forced to go to war, and after taking Amaziah prisoner he demolished a large section of the wall of Jerusalem, going home with hostages and loot (14:11-14).

JOB. Possibly meaning *No father,* i.e. an orphan.

We speak of having the patience of Job, whereas Job was in fact a most impatient man. The contradiction is due to a change in the English meaning over the years. When the KJV translators wrote the words in James 5:11, they intended the same as the RSV, 'steadfastness', or 'perseverance' or 'endurance' as in other translations. The whole significance of Job's test was to show whether a man will still continue loyal to God when things go strangely wrong, or whether we serve God only for what we get out of him.

This was Satan's challenge in Job 1:9-11 and 2:4-5, and all through the book Job never turns from God, but rather to him (e.g. 16:18-22; 19:23-27), even though he was in an agony over the way God seemed to be treating him. Thus, when at the end he came face to face with God, as he had been demanding, he confessed to having spoken too brashly (40:3-5; 42:1-6). But still he was vindicated by God in contrast to his friends who had maintained, each from his own angle, that suffering and prosperity are in precise proportion to faithfulness (42:7-9), a belief that some Christians and non-Christians still share.

The scene of the book is Edom (Job 1:1), noted down the ages for its concern with wisdom (Jeremiah 49:7; Obadiah 8). When Job suffered the loss of his possessions and his family, except for his wife, and was struck down with what was probably elephantiasis, three friends came to comfort him, each from his own angle (see **Bildad, Eliphaz, Zophar**). Obviously a crowd of spectators gathered to listen to the entrancing debate, one of whom, **Elihu**, later joined in. The present form of the book records in poetical form what was certainly hammered out in prose (compare Shakespeare's use of Holinshed's Chronicle), and the book ranks as one of the literary masterpieces of the world.

Each friend accuses Job, and is answered in turn. Gradually they fall silent, and in the third round of speeches only Eliphaz stays the course. Bildad is content with a few platitudes (Job 25), and Zophar says nothing. It is astonishing how some commentators, lacking a sense of what happens in real life, quite apart from literary skill, try to manipulate the third round chapters so as to introduce all three speakers.

When young Elihu speaks (chapters 32-37), Job ignores him, but he is confronted by a vision of God (chapters 38-41). God does not explain, but describes in astonishing pictures the universe and the earth with its animal inhabitants, all of whom he upholds in life. The implication is, Can you, Job, not trust me without wanting to argue with me? (e.g. Job 10; 23:1–24:1).

Eventually Job comes into smooth waters again (Job 42:10-16), but until the scene in heaven and Satan's challenge were revealed by God to the recorder of the debate, whose date we do not know, nobody knew what an amazing victory Job had won in the long conflict with Satan. He well deserves the rank that God gives him in Ezekiel 14:14,20 with Noah and Daniel.

JOCHEBED. *Jehovah is glory*
Mother of Moses and Aaron. She is mentioned only in Exodus 6:20 and Numbers 26:59, but the reason for including her here is

that she has a name which contains Jehovah in the first syllable. This demonstrates, apart from the Genesis records, that Exodus 6:2 cannot mean that the name of Jehovah was now made known for the first time (compare Exodus 3:13-16), but rather that it was not previously revealed in covenant significance.

JOEL. *Jehovah is God*

Author of the book of prophecies that bear his name. Its date is unknown. Commentators vary between making it the earliest of the prophetic books, say in the time of Joash before 800 BC, or at some date after the return from exile. It cannot be during the exile, since the temple is standing (Joel 2:17). Joel sees a recent locust devastation as symbolizing an actual invasion by a hostile power, which could be turned back by sincere prayer. Joel is one of the prophets who were given a vision of the coming of the Holy Spirit at Pentecost (Joel 2:28-29, compare Jeremiah 31:31-34; Ezekiel 36:25-27).

Joel links Pentecost with the portents in heaven and on earth that occurred at the crucifixion. To make these refer to the Second Coming of Christ would be to rob Peter's quotation in Acts 2:19-21 of all significance. Peter appealed to the darkening of the sun, and the earthquake with its dust changing the colour of the moon and causing fires in the city, events of which his hearers were aware.

JOHANAN. *Jehovah is gracious*

A shortened form of Jehohanan. Out of the many who bear this or an equivalent name (compare English *John*) we note the Johanan who joined the governor, Gedaliah, after the destruction of Jerusalem, and warned him of a plot to kill him. Gedaliah was murdered by a distant member of the royal family, Ishmael, who then carried off a number of prisoners. Johanan followed and rescued them, though Ishmael escaped. Unfortunately, Johanan then took the lead in advocating an escape to Egypt by as many Jews as wished to leave the country, in spite of a warning by Jeremiah. Presumably he died in Egypt (Jeremiah 40:13–43:7).

Another bearer of the name was the high priest, grandson of Eliashib, and son of Joiada, also called Jonathan in the list in Nehemiah 12:11,22. We know nothing more of him from the Bible, but Josephus says that he murdered his brother whom he feared as a rival for the high priesthood. A Jewish settlement at Elephantine on the Nile appealed to him for help when their temple was destroyed in 411 BC. The Jehohanan who gave hospitality to Ezra in 458 BC (Ezra 10:6) would be the uncle of the later high priest through his brother Joiada.

JOHN ^{NT}. *Jehovah has been gracious*
1. John the Baptist. The son of old parents (Luke 1), he emerged as a powerful preacher about AD 27 (Luke 3:2-3). He knew that he was called to be the promised forerunner of the Messiah (Isaiah 40:3-5; John 1:23) in the line of Elijah (Malachi 4:5-6; Luke 1:17). He centred his mission in the Jordan valley, and linked his preaching with baptism that would signify repentance, dedication, and readiness for the Messiah (Luke 3:3-17). He may well have mixed with the strict Essenes of Qumran whose literature has now come to light. The identity of the Messiah was disclosed to him when his cousin Jesus came for baptism, not for repentance, but as a dedication to the Messianic kingdom (Matthew 3:13-17). When the Spirit descended as a dove and the voice of God was heard from heaven, John knew Jesus as the Messiah (John 1:32-34).

John had a few close disciples, several of whom left him to follow Jesus (John 1:35-42). Now that John had seen the purpose of his mission fulfilled, he was not jealous (3:30), but he became puzzled when nothing spectacular happened, and he himself was imprisoned for rebuking Herod Antipas over his marriage. (See **Herod**). He sent two of his followers to get a direct answer from Jesus about his claims. The answer from Jesus demonstrated his claims by works of mercy and by preaching God's good news (Matthew 11:2-6). Jesus then extolled John as the last and greatest prophet (or perhaps the greatest man) of the fading Jewish era (Matthew 11:7-15). He referred to the extreme asceticism of John, which some think he learnt from the Essenes in the Dead Sea area. Jesus himself lived simply, but enjoyed the good things of life (Matthew 11:16-19).

John was beheaded in prison through the influence of Herod's wife (Matthew 14:1-12). Josephus says that this happened at the fortress of Machaerus, east of the Dead Sea. A number of John's followers became preachers of the coming Messiah without knowing that the Messiah had come (Acts 18:24–19:7).

2. John the Apostle. For his parentage, possible relationship to Jesus, and association with his brother during the ministry of Jesus. (See **James**). He was linked with Peter in the arrangements for the Last Supper (Luke 22:8-13). He is not mentioned by name in the fourth Gospel, of which he is traditionally the author, but he is likely to have been the anonymous disciple in John 1:35-40, the disciple who was allowed to follow Jesus into the high priest's court (18:15), and 'the disciple whom Jesus loved' (13:23) who was given the care of Jesus' mother (19:26-27), and who ran with Peter to the empty tomb and realized the significance of the grave clothes which remained as though the body of Jesus had risen through them (20:3-8). 'The disciple whom Jesus loved' was also present when Jesus appeared by the Sea of Tiberias, and on this occasion it is specifically said that the sons of Zebedee were there (21:2,7). In 21:20-24 it is implied that he would live to a considerable age.

In the Acts John was present in the Upper Room at Pentecost (Acts 1:13-14), and soon afterwards was arrested with Peter for provocative preaching of Jesus as Messiah, although both were released after trial (chapters 3 and 4). He and Peter were sent as the representatives of the Jerusalem church to acknowledge the Samaritans as full members of Christ by laying hands on them, thus opening the door for the Samaritan Pentecost (8:14-17). Some years later he and Peter and James (the Lord's brother) discussed with Paul about the special nature of ministry to the Gentiles, to which they themselves were not primarily called, although there was no difference in the gospel message (Galatians 2:7-10).

Nothing more is said in the Bible about John's movements, but there is a strong tradition that he lived and died at Ephesus. Both Polycrates, Bishop of Ephesus about AD 190, and Irenaeus about the same date, refer to his residence there.

As author, he is traditionally credited with the fourth Gospel, the three Epistles that bear his name, and Revelation. The total omission of John's name in the fourth Gospel is puzzling if the Gospel came from another hand, but understandable if John is indicating his presence while modestly refusing to name himself. Differences from the other Gospels are partly explained by John's deliberate supplementing of the first three Gospels with occasions of which he had special memory and knowledge. For example, he records events and talks when Jesus visited Jerusalem on several occasions, and it may be that John, who had links with Jerusalem and possibly a house there (John 18:15; 19:27), accompanied him alone.

One naturally contrasts the more mystical talks in the fourth Gospel with the more down-to-earth sayings in the Synoptics (the Gospels of Matthew, Mark and Luke). But since Christ was perfect Man and spoke for all mankind, it would be extraordinary if he did not speak at all levels of spiritual understanding. John had an ear for these talks, whereas Matthew and Peter did not at the time see the same significance in them. Today, even an imperfect Christian may be both an evangelist, a social reformer and a deep conference teacher, and attract a different type of audience on each occasion. Certainly the Gospel writer presents his subject as an eyewitness, and attention is called to this in John 20:30; 21:24. The title 'The disciple whom Jesus loved' may have been the name by which he was known at Ephesus, indicating that he was the last surviving member of the Twelve.

The three Epistles have the same style of writing as John had learnt from Jesus, and emphasize positive love and negative sin. The first again claims to be written by one who had close contact with Jesus on earth (1 John 1:1-3). The authorship of the Revelation (Revelation 1:1-2,9) is puzzling in view of the crudeness of its Greek. Yet there is very strong early tradition that the author was John the apostle. If so, we may suppose that John, whose native language was Aramaic, was a poor Greek speaker. This could have been one reason why he was led to a ministry among Jews rather than Greek-speaking Gentiles (Galatians 2:9). When he wrote his Gospel and Epistles, he would have employed a bilingual amanuensis, or secretary, who would have set down his words (whether Aramaic or rough Greek) in the elegant language that we now have. But on Patmos John had no amanuensis, and had to manage as best he could.

JONADAB. *Jehovah is bounteous*
Founder of an ascetic movement. Jehu thought it would be a good boost to his abolition of Baal worship if he could enlist Jonadab's support as being a good Jehovah man (2 Kings 10:15-17). He named his movement after his father Rechab, and decreed no wine, no agriculture, no houses, but only the simple life in tents, as a protest against the eroding luxury that had crept over the land (Jeremiah 35:7-10). When Nebuchadnezzar invaded the country, the contemporary Rechabite community felt it right to move into the city (35:11), but they refused Jeremiah's offer of wine (35:1-6). Jeremiah used this as God's object lesson. These men were loyal to the command of an earthly founder, whereas Judah paid little attention to the commands of God (35:12-19).

JONAH. *Dove*
Jonah lived in the reign of Jeroboam II (793-753 BC). His home was in Galilee. He foretold the restoration of some conquered Israelite territory (2 Kings 14:25). He is mainly known through the book that bears his name, whether or not he was the author. On being told by God to go to Nineveh, he abandoned his right to stand in the presence of God as a prophet (Jonah 1:3, compare 1 Kings 17:1), and took ship in the opposite direction. A disastrous storm threatened to sink the ship, and Jonah eventually induced the sailors to throw him into the sea to expiate his guilt. The

waves died down, and the Lord, for whom suicide was not the way out for disobedience, caused a great fish, or maybe a type of whale, to swallow the prophet (Jonah 1).

Now repentant, Jonah began to pray in snatches of Psalms that came to his mind, and the fish disgorged him near enough to the shore for him to scramble on to dry land (Jonah 2). Now Jonah obeyed, and went to Nineveh. He walked through the city and its extensive suburbs with a message of destruction for the wicked Assyrian capital within forty days. Prophets were universally respected, and the king and his people prayed to God for mercy and turned to him in repentance, with the result that Nineveh was spared (Jonah 3).

It now becomes clear why Jonah had been reluctant to go on God's mission. He would like to have seen Nineveh destroyed, but knew that God was a merciful God (Jonah 4:1-4). He sat half hopefully in a safe place, but God used a shady plant and a destructive grub to teach him a lesson. Jonah professed to be sorry for the poor plant for which he had no responsibility. Surely then God should care for those whom he had created (3:5-11). God's mercies extend to the Gentile world. But repentance did not last. Assyria became more and more brutal, and Nineveh was eventually destroyed in 612 BC.

The story is certainly full of moral and spiritual significance, but need not be only an allegory. Jesus spoke of it as though it was historically true, and said that the Ninevites would be vindicated at the judgment (Matthew 12:38ff). There are two modern accounts of men who have been swallowed by whales, and who have emerged alive. James Bartley in 1891 was swallowed one evening when his boat was upset, and next morning was found alive in the carcase of the whale[*]. The other case was an Arab who was swallowed by a killer whale in the Gulf

---

[*] Recent research has failed to verify the Bartley account, showing it to be almost certainly fabricated shortly after the alleged event. This does not challenge the scriptural story in any way. However, stories such as the one about James Bartley, which are still widely circulated, have not measured up to a standard of reliable evidence.

of Aqaba, and who escaped by cutting his way out with his knife. The second, less well known, has eyewitness testimony in the *Bible League Quarterly,* January 1959.

JONATHAN. *Jehovah has given*
A frequent name in the Old Testament, sometimes as the equivalent of **Johanan** (e.g. Nehemiah 12:11,22). The best known is Saul's son. By a clever feat of mountaineering, Jonathan and his armour bearer successfully attacked a Philistine outpost (1 Samuel 14:1-23), but Jonathan inadvertently broke a rather foolish taboo that Saul had placed on touching any food during the battle that followed. Only popular outcry prevented Saul from putting him to death (1 Samuel 14:24-46).

After David had killed Goliath, he and Jonathan made a compact of healthy friendship (1 Samuel 18:1-4, compare 20:17) as a result of which Jonathan acted as a buffer between David and Saul's crazy anger (19:1-7; 20:1-42) even though he realized that the Lord had chosen David and not himself to be Saul's successor (20:14-16,31). Jonathan and his brothers fell in battle when their father also died at the hands of the Philistines on Mount Gilboa (31:2). David's lament for Saul and Jonathan is a classic (2 Samuel 1:17-27).

JORAM.
See **Jehoram**.

JOSEPH[OT/NT]. *May He (God) add*
1. Joseph[OT], son of Jacob. At last, Rachel, the wife whom Jacob really loved, had a son, and in the hope of yet another, she gave him this name (Genesis 30:22-24). She did have one more, Benjamin. Joseph is in the centre of the picture in chapter 37 to 50. He incurred the jealousy of his brothers through his father favouring him (37:2-4) and through his tale-bearing (37:2), and dreams in which he foresaw the whole family bowing down to him (37:5-11; from verse 10 we gather that Benjamin was not yet born, since Rachel died in giving him birth 35:16-20).

Joseph's brothers saw an opportunity of getting rid of him, first by leaving him to die in a deep pit, and then by selling him as a slave (Genesis 37:12-36). (See **Reuben**). He was sold in Egypt to Potiphar, the captain of Pharaoh's guard, who soon came to trust him absolutely with the administration of his household (39:1-6). Potiphar's wife did her best to seduce him, but Joseph's moral resistance had not been sapped by contemporary literature and drama, and he refused her. She then falsely accused Joseph, and his master had him committed to the royal prison, where again his responsible behaviour led the prison governor to appoint him warder (39:6-23).

Joseph won the confidence of the prisoners, so that two of them, Pharaoh's butler and baker, asked him about their dreams. Joseph interpreted them as precognitive, and his interpretation proved true (Genesis 40:1-23). When Pharaoh two years later had what seemed to him to be a significant dream, the butler remembered Joseph. Pharaoh summoned him from the prison, and Joseph interpreted the dream as foretelling seven years of plentiful crops to be followed by seven years of failure of the harvest. He added the advice to appoint a Minister of Food to be responsible for storing all the spare grain each year. Pharaoh surprisingly chose Joseph, and gave him his own signet ring of authority.

Pharaoh gave Joseph the additional name of Zaphenath-paneah. This name has puzzled commentators, since it is difficult to know how far the present Hebrew letters represent Egyptian equivalents. One suggestion is that it means, 'The one who supplies the sustenance of the land'. Another suggestion is '(Joseph) who is called Ip-ankh', this being a common Egyptian name. Pharaoh also married him to Asenath, daughter of the priest of the sun god at On, or Heliopolis. Asenath would naturally accept her husband's faith, and she bore two children, Ephraim and Manasseh (Genesis 41:1-52).

Joseph built vast storehouses, and Egypt held a monopoly of wheat when the years of famine came. Joseph's brothers were among buyers from neighbouring countries, and Joseph turned the tables on them by a series of frightening practical jokes (Genesis 42 to 44), which nearly killed his old father (42:36-38; 43:13-14). But all ended happily, with Jacob and his sons joining Joseph in Egypt and being well received by Pharaoh, who settled them in the land of Goshen, the north -eastern section of the Nile delta. Meanwhile Joseph drove hard bargains on Pharaoh's behalf with the Egyptians who became desperate for corn as the famine continued (47:13-26).

On his deathbed, Jacob blessed Joseph's two sons, Manasseh and Ephraim, giving the elder's blessing to the younger son, Ephraim (Genesis 48). Joseph arranged for his father to be embalmed, and probably mummified, and taken back to Canaan for burial in the family vault (47:29-31; 50:1-14). His brothers now feared reprisals, and faked a message said to have been given by Jacob before his death. But Joseph was too big a man for petty revenge (50:15-21). On his death, Joseph also was embalmed. Much though he might have wished to be taken to Canaan for burial there and then, he charged the Israelites by an act of faith (Hebrews 11:22) to take his body with them when God should bring them back to the land (Genesis 50:24-26). This they did (Exodus 13:19) and Joseph was buried at Shechem in a patch of land that his father had bought (Joshua 24:32).

NB: Genesis 44:5. There is no evidence that Joseph used his cup for divination. The excited steward wanted to impress the brothers that his master had his ways of supernormal knowledge.

2. Joseph[NT], husband of the Virgin Mary. A carpenter of Nazareth (Matthew 13:55; Luke 2:4). He was of Davidic descent, so went to Bethlehem, David's city, for the census (Luke 2:1-5). Joseph was engaged to Mary, but the couple had not yet celebrated their wedding (Matthew 1:18). When he found that his fiancée was to have a baby, Joseph was profoundly shocked. A Jewish engagement was almost as binding as a marriage, and Mary could have been branded as a bad woman if she had been formally put away. Joseph, however, was sufficiently in love with her to arrange things quietly. Before matters reached the point of no return, God intervened in a vision to confirm Mary's story

J Stafford Wright

that she was indeed a virgin, and miraculously to be the mother of the long-promised Messiah, Emmanuel, 'God with us', who would save his people from their real enemies, the sins that pulled them down (Matthew 1:18-24). The twofold attestation of the virgin birth from two independent sources is a very powerful testimony to its actual occurrence.

After the birth of Jesus, the family remained for a time in Bethlehem. The implication of Matthew 2:11 is that when the wise men came, he and the family had moved into a private house; and since Herod selected two years and under as the age for the massacre of the babies in Bethlehem, Jesus may then have been at least eighteen months old. Joseph took the family to Egypt for perhaps two or three years (Matthew 2:13-23). By this time Jesus would have been old enough to be accepted as a true son of the marriage by friends and neighbours in Nazareth, without so much fear of scandal.

Matthew 1:25 implies that Joseph and Mary had other children after Jesus, and this is borne out by mention of the brothers and sisters of Jesus (13:55-56). It is a false idea of sex in marriage to suppose that these must be children of Joseph by a former marriage. Since Jesus on the cross commended his mother to John (John 19:26-27), we assume that Joseph had died before this. It is probable that his brothers were not yet believers (7:5), though James was at least on the verge of believing. (See **James**).

Both the genealogies in Matthew 1 and Luke 3:23-38 trace the descent of Jesus through Joseph. Joseph, of course, was legally the head of the family, but if both genealogies are his there would be no literal and physical descent of Jesus from David, which the Old Testament leads us to look for. Hence, we assume that one of the genealogies is that of Mary, although a woman was not usually reckoned in the line of descent. Because of this, the genealogy has to be taken up by Joseph, and it is probable that Luke, who writes from Mary's point of view, has given us what is essentially her line from David.

We know that Mary had a sister (John 19:25), but there is no evidence of a brother. According to the regulations in Numbers 27:1-11; 36:1-9, when only daughters survived, their possessions and family name needed a male relative to carry them on. Joseph was himself of the line of David, and could have been a distant relative of Mary. In marrying her, he became the son of her father, Heli (Luke 3:23). There are other suggestions, but this is a simple solution.

3. Joseph of Arimathea[NT], an unidentified place, but probably not far from Jerusalem. A wealthy MP (Matthew 27:57), who had refused to vote for the arrest of Jesus (Luke 23:50-51). He was in fact a secret disciple of Jesus, though we do not know whether he had any opportunity to talk with Jesus, as his friend Nicodemus had (John 19:38). After the crucifixion, Jesus would normally have been buried in a common criminals' grave, but Joseph secured his body for burial in a tomb which he owned (Matthew 27:60) thus fulfilling both parts of the prophecy about the Messiah's burial in Isaiah 53:9. 'They made his grave with the wicked and with a rich man in his death.'

The tradition that Joseph established the Christian church in Glastonbury in Somerset is not traceable earlier than about AD 1200, but it is strange that a famous old abbey should claim as its founder such a nonentity as Joseph rather than one of the apostles.

JOSHUA. *Jehovah is salvation*
1. Joshua, son of Nun, an Ephraimite. He was renamed Joshua from the simple Hoshea, 'Salvation' (Numbers 13:8,16). Moses appointed him as leader in the battle against Amalek, soon after coming out of Egypt (Exodus 17:8-15), but normally he was the personal servant of Moses, going with him at least part of the way up Mount Sinai (Exodus 24:13; 32:17), and looking after Moses' tent which was the centre of God's manifestation before the tabernacle was made (33:7-11). He was jealous for Moses' position when Eldad and Medad spontaneously received the Spirit directly and not through Moses as intermediary (Numbers 11:26-30). He was one of the party sent to spy out the land of

Canaan, but only he and Caleb refused to be discouraged by the difficulties ahead, Caleb being the spokesman on their return (Numbers 13:1-33; 14:38). These two survived the forty years of wandering. Ultimately Moses was told to appoint Joshua as his successor (Numbers 27:18-22; Deuteronomy 3:28). Joshua was humble enough to doubt his ability for the task, and needed to be encouraged both by Moses (Deuteronomy 31:7-8) and by God (Joshua 1:6-7,9) to be of good courage.

The book of Joshua records his invasion of Palestine. He first took Jericho, with the aid of an earthquake that dammed the Jordan, as has happened again in modern times (Joshua 3; 4), and in a second shock later threw down the wall of the city, the miracle being in God's use of natural forces at the right time (Joshua 6). A setback, due to Achan's sin, was followed by further victories (Joshua 7 and 8). In a series of strikes, Joshua defeated concentrations of Canaanites in every area of the land (Joshua 9-12), but the people did not at this stage occupy any of the conquered territory. This meant that a number of the cities were reoccupied by the Canaanites, and needed to be retaken when the land was divided among the tribes, as described in Joshua 13 to 22. Before his death, Joshua gave a powerful harangue to the leaders of the tribes assembled at Shechem, with as many of the ordinary folks as could come (Joshua 23 and 24).

Joshua's Long Day, described in Joshua 10:12-14, has no obvious explanation. Some have held that the near approach of some heavenly body put a brake on the rotation of the earth. If the 'great stones' of verse 11 were a shower of meteorites, meteoric dust in the stratosphere could have prolonged the daylight considerably by refraction, as happened in Europe in June 1908, after a heavy shower of meteorites in Siberia[*].

---

[*] In his book *Christians and the Supernatural* (White Tree Publishing 2011), the author points out that after the explosion of what is believed to be a huge meteorite in Siberia in June 1908, it was noticed that the refraction from the residual meteorite dust led to an extension of daylight in Europe. The Edinburgh Observatory at the time described the night as 'practically daylight, while in the north of England men are reported to have worked in the fields all night, getting in the hay'. (*Popular Astronomy*, Vol. 41, November 1933, page 477)

A very different interpretation ties up with the storm of Joshua 10:11, and with the literal meaning of the word translated 'stand still' in the first two occurrences in verses 12 and 13. The word means 'be silent', and would be more appropriate to a blazing sun whose heat was exhausting the Israelites. Hence Joshua commands the sun and moon to cloud over, and the storm was God's answer. The sun was blotted out, and did not drop below the clouds for the rest of the day. The significance of verse 14 is that Joshua spontaneously commanded the sun without any word from God; yet the Lord responded.

2. Joshua son of Josedech or Jozadak, also called Jeshua. He and Zerubbabel were the effective leaders of the return from exile under Sheshbazzar, and set out to erect an altar and rebuild the ruined temple in 536 BC (Ezra 3). Owing to opposition, little was done until 520, when Haggai and Zechariah stimulated a revival, and the work was completed in four years (Ezra 5 and 6). Some of the prophecies of Haggai and Zechariah survive, and Zechariah's references are particularly significant. It is clear that there are points in common between building a material temple and building the church as the living temple, as in Ephesians.

Priest (Joshua) and governor (Zerubbabel) work together, and in one place Joshua is crowned as symbolizing the Messianic Branch whose coming had been foretold in Jeremiah 23:5; 33:15 (where the same word is used), and in Isaiah 11:1 (where another word has the same meaning). Whatever may be the exact translation, the general meaning is that priest and king are to be as one (Zechariah 6:9-14), and Jesus Christ is both.

In Zechariah 3:1-5, Zechariah has a vision of Joshua accused by Satan before the court of God. Perhaps he represents the nation. Satan loses his case, and Joshua has his filthy clothes changed for clean high priestly garments. In 3:6-10 he is seen as picturing the Messianic Branch, who with his fellow priests has full access to God. The mysterious stone of verse 9 could be some jewel, but may well be the key foundation stone of the temple (compare 4:9). The reference to the removal of guilt in one day could have a fuller meaning in the light of the once-for-all death of the Branch upon the cross (compare 12:10; 13:1).

JOSIAH. *Jehovah supports him*

When his father Amon was murdered, Josiah, then eight years old, was crowned king (639-609 BC). He was converted at sixteen, and after two years of development he began a thoroughgoing destruction of the idolatry that was characteristic of so much of the nation (2 Chronicles 34:1-7). Six years later he turned his attention to necessary repairs to the temple. These were extensive, and unexpectedly brought to light a copy of the Pentateuch – the first five books of the Old Testament (2 Kings 22:1-10).

It is probable that such written copies as had been in the hands of the priests and the king, perhaps not more than two or three, had been destroyed by Manasseh (2 Kings 21), but this copy had probably been concealed in the temple by a priest who was martyred before he could pass on his secret. Or it may have been a copy that was buried in the foundations when the temple was originally built.

There is no need at all to suppose, as some do, that the book was a recently written forgery of what we now know as Deuteronomy, although the section of the book that was read aloud to Josiah may well have been Deuteronomy, since this was the popular summary of the law that had to be read periodically to the people (Deuteronomy 31:9-13), and copied out by the king (17:18-20).

The warnings in the book made Josiah realize how far the nation had fallen under his grandfather Manasseh, but the prophetess Huldah assured him that his repentance and his reform of the faith had for the time being averted the judgment, which might yet come if his successors again brought the nation down (2 Kings 22:11-20).

Josiah's next act was to collect the people to renew the covenant that had been made in the time of Moses (2 Kings 23:1-3) and to keep the Passover unitedly in Jerusalem (23:21-23). Although the popular idea is that all the northern kingdom had been taken into captivity (chapter 17), Josiah's reformation extended there (2 Kings 23:19-20; 2 Chronicles 34:33) and Israelites as well as the men of Judah joined in the united Passover (2 Chronicles 35:17-18).

In reading the account in 2 Kings 23, it is probable that verses 4-20 are in the nature of a parenthesis, summing up all the destructive side of Josiah's reforms before and after the covenant, thus including all that he had done ten years earlier (2 Chronicles 34:3-7).

Sadly enough, the people were only carried on the crest of emotion, and the book of Jeremiah shows how superficial the reformation was, although Jeremiah has the highest opinion of the king himself (Jeremiah 22:15-16).

The death of Josiah in a battle with Egypt at Megiddo is a puzzling feature. Why did Josiah oppose Pharaoh Necho II as he marched through to help the Assyrians against the Babylonians and Medes (2 Kings 23:28-29)? Perhaps Josiah feared being brought under Egyptian domination, as in fact happened to the country after his death. We learn from 2 Chronicles 35:21-22 that even advice from a potential enemy may be the message of God for us, and must be tested by common sense. Josiah's death was a tragedy, and Jeremiah and others kept his memory green (35:25).

JOTHAM. *Jehovah is perfect*
1. A son of Gideon, who alone escaped when his illegitimate half-brother, Abimelech, murdered the rest of Gideon's sons. When Abimelech proclaimed himself king, Jotham in the manner of a town crier shouted a rude parable about a bramble bush that wanted to be boss of all the trees. He then ran for his life before Abimelech could catch him (Judges 9:1-21). (See **Abimelech**.)

2. King of Judah, who first acted as regent during Uzziah's illness c. 750 BC (2 Kings 15:5). He was a good man, although he did not abolish those high places where Jehovah, not Baal, was worshipped (see **Jehoshaphat**). He built a new gate for the temple court, and fortresses in various parts of the land. He also made the Ammonites tributary (2 Kings 15:35; 2 Chronicles 27). His name occurs for dating purposes at the beginning of Isaiah, Hosea and Micah, but we do not know which prophecies belong to his reign.

JUBAL

A son of Lamech, who discovered the art of music on strings and wind instruments. Occasional simple bone whistles, and perhaps elementary pipes, have been found from the Upper Palaeolithic (Late Stone Age) period, say 30,000-10,000 BC, but we cannot say whether these were used for 'serious' music. Some have interpreted a picture dated to approximately 13,000 BC in Les Trois Frères cave in south west France as a man playing a pipe or twanging a curved bow, but since he is chasing two bison it is more likely that he is in fact preparing his bow to shoot.

JUDAH. *Praise*

Leah's fourth son (Genesis 29:35). In the story of Joseph, it is Judah who trades him to the Midianites to take as a slave to Egypt (37:26-27), and later he takes the lead when he and his brothers come to Egypt for corn (43:8; 44:14-34; 46:28). Earlier he had married a Canaanite girl named Shua, after an affair with another girl (38:1-2). The rather sordid story of his family told in Genesis 38 ends with Judah having twins by his daughter-in-law, Tamar, after she had offered herself to him in disguise as a prostitute, knowing his weakness for women. Significantly, this would have been at about the same time as Joseph in Egypt resisted the advances of Potiphar's wife (39:6-18).

Yet the ways of God are strange. One of the twins, Perez, is in the genealogy of Jesus (Matthew 1:3), and when Jacob blesses his sons, Judah is given the sceptre 'until he comes to whom it belongs' (Genesis 49:10; the NEB translation here is less likely). The tribe of Judah produced the line of David, and, as Jews, absorbed the other tribes in Palestine, and also the Philistines, Edomites and many of the Canaanites.

JUDAS^{NT}. *Praised*
See also **Jude**.
The name of a brother of Jesus (Matthew 13:55), also of one of the Twelve, son or brother of James (presumably the same as Lebbaeus [Matthew 10:3] or Thaddeaus [Mark 3:18]), who asked a question at the Last Supper (John 14:22). Also the name of a Galilean insurrectionist (Acts 5:37), mentioned by Josephus as making a disturbance in AD 6; also Judas Barsabbas, a prophet, carried the letter of the Jerusalem Council to the Gentile Christians (Acts 15:22-33).

The best-known Judas is Iscariot. The name Iscariot was also borne by his father (John 6:71), and probably indicates their home town, meaning 'Man of Kerioth'. One Kerioth was near Hebron (Joshua 15:25), another in former Moabite territory (Jeremiah 48:24; Amos 2:2). Some connect Iscariot with the Latin and Greek for *assassin,* and suppose that Judas was, or had been, a member of a nationalist gang of violent men, or Zealots, such as we also know only too well today (Acts 21:38).

It is one of the mysteries of the Bible why Jesus chose Judas as an apostle (Mark 3:19), knowing that in the end he would betray him (John 6:64). One may surmise that, since Jesus Christ came to live a fully human life, he deliberately chose involvement in the nastiness, as well as the pleasantness, of human relationships. Any public figure is liable to be dogged by a Judas. We need not suppose that in the end Judas was compelled by God like a puppet to betray Jesus, although it is certain that some close friend would have turned against Jesus, as so often happens with a perfectly good man (John 13:18). Having gone so far, Judas found it impossible to turn back. When at supper he spurned the final appeal of Jesus, he unwittingly opened himself to Satanic possession (John 13:21-27).

In modern times there has been much speculation about Judas' motives. His action has been justified by supposing that he wanted to force Jesus to set himself up as King, which presumably he would do rather than throw his life away on the cross. But it emerged afterwards that Judas was money-minded, and helped himself to cash from the common purse (John 12:6). The bribe of 30 shekels, the value of a slave (Exodus 21:32), and about the amount a working man would earn in four months, was too tempting for him (Matthew 26:14-16). He arranged the arrest of Jesus at a place and time that would give the minimum publicity. In the semi-darkness it was important that the right man should be arrested, and Judas identified him with a kiss (Matthew 26:47-50).

We must bring together Matthew 27:3-10 and Acts 1:18-19 for the account of his death, and may surmise as follows: Judas had negotiated with a potter to buy one of his fields with the blood money, but when he realized the enormity of his deed he flung back the money to the authorities, and hanged himself from a tree in the field that would shortly have been his. By the time the Passover was over, his body had begun to decay and fell to the ground with sufficient force to release its intestines over the grass. (NB: Luke, the doctor who recorded Acts 1:18 knew perfectly well that bowels do not 'gush out' in an ordinary fall.)

The potter complained to the authorities that his field would now be unsalable, so they wisely settled his claim by buying the land themselves as a cemetery for foreigners. A gentleman would refer to it as the Field of Blood (money) (Matthew 27:8), but ordinary folk spoke of it as the Bloody Field for more obvious reasons (Acts 1:19). The ascription in Matthew 27:9 of Zechariah 11:12-13 to Jeremiah may not be as difficult as it sounds. In making his quotations, Matthew sometimes names the prophet and sometimes merely says, 'spoken by the prophet'. In this case he probably wrote the latter, but a smart copyist, remembering Jeremiah's experience with a potter (Jeremiah 18), showed off his knowledge, which was unfortunately wrong.

JUDE[NT]
His name is a variant of Judas. The writer of the epistle of Jude calls himself 'brother of James'. He could be 'Judas of James' (Luke 6:16) if this means 'brother of James' rather than the more likely 'son of James'. But more likely the writer of the epistle of

Jude, like the James who also wrote an epistle, was the brother of Jesus (Matthew 13:55). Although Jude blasts a degrading heresy, he concludes with verses that are often quoted as an encouragement to Christians (Jude 20-25). He and Peter probably gathered information about this particular heresy from the same source, since there are similarities between Jude and 2 Peter. Writers on heresies today commonly gather information from others who have made a special study of the heresy in question.

JULIUS[NT]
Commander of an auxiliary force known as the Augustan Cohort. On technical grounds it is thought that Julius received his Roman citizenship for services rendered. Appointed to escort Paul and other prisoners to Rome by boat (Acts 27:1-2), he naturally preferred the advice of the captain to advice that Paul gave (27:9-11). But he summed up Paul's character sufficiently well to allow him to visit his friends when the ship called at Sidon (27:3), and to co-operate with him when his keen observation and common sense saved everyone's life at the time of the shipwreck (27:30-32, 42-44).

KETURAH. *Perfumed*
Abraham's wife after the death of Sarah (Genesis 25:1). In 1 Chronicles 1:32 she is called his concubine, and it may be that Genesis also means that she did not have the status of a proper wife, since 1 Chronicles 25:6 refers to 'the sons of his concubines', obviously meaning the sons of Hagar and Keturah. A concubine had her own status, and the relationship was not adultery or fornication.

KORAH. Perhaps, *Baldness*
The ringleader in a revolt against the authority of Moses and Aaron (Numbers 16). As a descendant of Kohath, he already had important duties in connection with the tabernacle (4:37; 7:9). His fellow conspirators, **Dathan** and **Abiram**, showed less

enthusiasm (16:12-14), but others accepted the test that Moses proposed, and Korah mobilized a crowd of 250 to come to the tabernacle with censers in their hands and offer incense as though they were priests. But a sudden blaze from the shekinah glory destroyed them, while an earthquake split the ground round the tents of Dathan and Abiram (see Abiram) NB: Jude 11.

It is good to find that Korah's descendants became singers and musicians when David settled the ark of the covenant in Jerusalem (1 Chronicles 6:31-38). Although some think that these were descended from another Korah, both Numbers 16:1 and 6:37-38 speak of Izhar as the father. The sons of Korah appear in the titles of Psalms 42, 44-49, 84-85, 87-88, probably as authors.

LABAN. *White*
Son of Bethuel, who was Abraham's nephew (Genesis 22:20-23). His branch of the family had remained at Haran, in the Padan-aram district of northern Mesopotamia, when Abraham moved into Canaan. Abraham sent his servant back there to find a wife for Isaac (Genesis 24), and Bethuel and Laban allowed Rebekah to return with him (24:50-51).

Laban next appears when Jacob arrived, also looking for a wife (Genesis 28:1-5). For the account of their fascinating attempts to trick one another, see **Jacob**.

LAHMI
Brother of Goliath (1 Chronicles 20:5). See **Elhanan**.

LAMECH. Possibly, *Strong young man*
1. A descendant of Cain (Genesis 4:18-24), who had two wives, Adah and Zillah, and three brilliant sons (see **Jabal**, **Jubal**, **Tubal-Cain**). His words to his wives (verses 23-24) are most naturally interpreted of his having to kill a young man in self-defence. If Cain was protected by God in spite of the deliberate murder of his brother (4:15), how much more Lamech who had killed in self-protection.

2. Although the first Lamech was the son of Methushael (Genesis 4:18) and the second the son of Methuselah (5:25-31), the resemblance of the fathers' names is probably coincidental, and does not mean that there has been some confusion in the genealogies. The second Lamech was descended from Seth, not Cain. Having experienced the hard struggle that God had decreed for agriculture after the Fall (3:17-19), he names his son Noah *(Rest* or *Relief)* in anticipation that he will make things easier for his old father, who was at that time 182, and had many years ahead of him, if we take the genealogies at their apparent face value (see discussion under **Methuselah**).

LAZARUS[NT]. Greek equivalent of Eleazar, *God is helper*
Brother of Martha and Mary, whose home was in Bethany. John 11 gives the dramatic account of how Jesus raised him from the dead after three or four days in the grave. The details bear all the marks of an eyewitness who was with Jesus when the sisters sent for him. Others also were present (12:17). The emotions roused by the event made the authorities think seriously of putting Lazarus to death again (12:9-11).

The reason why the story is not related by the other Gospels may be that Lazarus was still alive, and they did not want him to be plagued by visitors and interviewers trying to find out what it was like after death. When John wrote later, Lazarus would be dead. Browning's remarkable speculative poem, *An Epistle of Karshish* (from his *Men and Women),* is a doctor's puzzled description of how he met Lazarus in his travels.

It is impossible to suggest why the beggar in the story in Luke 16:19-31 has the name of Lazarus. Because of this second man, from the 14th century the term Lazar came to be used of a leper or other person with plague or skin disease, and a lazar house was set apart as a place of quarantine.

LEAH
Laban's elder daughter, less good-looking than her sister Rachel.

Laban managed to marry her off to Jacob by a trick, when he thought he was marrying Rachel (Genesis 29:15-28). In the end, Jacob had both sisters, but it cannot have been very pleasant for Leah. God, however, gave her the only sort of compensation open to her, and she produced four sons before Rachel became a mother at all (29:31-35). Now it was Rachel's turn to feel inferior, but the best she could do was to let Jacob give her children through her personal maid, Bilhah.

When Bilhah had had two sons, Leah once more joined in the mad race for children, and her maid Zilpah gave Jacob two more sons. Then Leah tried a love potion and became the mother of two more sons and a daughter. Only then did Rachel become the mother of Joseph, and in spite of all Leah's efforts, Joseph became Jacob's favourite son (Genesis 30:1-24). For marriage customs, see **Asher**. Leah returned with Jacob and Rachel and all the children to Canaan. Nothing more is known about her. But she did have the last word over her sister. She lies side by side with Jacob (49:31), while Rachel has a grave on her own (35:19-20).

LEBBAEUS[NT]

His name occurs in some manuscripts of Matthew 10:3 as a second name for Thaddaeus. (See **Judas**)

LEMUEL. *Devoted to God*

A king of Massa, probably in North Arabia. In Proverbs 31 he relates what his mother had told him about wine, women and the underdog. Rabbinic tradition identified Lemuel with Solomon, and indeed there was an idea that Bathsheba composed Proverbs 31:10-31 as a wedding present for him. But the identification is unlikely, compare 30:1. One can hardly imagine the princess of Egypt (1 Kings 3:1) making Solomon's shirts (Proverbs 31:13,19) and getting up early for bargains in the supermarket (verse 15).

Since verses 10-31 are in the form of an acrostic poem, they may not be Lemuel's words, but a separate contribution to the book, praising the ideal housewife. Curates and young ministers used it in the past at Mothers' Meetings to the indignation of the members!

LEVI. *Joined*
Leah's sad hope of winning Jacob's love by bearing him sons (see **Leah**) is shown by the name she gave to Levi, feeling that after this third baby Jacob would be joined to her. He grew up to be one of the least pleasant of the sons. He and his brother Simeon, no doubt with the help of their servants, made a vicious attack on the men of Shechem, after persuading them to be circumcised in good faith. They killed them all and plundered the city. This was in revenge for the rape of their sister Dinah by the son of the king, even though he immediately asked to marry her (Genesis 34).

Unlike Reuben and Judah, Levi made no attempt to save Joseph's life in Genesis 37. It seems from Jacob's summing up of their character in 49:5-7 that Levi and Simeon engaged in brutalities on other occasions also. Jacob's prediction that God would divide and scatter their descendants among the tribes was fulfilled when the Levites were given cities up and down the land (Joshua 21). It is strange that their savage ancestor fathered a peaceful line who supplied priests, temple attendants and teachers. This was after they had struck one more fierce blow, this time as the executioners of the men who had gone back on all that the Lord had shown them, and had flung themselves into the orgies of the golden calf (Exodus 32:25-29).

For the New Testament Levi, see **Matthew**.

LINUS[NT]
One of Paul's associates during his imprisonment in Rome (2 Timothy 4:21). Irenaeus (c. AD 180) says that Linus was given the oversight of the church in Rome by Peter and Paul. For a possible link with Britain see **Pudens**, who is here mentioned with him.

LOT. Perhaps, *Covering*
Nephew of Abraham (Genesis 11:27-29), who first moved from Ur to Haran with his grandfather, and then came with Abraham

into Canaan (11:31-32). It seems that he was already a man of some wealth (12:5), and he and Abraham accumulated more in the new land. In the end their herdsmen were continually falling out over pasture for their owners' cattle, so Abraham and Lot agreed to separate (13:6-7). Abraham gave Lot the choice of territory, and Lot picked the Jordan valley as being the best (13:8-12).

Little by little Lot grew tired of the simple life, and whereas in Genesis 13:12 he was still happy to live in a tent, we next find him in a house in Sodom (14:12; 19:3). He had a narrow escape when he and his property were captured in a sudden invasion by a northern army, and it was not until he had marched with the other prisoners for over 150 miles that Abraham, with 318 members of his household, caught up with them and rescued Lot and the others. Lot was perhaps surprised that his uncle refused to accept any reward from the king of Sodom (14:1-24), but he himself had his own possessions back, and settled down comfortably in Sodom once more.

Sodom was a place of bad reputation (Genesis 13:13; 18:20-33), and, although Lot tried to keep up standards, he carried no weight when he tried to protect the two angels whom God sent disguised as men to warn him of what was to happen to the city (19:1-9). Angels or no angels, Lot was not sure whether to believe them, unlike his uncle Abraham who had agonized in prayer over the coming fate of the city (18:22-33).

Lot was not helped by the fiancés of his two daughters, who treated him as a silly old man when he tried to get them to leave the city with him (Genesis 19:14). While he was still in two minds, the angels seized him and his family by the hand and hurried them out of the city, urging them to escape to the hills. But Lot had lost his taste for the country, and begged successfully to be allowed to take refuge in the small town of Zoar. Only his wife kept stopping to look back on all the attractions of Sodom, and she was still far behind when Lot and their daughters reached Zoar. Then a sudden earthquake released underground gas which caught fire and hurled clouds of chemical dust into the air. As Lot's wife looked back the clouds swept down on her, and in death she was covered from head to foot with deposits that hardened round her. Lot watched with equal horror from the safety of Zoar, which God had placed outside the circle of destruction (19:15-29).

Now this man, who had always enjoyed the luxuries of life, suffered a strange psychological reaction. He became jumpy in case Zoar should suffer a like fate, dragged his daughters up into the hills and settled down with them in a cave. The repressed sense of guilt that had once led him to offer his daughters to the men of Sodom (Genesis 19:8), and the hidden resentment against their fiancés who had humiliated him (19:14), were perhaps the factors that made him isolate the girls from all social contacts (19:31). But the girls, who had absorbed the moral standards of Sodom, made their father drunk and induced him to father two more children by each of them in turn. The children were Moab and Ben-ammi *(son of my people)* and their descendants headed Moab and Ammon, two nations that were a sad trouble to the Israelites later (19:30-38).

Jesus Christ used the story of Lot and his wife and Sodom as a warning to be ready for his Second Coming in judgment (Luke 17:28-32).

Although this summary of Lot's behaviour and character arises naturally from the Genesis account, we must not forget the reminder in 2 Peter 2:7-8 that he did try to keep up his standards, and Abraham's prayer in Genesis 18:22-33 undoubtedly assumed that Lot and his family would be among the few righteous people in Sodom. But even so, the picture in 2 Peter 2:7-8 is a somewhat pathetic one of a man who opened his local paper each morning, read out the fresh scandals to his wife, said 'Dear me, what times we live in!' and went on with his breakfast. He made no impression on his neighbours (Genesis 19:9), and might as well have gone elsewhere.

The site of Sodom is unknown as yet. Traditionally it was just south of the Dead Sea, but it might have been in the flooded area to the north. Four cities are mentioned as being destroyed at this time, Sodom, Gomorrah, Admah and Zeboiim (Deuteronomy 29:23; Hosea 11:8). Zoar, a small village, was just outside the affected area (Genesis 19:20-23). Doubtless all these places had similar moral standards, but Sodom and Gomorrah are repeatedly quoted in the Old Testament as examples of degradation and as warnings of judgment (e.g. Isaiah 1:9-10; Jeremiah 23:14).

Sodom has special mention for the high standard of living demanded by its upper classes to the detriment of the poor (Ezekiel 16:49), but this reference is set in a passage that speaks of its sexual abominations also, and these, particularly practising homosexuality, come out in Genesis 19:1-11. (For the 'blindness' in Genesis 19:11, see **Elisha**.) In Revelation 11:8 the names of Sodom and Egypt are given allegorically to the Jerusalem that crucified Jesus Christ.

LUKE[NT]

There is no reason to doubt the uniform tradition that Luke wrote the Gospel that bears his name, and also Acts. The second is a deliberate continuation of the first, as is shown by the opening dedication to the unknown Theophilus. Luke had every opportunity to obtain first-hand and second-hand information (Luke 1:1-4), since it is clear from Acts that he travelled extensively with Paul, and must have met all the main characters who figure in the Gospel story.

We can follow some of Luke's travels by noting the passages in Acts where he writes in the first person plural (16:10-16; 20:5-15; 21:1-18; 27:1–28:16), but it is obvious that in the sections in between, Luke must often have been with Paul. In Colossians 4:14 he uses Paul's letter to send greetings from Rome and is referred to as 'the beloved physician'. In Philemon 24 Luke is one of Paul's 'fellow workers', and in 2 Timothy 4:11 he is Paul's sole companion. He often uses the precise medical terminology of the day, and his Greek style is excellent. It is significant that God chose a medical man to write in detail about the virgin birth of Jesus Christ. He had plenty of opportunity to meet Mary while

Paul was in prison in Caesarea (Acts 24:27).

In writing his Gospel, Luke goes as near as makes no difference to claiming absolute accuracy as the result of his careful interviews with those who were eyewitnesses of the events (1:1-4). He clearly made use of Mark's Gospel and probably of a collection of Christ's teachings, referred to as Q, which may have been compiled by Matthew (see **Matthew**). There are, however, a number of sayings and parables that occur in Luke's Gospel alone. Luke presents Jesus Christ as the Redeemer and Saviour of people of all kinds.

There is no evidence for the suggestion that Luke was one of the Seventy (Luke 10:1), or one of the two who walked to Emmaus (24:13), or one of the Greeks who came to Jesus (John 12:20). Nor is his name in Greek, *Loukas,* an equivalent of *Lucius* (Acts 13:1).

LYDIA[NT]

Paul's first convert when he crossed from Asia to Europe (Acts 16:14). Lydia was already a Jewish proselyte. Although she was a native of Thyatira in Asia Minor, she had settled in Philippi as a trader in purple cloth. She had her own household servants, and was probably a well-to-do widow. She welcomed Paul, Silas and Luke into her house (16:15).

Purple dye was an expensive commodity, coming chiefly from the coast around Tyre. It was extracted from the shellfish *murex*. The shells were smashed and the fish were put in vats. As they putrefied, they produced a yellowish liquid which was diluted in varying degrees for the required shades, varying from rose colour to dark violet. Exposure to the sun produced darker tones. It is interesting to find that Canaan got its name from a Mesopotamian Semitic word *kinahhu,* meaning *purple,* so means Land of the Purple. Similarly Phoenicia is named from the Greek *phoinix,* which also means *purple.*

Some think that Lydia is not intended as a proper name, but that since this woman came from the borders of the kingdom of Lydia, Luke refers to her as 'a Lydian woman'. One can then go on to surmise that she was either Euodia or Syntyche of Philippians 4:2. But Luke refers to her literally as 'a woman by name Lydia', and Lydia was a reasonably common name.

LYSANIAS[NT]
Tetrarch of Abilene, about eighteen miles [29 km] north-west of Damascus, when John the Baptist began to preach (Luke 3:2). Although literally *Tetrarch* should mean *Ruler of a fourth part,* it was applied to the person in charge of any small territory. An earlier Lysanias was in charge of the area in 40-36 BC, but an inscription on a temple between AD 14 and AD 30 refers to its dedication by a freedman of Lysanias the tetrarch. Lysanias was presumably a Roman or a Greek.

LYSIAS[NT]
See **Claudius**.

MAACAH, Maachah. *Oppression*
The name of some ten people, the curious thing being that some are male and some female. None is of sufficient importance to have special treatment here. Similarly there are some twenty men named **Maaseiah**, *Work of Jehovah,* and again we have insufficient information about them for an article. We may wonder why God included names of this kind in the Bible. One answer is that the Bible was not written for ourselves alone. Many Jews in Old Testament times and since have been reminded of their ancestors through the records, however brief. Moreover we need continual reminder that it is not only the 'great' men and women for whom God has special concern. 'Even the hairs of your head are all numbered' (Matthew 10:30), although they are less exciting than the heart.

MACHIR. *Sold*
1. Joseph's grandson, son of Manasseh. His children were born in Egypt (Genesis 50:23). His descendants occupied Gilead

(Numbers 32:39-40), and perhaps at this time renamed it after Machir's son, Gilead (Numbers 26:29).

2. Among so many great, and not so great, warriors, it is pleasant to find a gentle and quiet man who looked after Jonathan's crippled son Mephibosheth (2 Samuel 9:3-5), and later brought food and camping equipment for David when he was escaping from Absalom (17:27-29). His home was at Lo-debar, possibly Debir, east of the Jordan.

MAGOG

Son of Japheth, who seems to have given his name to peoples in the north (Genesis 10:2). The name is of special interest because of its association with Gog in Ezekiel 38 and 39, and Revelation 20:8. Although Gog is not the name of any known person or tribe, he is spoken of as the leader and is called 'Gog of the land of Magog' (Ezekiel 38:2). In Ezekiel, Gog from Magog, with other peoples from every quarter (38:1-6), swoop upon undefended Israel, but are destroyed by God's intervention.

In Revelation, Satan gathers Gog, Magog and other nations against what has been the centre of God's government during the Millennium, but again they are destroyed by God (Revelation 20:7-10). Commentators vary over the interpretation of this. Some look for an invasion of Israel by northern powers shortly before the return of Christ. Others identify the Ezekiel invasion with that at the end of the Millennium. Others look for a double fulfilment. There are, of course, differing interpretations of the nature of the Millennium, but fortunately the Second Coming and its accompaniments are *facts* known to God and do not depend on a majority vote of theologians and commentators.

The names of Gog and Magog have captured imaginations. One story goes that when Brut, great-grandson of Aeneas of Troy, came to Britain and named it after himself, he and his fellow Trojans killed the few giants that occupied the country, except for Gog and Magog. These were taken to the new town of London and made to work as porters in Brut's palace on the site of the present Guildhall. They were commemorated by the two figures on the Guildhall. The originals were destroyed in the Fire of London (1666), and their replacements were destroyed in the blitz of World War II. Fresh figures in lime wood were placed on either side of the minstrels' gallery in 1953.

MAHER-SHALAL-HASH-BAZ

One of Isaiah's two sons. Isaiah gave both of his sons symbolic names to illustrate the themes that God had given him to preach (see also **Shear-jashub**). The name means *The spoil speeds, the prey hastens.* Isaiah first writes the words on a large tablet (Isaiah 8:1). Then his wife 'the prophetess' (i.e. Mrs Isaiah) bears him a son, to whom he gives this name. It was at a time when Syria and Israel were invading Judah, and King Ahaz was about to appeal to Assyria for help. Isaiah warned Ahaz against this on the ground that he would be putting himself and his own country under the domination of Assyria.

Isaiah first spoke of the Messiah who would be born of a virgin, and described his upbringing in poor surroundings (for 'curds and honey' in Isaiah 7:15 compare poverty in 7:21-25). He implies that the new policy of appealing to foreigners would be carried on until the land was always dominated by others. Yet, if Ahaz would only wait quietly upon God, he would see his immediate enemies swept away within the time that it takes for a baby to grow to years of moral discretion (7:14-17). Then he reiterates the message in his own child. This time there is no question of a virgin. Although the Hebrew word in 7:14 does not emphasize virginity (for which there is another word) it is always used elsewhere in Scripture of one who is unmarried, or presumed to be so. It could not apply to Isaiah's wife, who already had a son old enough to walk around with his father (7:3).

MAHLON. *Sick*
See **Ruth**

MALACHI. *My messenger*
It is possible that this is not a proper name belonging to the writer of the last book in the Old Testament, but may be a descriptive title taken from 'My messenger' in Malachi 3:1. We know nothing about the background of the prophet except that the temple was standing when he wrote, and there is mention of a governor, not a king (Malachi 1:8). Thus the book belongs to a time after the return from exile, perhaps in the period between the rebuilding of the temple (516 BC) and the coming of Ezra (458 BC), when mixed marriages were already a problem (Malachi 2:10-16; Ezra 9:1ff).

The book is a scathing comment on the casual behaviour of the priests, either as compared with the sincerity of the Gentiles, as some interpret Malachi 1:11, but more probably as compared with the sincere devotions of Jews who were still scattered in Gentile lands. Malachi 2:5-7 gives a superb description of a man of God called to be a leader, and deserves comparison with the picture shown to Christian in the Interpreter's house in Bunyan's *The Pilgrim's Progress:* 'He had eyes lifted up to heaven, the best of books in his hand, the law of truth was written upon his lips, the world was behind his back; he stood as though he pleaded with men, and a crown of gold did hang over his head.'

Malachi turns to the mixed marriages, which were a problem in the time of Ezra and Nehemiah, but stresses the nastiness of the divorce of Jewish wives in order to marry pagans (Malachi 2:10-16). Then comes the call to live in the light of eternity. God will send his messenger (John the Baptist; Matthew 11:10) to prepare for his own coming to cleanse and purify (Malachi 3:1-5). Meanwhile live as those who treat God as real (3:6-12), even though you face the age-old problem of the suffering of the righteous and the prosperity of the wicked. One day God will vindicate himself with both, but in the meantime one must find fulfilment in true fellowship and mutual help (3:13–4:3). The book closes with a further reminder of how John, the Elijah-type prophet, will come to prepare for the Messiah (Malachi 4:5, compare Luke 1:16-17).

In reading Malachi in their services, the Jews close by rereading Malachi 4:4, so as to avoid the nasty taste left by the threat to 'smite the land with a curse'. But it is significant that the Old Testament ends with the promise that the curse which came on the human race at the Fall (Genesis 3) will be removed by the mystery of the coming of God himself. None could realize what form this would take, nor how the God-man Christ Jesus would take the curse upon himself (Galatians 3:13; 2 Corinthians 5:21).

MALCHUS[NT]
Caiaphas' slave, whose ear Peter cut off. John alone names him (John 18:10), probably as a mutual friend in the servants' hall (18:15). Dr Luke checked, and writes that Jesus healed him (Luke 22:51).

MANAEN[NT]. Greek equivalent of Menahem, *Comforter*
A disciple at Antioch who is described as a *syntrophos* of Herod (Antipas). The word can be translated 'foster brother', and denotes one who as a boy had been brought up in the court as companion to the royal children.

MANASSEH. *Making one forget*
1. Joseph's first son, the reason for his name being given in Genesis 41:51. He had an Egyptian mother. When Jacob blessed his two grandsons, he was shown that the descendants of the younger son, Ephraim, would become the more important (see **Ephraim**). In the allocation of territory, the Manasseh tribe was divided and was given land on the east of Jordan (with Reuben and Gad) as well as on the west.

2. Son of the good king, Hezekiah. He was only twelve when he began to reign (2 Kings 21:1), but it is difficult to sort out the chronology of this period, and it may be that for a time he was joint ruler with his father. In giving him this name, what was Hezekiah commemorating? Did the birth of his son make him forget his severe illness (2 Kings 20)? Or, after the miraculous deliverance from Sennacherib (chapter 19), could he now forget the Assyrians?

Sadly enough, Manasseh proved to be the worst king that Judah ever knew. Even in the northern kingdom, Ahab had simply consented to the deliberate attempt of his wife Jezebel to stamp out the worship of Jehovah in favour of Baalism, whereas Manasseh not only went back on the sweeping reforms of his father, but offered his own sons as a human sacrifice, and became a devotee of the black arts (2 Kings 21:6; 2 Chronicles 33:6). He turned the temple into a shrine of idols, including a particularly monstrous figure (2 Chronicles 33:7).

The rare Hebrew word used here occurs again in Ezekiel 8:3,5, and although 2 Chronicles 33:15 says that the image was thrown out of the city, it was probably rescued by sympathizers and later set up again. Manasseh's purge included the murder of those who resisted him (2 Kings 21:16), possibly including Isaiah (see conclusion of **Isaiah** entry), and evidently involved the destruction of such copies of the law of Moses as he could lay his hands on. Possibly only a single copy survived (see **Josiah**)

In 2 Chronicles 33:10-13 there is a record of Manasseh's temporary imprisonment in Babylon, and subsequent return after he had confessed his sins to God. King Ashurbanipal of Assyria, who would have been his captor, treated Neco of Egypt in the same way, reinstating him after extracting an oath of loyalty. The reason why there is no reference to this in the Kings account may be that his repentance was superficial. As we have seen, Chronicles does not record that he smashed the idols when he threw them out of the city (2 Chronicles 33:14-17), and his son Amon was able to restore them (2 Kings 21:21; 2 Chronicles 33:22). There is a lesson here.

MARK[NT]

In referring to this man, the New Testament uses both his Latin name Marcus, and his Jewish name John, sometimes using both together (e.g. Acts 12:12,25). It is usually thought that he includes himself in his Gospel as the young man who was nearly arrested in Gethsemane (Mark 14:51-52). In Acts 12:12 his mother's house is the centre in Jerusalem where Peter expected to find Christians gathered for prayer.

If we want to try a piece of detective work, we can ask a few questions. Was this house the same as the one in which the disciples were gathered at Pentecost (Acts 2:1-2)? Once they had found a house with ample accommodation, they would be likely to continue to use it as a centre. Was the Pentecost house the one with the upper room in which the disciples stayed between the ascension and Pentecost, which could accommodate over 100 people (1:13-15)? The sequence in Acts 1 and 2 makes this a virtual certainty.

Then was this upper room the one in which Jesus had met with his disciples for the Last Supper, which Mark describes as 'a large upper room furnished and ready' (Mark 14:15)? Then was Mark present at the supper, probably serving? This would account for his presence in the garden immediately afterwards (14:51-52). Was Mark the man carrying a jar of water (14:13)? Or was he 'the householder' (14:14), since the house in Acts 12:12 is 'the house of Mary', showing that Mark's father was dead? Such speculation stimulates thought, but must be treated as no more than an interesting theory.

Mark was the cousin of Barnabas (Colossians 4:10) and if we may again make a guess, it was Barnabas's mother who was the sister of one of Mark's parents, since Barnabas's father was probably a Cypriot Jew (Acts 4:36), while Mark's family was firmly entrenched in Jerusalem. Barnabas would naturally stay in his mother's old home whenever he visited Jerusalem, and the time came when Barnabus asked Mark to leave his mother and join him and Paul in Antioch (Acts 12:25).

From there he was called to accompany Barnabas and Paul on their first missionary journey through Cyprus and parts of Asia Minor (Acts13:1-4). After a time, Mark suddenly left the others (13:13). No reason is given. He had not encountered the mob violence that Paul and Barnabas suffered in Asia so he had no reason to be afraid. Perhaps he could not get on with Paul. Certainly when the two men were called to go on another missionary tour, Paul refused to take Mark, and Mark went with Barnabas alone (15:36-41).

Both leaders were right. Paul could not risk the Lord's work being damaged, while Barnabas believed that Mark could redeem his past failure. It is good to see a fine, though rare, example of a quarrel being completely made up. When Mark joins Paul in prison in Rome (Philemon 24), he is commended by Paul to the church in Colossae (Colossians 4:10), and is actually sent for by Paul on the ground that 'he is very useful in serving me' (2 Timothy 4:11). Such a complete reconciliation needed much grace on both sides.

Mark himself was not in prison, but Paul was allowed visitors, who by coming identified themselves as Christians. Mark also assisted Peter, and when Peter calls him 'my son' some think that this means that Mark was converted through Peter, and at this time was with him in Rome, if this is what Peter here indicates by 'Babylon' (1 Peter 5:13).

Two traditions are interesting. Mark is said to have gone to Egypt and been responsible for the beginnings of the church in Alexandria, which became an important centre of Christianity. The earliest reference is in Eusebius, about AD 300, but Clement and Origen, both stalwarts in the church in Alexandria shortly before this, make no mention of Mark, though they do not claim anyone else as the founder.

The other tradition appears in the writings of Hippolytus of Rome, about AD 230. He speaks of Mark as being 'stumpy fingered'. This is such an extraordinary description of a person who writes that it is unlikely to have been invented. Might it be linked to his Latin name, Marcus, which means *hammer,* just as we speak of a permanently bent toe as a hammer toe? This does not mean that every Marcus was deformed, but out of the available names this was chosen as an obvious one, perhaps beginning as a nickname in place of his name John.

Some think that Hippolytus uses the adjective metaphorically of Mark's short Gospel for brevity of style, but it is most unlikely that he would actually invent a double-barrelled adjective, which does not occur in any extant Greek literature, for this purpose. So we may picture Mark with some deformity of the fingers of one hand, but able to write with the other.

Certainly Mark did write, and there is no reason to doubt his authorship of the Gospel that bears his name. It is the shortest, and is normally regarded as the first written of the four. Irenaeus, who died about AD 200 says that 'Mark the disciple and interpreter of Peter delivered to us in writing the things that were preached by Peter', and Papias (c. AD 140) is quoted by Eusebius (c. 300) in very similar terms. We have seen that Mark was helping Peter, and it is easy to imagine Peter as the eyewitness behind the stories and teachings as Mark sets them out. They are remembered incidents rather than elaborated history.

Mark may have had the idea of setting something down in writing long before compiling his Gospel between, say, AD 55 and 70. When he is taken on the First Missionary Journey by Paul and Barnabas, Luke says, 'They had John also as *Hyperetes.*' This word certainly means *servant,* but in the two places where Luke uses it in his Gospel it has a more technical sense. In Luke 4:20 it describes the official in the synagogue who, among other duties, had the position of village schoolmaster. In 1:2 Luke says that he obtained accurate information from 'eyewitnesses and *ministers* of the word'. Eyewitnesses might or might not be ministers of the word, but the latter were evidently what we might call *catechists,* i.e. instructors who passed on what they had seen or what they had been given by those who had seen.

In those days, religious instructors in the synagogues and elsewhere did not adapt original stories, but taught according to a pattern, passing on exactly what they had received. We may compare what happens in a family when something interesting has happened. Mother or father tells the story to every neighbour and friend who comes in. After the story has been told two or three times, the children know exactly what is coming next, down to the actual words and phrases. This is how Mark obtained material for his Gospel. If he was catechist for new converts, he would have learnt his material with the disciples in Jerusalem.

Before he actually wrote his Gospel, Mark would be familiar with Peter's oft-told stories. Thus, although a long time elapsed between the ministry of Christ and its committal to writing, the records were passed on orally and accurately.

MARTHA[NT]. From the Aramaic, *lady* or *mistress*
The down-to-earth sister of Mary and Lazarus. In Luke 10:41 she is gently reminded that there are occasions, such as the visit of Jesus to her house, when the opportunity should be taken to receive and not only to give. A good simple meal would have given her the opportunity to listen with Mary, but she was determined to turn out an elaborate sample of her cooking. After the death of her brother Lazarus, it was Martha who went out to meet Jesus and to hint that he might even raise him from the dead (John 11:20-27). In 12:1-2 Martha is still the one who is active in getting the meal.

There are two puzzles to which we do not know the certain answer. In John 11:1 Martha, Mary and Lazarus are living in Bethany, near Jerusalem, but the account in Luke 10:38-41 occurs during the Galilean ministry. Luke, however, does not locate the village, and the incident may well have happened during one of Jesus' visits to Jerusalem recorded by John (e.g. John 7:10). Jesus' close friendship with the family (11:5) shows that he had known them for some time.

The other puzzle is whether Martha was unmarried, or the wife or widow of a man called Simon the leper. When Mary anointed Jesus, this was in the house of Simon the leper in Bethany (Matthew 26:6). It is easy to read John 12:1-7 as though the incident took place in the house of Lazarus, but John says no more than that it took place in Bethany. Indeed, it would be pointless to say that Lazarus was present at the meal if it was in his own home (John 12:2). Obviously Lazarus and his sisters were asked to bring Jesus and his disciples, who were probably staying with them, just as Mary was asked to bring them to the wedding in Cana (2:1-2). This is simpler than supposing that Martha was the wife or widow of Simon the leper. (See **Mary**)

MARYᴺᵀ. Greek equivalent of *Miriam,* meaning uncertain

1. Following on the previous entry, we may take Mary of Bethany first, without repeating facts common to both sisters. Mary was the more emotional of the two. Although John alone names her as the woman who anointed Jesus shortly before his death (John 12:3), it would be too much of a coincidence to suppose that another woman in Bethany was moved in the same way at the same time (Matthew 26:6-13; Mark 14:3-9), whatever may have happened earlier (see **Mary Magdalene**), Matthew and Mark do not name her because she has not figured in the story before. While Matthew and Mark speak of the head and John of the feet, it is clear from Mark 14:8 that the woman anointed Christ's whole body.

2. The mother of John Mark. (See **Mark**.)

3. Mary Magdalene, i.e. from Magdala on the south-western edge of the Sea of Galilee. She had been heavily possessed by evil spirits but Jesus had freed her, and she joined other women who were looking after the material needs of Jesus and his disciples (Luke 8:1-3). She next appears at the crucifixion (Matthew 27:56; Mark 15:40; John 19:25), and noted carefully where Jesus was buried (Matthew 27:61; Mark 15:47). Early in the morning of Easter Day she and other women went to the tomb to add additional spices and oils to the body of Jesus (Matthew 28:1; Mark 16:1-2; John 20:1). As soon as Mary saw that the stone had been rolled away, she ran back to Peter and John with the news that someone had violated the tomb and stolen the body.

Peter and John ran to see for themselves, but Mary was too exhausted to cover the distance at their speed, and by the time she reached the tomb, Peter and John had vanished. On looking in, she saw two angels sitting there, but evidently did not recognize them as angels, anymore than at first she recognized Jesus who now stood behind her as she turned away. As Jesus spoke, she knew him, but Jesus forbad her to cling to him since from now onwards he would be disentangling his disciples from the old earthly relationships to the new relationship with him as the ascended Lord (John 20:1-18).

In Luke 7:36-49 there is the story of a prostitute who anointed the feet of Jesus in the house of a Pharisee named Simon. An extraordinary sequence of reasoning has been built up. First, this anointing has been equated with that by Mary of Bethany (see above), and then the name of Mary has been equated with that of Mary Magdalene. Hence Mary of Bethany, Mary Magdalene and the woman who was a sinner, have been lumped into one. This was the official identification by Pope Gregory the Great (c. AD 600).

The reformers challenged this, but unfortunately there is still a tendency to identify Mary Magdalene with the prostitute, forgetting that once the latter's action is separated from the later anointing by Mary of Bethany, her name is unknown, and there is no reason at all to suppose that she was Mary Magdalene. Indeed Luke would surely have called attention to her action when he mentions her, two verses after the anointing (Luke 8:2). Mary Magdalene is thus one of the most wronged women in the Bible, and from the 17th century gave her name to reformed prostitutes in England. Colleges at Oxford and Cambridge have restored her lost dignity, although the Oxford College has dropped the final 'e' and is pronounced *Maudlen*. This links up again with the now old-fashioned English word *maudlin,* since both the unnamed woman and Mary Magdalene in the garden are described as weeping (Luke 7:38; John 20:11).

4. Even if we are wrong in identifying Mary the mother of James and Joseph (Joses) with Mary the wife of Clopas, no great harm is done. The former is named as being at the cross in Matthew 27:56 and Mark 15:40, while the latter is similarly named in John 19:25. This James may be James the son of Alphaeus (Matthew 10:3) since Alphaeus and Clopas could be alternative transliterations into Greek of a Hebrew name *khalphai.* Some have read John 19:25 as though Mary the wife of Clopas was the sister of the mother of Jesus, but it is unlikely that two girls in the same family would be given identical names. It is more likely that the sister left unnamed is the mother of James and John, who certainly was present at the cross (Matthew 27:56). The other Mary was also one of those who went to the tomb on Easter Day (Matthew 28:1; Mark 16:1; Luke 24:10). (See **Clopas, James**).

It has been suggested that the women went to the wrong tomb in the early morning darkness, and naturally found it empty because it was still unused. This is a desperate attempt to evade the evidence of the empty tomb. Obviously the other disciples, and the women also, would have gone again during the day to check for themselves, and they could not all have gone to the wrong place.

5. The Virgin Mary. She was almost certainly descended from David, so that Jesus, according to prophecy, was physically the son of David as well as legally his son through Joseph. It is likely that the genealogy in Luke 3:23-38 is hers (see **Joseph**). The same angel Gabriel, who had spoken to Daniel of the coming Messiah (Daniel 9:20-27), was sent by God to tell Mary that she was to be his mother (Luke 1:26-38). Although Mary was engaged (1:27), she was not yet married, and there was something in Gabriel's words and manner that made her see that the conception of the child would take place very soon if not immediately (1:34). But Gabriel assured her that the child would be conceived by the miraculous agency of the Holy Spirit (1:35). He also told her that her cousin Elizabeth would shortly have a son in her old age (1:36-37).

Mary lost no time in visiting Elizabeth, and even at this early stage in Mary's pregnancy Elizabeth's unborn son moved violently within her, as it were leaping for joy at the greatness of Mary's child (Luke 1:39-45). Mary was moved to praise, and spoke out the poem that we call the Magnificat. She evidently knew her Bible well, and her poem contains reminiscences of Hannah's words when she gave thanks for the unexpected gift of a son (Luke 1:46-55, compare 1 Samuel 2:1-10). Matthew takes up the story when Joseph, her fiancé, was shocked to learn that Mary was to have a child. An engagement was a solemn act, though less binding than a marriage, and Joseph believed it right to break the contract, though with the minimum of publicity. At this point he also was visited by an angel, who assured him that this was through the hand of God (Matthew 1:18-25).

A census required Joseph and Mary to go to David's town of Bethlehem, and here Jesus Christ was born in a stable (Luke 2:1-7). The visit of the shepherds and the wise men set a further seal on God's miracle. (For the sequence of events, see **Joseph**.) Luke records visits to Jerusalem, first after about forty days for Mary's purificatory offering (Luke 2:22-38; Leviticus 12:1-8), and then annually for the Passover, taking Jesus at the age of twelve, when he stayed behind in the temple precincts for three days (Luke 2:41-51). Mary had other children before Joseph died (e.g. Matthew 13:55-56).

At the age of twelve Jesus indicated to Mary and Joseph that he had special obligations to his heavenly Father (Luke 2:49), and when he was about to begin his ministry he gently reminded his mother at the wedding in Cana that he must be guided in everything, not by her, but by his Father (John 2:4). His address to her in this latter verse is not rude, and the word 'Woman' is misleading today in this context; it is the equivalent of 'Sir', as used by sons to their fathers in the old days (NB: also John 19:26; 20:13,15). After Jesus had begun his ministry it may well be that Mary was afraid for her son, and by linking up Mark 3:21 (NEB has 'his family', JB 'relatives') with Mark 3:31 we may wonder whether she tried to persuade him to come back home.

We hear no more of Mary until we find her at the cross. She may not have come up to Jerusalem specially, in view of her son's danger, but followed her usual practice of being in Jerusalem for the Passover (Luke 2:41). In her agony she must have wondered where all the early promises had gone. Jesus commended her to John's care, John probably being her nephew (see James), and John took her home to his house in Jerusalem (John 19:26-27). We last hear of her with the disciples after the ascension, together with her sons (Acts 1:14), and we presume that she received the Holy Spirit at Pentecost, thus becoming a member of the church, the body of Christ. The Bible tells us nothing more of her life, but presumably John continued to look after her in

Jerusalem. Where the Bible is silent about her earlier life, some bogus writings such as apocryphal gospels fill the gaps with fanciful stories of the type that is incorporated in the Cherry Tree carol.

We may note very briefly some further ideas that have found their way into the teachings of the Roman Catholic Church.

A. The Immaculate Conception. It is argued that, as Jesus Christ was born free from original sin, Mary herself must have been free from original and actual sin. But then logically we should have to argue that Mary's parents and all her ancestors back to Adam and Eve must have similarly been sinless. This doctrine was a matter for discussion in the Roman Church until 1854, when the pope declared it an official dogma. This means that the Roman Church ranks it with such doctrines as the Deity of Christ as something that must be believed by all Roman Catholics.

B. The Assumption of the body of Mary to heaven after her death. This again was declared a dogma of the Roman Church in 1950. There is no historical justification for this belief.

C. The virgin birth. Protestants usually do not realize that technically there is a difference between the virginal conception, in which Protestants and Roman Catholics both believe, and the virgin birth. Roman Catholics hold that the actual birth was miraculous, so that if Mary had been medically examined afterwards she would have been pronounced *virgo intacta*. The story of how the midwife came to this conclusion comes from an apocryphal gospel called the *Protevangelium of James*. Its date is uncertain, but it was condemned as a forgery by three popes between 382 and 496. It was, however, re-edited as a Gospel ascribed to Matthew, which appeared in the 6th century. Even Protestants have drawn on this, though harmlessly, since Pseudo-Matthew was the first to describe how 'ox and ass before him bow' in the manger! In spite of what we have said, Protestants will rightly continue to use the term virgin birth in the commonly accepted sense.

D. The perpetual virginity of Mary. This belief gradually arose among some theologians who felt that there was something derogatory in sex relations, so that one cannot suppose that Mary and Joseph lived a normal married life after the birth of Jesus. Since the Gospels clearly speak of the brothers and sisters of Jesus (Mark 6:3), the idea arose of Joseph as a widower who already had children by a former marriage, so that they became the half-brothers of Jesus. There is no hint of this in the New Testament, and the phrase in Matthew 1:25 ('knew her not until she had borne a son') is extremely difficult to interpret of perpetual virginity.

E. Devotion to Mary. Many Roman Catholics today admit that expressions of devotion to Mary have tended to get out of hand. Contrary to the belief of some Protestants, the Roman Catholic Church forbids worship of Mary, but prayers can be addressed to her, as to other saints. There is no example of similar prayers anywhere in the New Testament.

We must conclude with a brief reference to the virgin birth, or virginal conception. The evidence for this comes from two independent sources, Matthew and Luke, and Luke was a doctor who had opportunities to talk with Mary herself. It is often argued that there is no other evidence in the New Testament. Mark begins his Gospel not with the birth of Jesus but with John the Baptist; yet it is significant that in Mark 6:3 he quotes people as saying 'Is not this the carpenter, the son of Mary?', whereas Matthew and Luke, having already related the story of the virgin birth, have 'Is not this the carpenter's son?' (Matthew 13:55) and 'Is not this Joseph's son?' (Luke 4:22).

In Galatians 4:23 Paul speaks of the birth of Ishmael, and uses the normal word, which has overtones of the father's part in begetting. But when a few verses earlier he speaks of Jesus as 'born of a woman' (4:4), he uses a very general word which means literally *becoming* or *coming to be*. He uses the same word on the two other occasions when he speaks of Christ's birth (Romans 1:3, Philippians 2:7). One can often tell a person's basic belief from the type of expression that he uses, and there is every likelihood that Paul, who travelled with Luke, knew of the virgin birth. It is probable also that John shows his awareness of the virgin birth when he records the Jews as saying to Jesus, 'We were not born of fornication' (John 8:41), with the suggestion that there were suspicious circumstances surrounding his birth. The reason why the virgin birth did not form part of the public preaching in the early days was undoubtedly respect for the reputation of Mary, who was still alive, but the evidence for it is very strong.

One cannot see how the pre-existent Son of God could have become man apart from a miraculous conception. If, for example, Joseph had been the father, there would have been a complete potential human being from the instant of conception. The person of Christ would then have had to be somehow attached to this foetus as a kind of extra. We know today that before conception there are 23 chromosomes in the male sex cell and 23 in the female, and these come together to form the 46 that are in every cell in the body as the person grows. The Holy Spirit supplied the male element of a kind that could be a vehicle for the Son of God to unite with the ovum within Mary's body.

We cannot plumb the mystery of the incarnation, but we cannot solve it by rejecting the virginal conception. The Council of Ephesus in AD 431 said the same thing by calling the Virgin Mary *Theotokos,* for which there is no slick English translation. The word means that from the moment the cell came alive as a potential child, that child was God as well as man. Unfortunately the translation *Mother of God* has conveyed the idea that Mary, as mother, can influence her divine son if Christians send their prayers up to her.

Mary has been much commemorated, by places such as Marylebone and by flowers such as marigold and lady's bedstraw (Mary being known as Our Lady). One of the most pleasing commemorations is in the Lady Chapel of Llandaff Cathedral, Cardiff. Twelve coloured bronze panels depict twelve flowers whose Welsh names include Mair (Mary).

MATTHEW[NT]. Meaning uncertain. Perhaps *True*

One of the Twelve chosen by Jesus as apostles (Mark 3:18). His call is described in Matthew 9:9; Mark 2:14; Luke 5:27. The account is similar in all three, but Mark and Luke call him Levi the son of Alphaeus. It is unlikely that this is the same Alphaeus as the father of James, since although Matthew and James come together in the list in Matthew 10:3 they are not said to be brothers as are Peter and Andrew, James and John, in verse 2. Like others in the New Testament, Matthew evidently had two names.

He was a tax gatherer (Matthew 9:9, etc.), an unpopular office, since the taxes were paid to Rome, the occupying power, and it was recognized that the tax gatherers could overcharge and take as much for themselves as they dared (Luke 3:12-13; 19:2,8). One of Matthew's first acts was to invite Jesus and his disciples to a magnificent meal in his home (Luke 5:29), with other tax collectors and people who did not mind associating with them as fellow guests.

From then onwards Matthew is totally unknown in the New Testament, so it is all the more significant that he was universally accepted as the author of the first Gospel. A statement ascribed to Papias (c. AD 100) says, 'Matthew wrote the *logia* in Hebrew (i.e. Aramaic, the language of Jesus), and everyone interpreted them as he was able'. The last phrase would obviously include translation.

A difficulty is that it is commonly, though not universally, accepted that much of Matthew's Gospel is based on Mark. We may, however, assume the following: Matthew, who was well used to writing, jotted down the teachings of the Lord, which were in Aramaic, during his ministry, and afterwards circulated these. These would be the *logia,* or sayings. At some stage Matthew or another person translated these into Greek, and when Matthew decided to produce a fuller history of the life of Jesus he incorporated Mark's version, with some expansions or clarifications based on his own memory of the events. Meanwhile it is likely that Luke made extensive use of Matthew's original record of Christ's teachings. Students of the Synoptic problem will see that we are identifying Matthew's *logia* with the alleged document Q. They will also realize that we have taken only one out of several theories of the Gospel, but this seems the simplest use of the available evidence.

MATTHIAS[NT]. *Gift of Jehovah*
After the ascension the disciples decided to fill the place of Judas among the Twelve (Acts 1:15-26). The candidate must be one who had been in their company from the beginning. They selected two who appeared to have equal claims, Matthias being one. They decided to ask the Lord to make the final decision and prayerfully drew lots, as used to be done with the Urim and Thummim in the Old Testament (1 Samuel 14:41. RSV and other modern translations). The lot fell out for Matthias, but he plays no further part in the New Testament. It is often thought that if the choice had been made after Pentecost, the Holy Spirit would have guided directly without the use of the lot (compare Acts 13:1-3).

John Wesley, however, copied the Moravians in occasional use of the lot when careful consideration showed that two choices were exactly balanced, either by drawing lots in the usual way, or by opening the Bible at random to see what text met the eye, a practice still occasionally followed as a short cut to guidance, although one would not recommend it for regular use.

MEDAD. *Affectionate*
See **Eldad**.

MELCHIZEDEK
His name can be interpreted in two ways, either *Zedek is my king,* or *King of righteousness* (Hebrews 7:2, see also **Adonizedek**). The second interpretation is likely in view of the fact that he is priest of God Most High rather than of a god Zedek (Genesis 14:18). He is also king of Salem, i.e. Jerusalem. He offers bread and wine to Abraham, and blesses him, after

Abraham had retrieved prisoners and property from invading armies (see **Lot**). Melchizedek had taken no part in the earlier battle. Abraham gives him a tenth of all that he had taken.

There is no doubt that Melchizedek was a monotheist who recognized that he and Abraham worshipped the same God. He was both king and priest, and, after David had captured Melchizedek's city of Jerusalem he was promised that his 'lord' would enjoy the king-priesthood for ever (Psalm 110:1,4). The New Testament quotes the opening verse of this Psalm more often than any other text.

The Melchizedek promise is expounded in Hebrews 5-7. The writer takes the promise and relates it to the perpetual priesthood of Jesus, as opposed to the changing succession of Levitical priests. Since we have no information about Melchizedek apart from the few verses in Genesis 14:17-20, we have to ask why he has been selected in the Psalm as a picture of Christ.

Obviously we must look for similarities in what is actually said in Genesis. Thus he is king of righteousness and king of peace (Salem). He suddenly appears in Scripture, with nothing said of his ancestry or of the close of his life. May we not therefore, taking Scripture as it stands, and looking for a comparison with Jesus Christ, compare him with the eternally existing Son of God (Hebrews 7:2-3)? The writer of Hebrews is concerned with what is actually said about him rather than with what archaeology might show him to have been.

MENAHEM. *Comforter* or *Comforted*

Shallum assassinated King Zechariah of Israel, but after a month was himself assassinated by Menahem, who then crushed resistance with extreme brutality (2 Kings 15:13-22). The date was about 752 BC.

He strengthened his position by taxing the rich to get the support of the king of Assyria, Pul or Tiglath-Pileser III.

MEPHIBOSHETH

For the reason why his original name of Merib-baal (1 Chronicles

9:40) *(The lord contends)* was rendered by copyists as Mephibosheth (perhaps *One who cuts the shameful thing in pieces*) see **Ishbosheth**.

Apart from a single mention of a son of Saul with this name (2 Samuel 21:8), the man of importance here is the son of Jonathan. He was lamed for life at five years old, when his nurse dropped him (4:4). We hear nothing about him during the first part of David's reign, except that he was looked after by a pleasant man named Machir on the east of Jordon (see **Machir**).

One of Saul's servants, Ziba, knew where he was, and when David enquired whether any sons of Jonathan remained he traced him through Ziba, brought him to court, and gave him back lands that had belonged to Saul (2 Samuel 9:1-8; NB: David's promise in 1 Samuel 20:16, 17, 42). Mephibosheth's son, Mica, apparently joined him, and Ziba and his family were appointed to work the fields for him (2 Samuel 9:9-13).

It is difficult to decide the rights and wrongs of what happened when Absalom rebelled. David left Jerusalem, and Ziba came along with food and drink for his army, with the story that Mephibosheth had gone over to the other side in the hope of being made king himself (2 Samuel 16:1-4). But when David returned after the battle, Mephibosheth had a very different story. He said that Ziba had taken advantage of his lameness, made off with the asses on which Mephibosheth might have ridden, and left him in Jerusalem (2 Samuel 19:24-27).

On the whole, one is inclined to accept this account, since Mephibosheth had made it obvious to everyone that he was in mourning for David during his absence (2 Samuel 19:24). David found it difficult to make a decision, since he had already promised Mephibosheth's lands to Ziba (16:4). In the end he divided the lands equally between them (19:29). Later, when the Gibeonites demanded the execution of seven sons or grandsons of Saul, David refused to include Mephibosheth among them (21:7). (For this see **Rizpah**)

MERAB. Perhaps, *Increase*

The elder of Saul's two daughters, one of whom her father promised in marriage to anyone who killed Goliath (1 Samuel 17:25) Saul out of jealousy refused to give her to David until he had proved himself further against the Philistines, hoping that he would lose his life in doing so. But he broke his promise, and married Merab to a man named Adriel (18:17-19). Most modern translations assume a copyist's error in the normal Hebrew text of 2 Samuel 21:8, and read Merab in place of Michal. (See also **Michal**.)

MEREMOTH. *Heights*

A priest who returned with Ezra and who checked that none of the donations of silver and gold had gone missing during the journey from Babylon (Ezra 8:33). He joined Nehemiah in building the wall of Jerusalem, and was one of the more energetic leaders who undertook two sections (Nehemiah 3:4, 21). He naturally was one who set his seal to the fresh covenant drawn up by Nehemiah (10:5). In Ezra 8:33 and Nehemiah 3:4 Meremoth is specifically described as the son of Uriah, showing that it is the same man in both cases. This is important evidence against those who wish to change the biblical order and make Ezra come to Jerusalem nearly fifty years after Nehemiah. This Meremoth is obviously not one of the sons of Bani who had married a pagan wife (Ezra 10:36).

MERODACH-BALADAN

Also rendered into Hebrew as Berodach-baladan. A king of Babylon, Marduk-apla-iddina II, who claimed the throne while Babylon was under the Assyrian empire (c. 721-698 BC). He had up-and-down brushes with the Assyrians, and his approach to Hezekiah (2 Kings 20:12; Isaiah 39), while nominally to congratulate him on his marvellous recovery, was undoubtedly to draw him to lead a resistance movement to Assyria in Palestine. Isaiah squashed the plan. Eventually Merodach-baladan was deposed by Sennacherib of Assyria.

MESHA

A king of Moab, who was thoughtful enough to leave us his version of his revolt against Israel recorded in 2 Kings 3. The account is cut into the so-called Moabite Stone erected in 850 BC, which is some 44 by 27 inches (1.1 x 0.7 metres) and thus has room for quite a long inscription. After its discovery in 1868 it was unfortunately deliberately smashed in a dispute over ownership, and some pieces lost. The repaired original is in the Louvre and a cast of it in the British Museum. Mesha describes how Omri dominated Moab for forty years until halfway through his (grand)son's reign. Mesha records how on the death of his father he successfully resisted Jehoram, Omri's grandson, and followed up his victory with raids on Israelite territory, which he describes in detail. He ascribes his success to the Moabite god, Chemosh, and in characteristic style adds that 'Israel perished utterly for ever'.

The language is very close to Hebrew. There is no factual contradiction between the Moabite Stone and the Bible, provided that King Mesha's reference to Omri's son is taken as equivalent to grandson. In fact, unless this is so, the stone contradicts itself in saying that the domination lasted forty years. Halfway through Ahab's reign (son of Omri) would have been between ten and twenty years (2 Kings 3:5).

The expedition against Mesha's city of Kir-hareseth is described in 2 Kings 3. The kings of Israel, Judah and Edom took part. A sudden flood with the sun shining red upon it was taken by the Moabites as a good omen, signifying that the kings had fallen out with one another and shed each other's blood. But they had misread the signs and were thrown back into the city. Mesha tried to break out to the Edomites, perhaps hoping that they would desert and come over to him, but they stood firm. Finally, in desperation he offered the heir to the throne as a public sacrifice on the city wall. This roused his men to such violent anger that they flung themselves on the enemy and this time forced them to withdraw and abandon the campaign.

MESHACH
One of Daniel's three friends, whose name Mishael (*Who is as God is?*) was changed to Meshach (meaning unknown) (Daniel 1:7). (For the three friends see **Abed-nego**.)

METHUSELAH. Perhaps, *Man of the javelin*
A rare, perhaps unique, example of a name in a genealogical list becoming known throughout the English-speaking world, and presumably in other languages also. 'As old as Methuselah' is a happy description for a long life of 969 years (Genesis 5:25-27). Although some interpret the long lives in these Genesis tables as representing the domination of clans or tribes rather than individuals, one need not dismiss the literal interpretation too readily.

Nobody has yet solved the mystery of ageing and longevity, but in our own generation we have seen the expectation of life extended further and further, and scientists are hopeful of taking it further still. It may well be that good men who lived nearer to the original Adamic creation retained a tremendous vitality, which gradually ebbed away in their descendants. Thus the average age of the characters in Genesis 11 is much less than that in chapter 5.

We may, however, fairly introduce the idea of clans or tribes in part. Devout Bible students, such as Archbishop Ussher (1581-1656), added up the figures in chapters 5 and 11 to calculate the date of the creation of Adam as 4004 BC, and these dates were given in the margin of the KJV until recent times. Our present knowledge of the antiquity of man, though limited (see **Adam**), has forced us to have a fresh look at the figures to see whether any interpretation is possible other than what appears to be their face value. Of the various suggestions a hopeful one is that in these lists we have the names of prominent men of old, with the omission of the less important, and with gaps between 'father' and 'son'.

Thus, for example, we might paraphrase Genesis 5:21-22 somewhat as follows: 'When Enoch had lived sixty-five years he started the line that eventually produced the next head of a clan, Methuselah; Enoch had other sons and daughters, but none of these were ancestors of any of the other great heroes of old.' The advantage of this type of interpretation is that we do not have to suppose that the named son was the eldest and was not born until his father was of a considerable age. Nor do we know how many decades or centuries passed before the new line threw up a prominent leader, who virtually became the father of a clan, tribe, or group. A special example would be Eber in 11:16, the father of the Hebrews (see **Eber**).

A suggestion communicated personally to the author keeps the idea of clan leaders, but removes the undue longevity of individuals by supposing a misunderstanding and consequent adaptation by copyists. Thus the original would be somewhat as follows: 'A lived 70 years. He begat (i.e. was the ancestor of) B. From the days of A to the emergence of B there were 800 years.' Through a misunderstanding, the clan years were taken to be the years of A, and the text was emended accordingly.

MICAH. The name is also rendered **Micaiah**, *Who is like Jehovah?*
1. The subject of an extraordinary story in Judges 17, 18. Micah helped himself to 1100 pieces of silver from his mother's savings. His mother put a curse on the thief; whereupon Micah confessed and handed the money back. His doting mother hurriedly changed the curse into a blessing, and arranged with the local silversmith to turn 200 pieces of the silver into a couple of images, which she then dedicated to Jehovah in memory of her son's generosity. Micah decided to go in for idolatry in a big way, and made a private chapel in his house, with further images of his own to accompany those given by his mother. He made one of his sons priest of the chapel temporarily.

Presently a young Levite came along. The Levites lived among the tribes, and were intended to be the spiritual leaders of the neighbourhood with a special knowledge of the law of God (Deuteronomy 31:9-13). This Levite's family lived in Bethlehem, but he himself had itchy feet and wanted to better himself. Micah offered him the post of priest, which he was delighted to accept, as the door to the legitimate priesthood was not open to him. Micah, knowing that the Levites were set apart for the Lord's service, even though only the sons of Aaron could actually be priests, felt that his chapel of gods was now really something. If this man was the first of his kind, he certainly was not the last, since Ezekiel 44:10-12 speaks of many others who set themselves up as idolatrous priests, with the outlook of Milton's Satan, 'Better to reign in hell than serve in heaven'.

Micah's chapel, images and priest attracted the attention of the tribe of Dan who were moving north, and Judges 18 vividly describes how the place was robbed, and the Levite was given an attractive invitation to become priest to the whole tribe of Dan instead of simply to Micah's little chapel. Micah and his neighbours, members of his congregation, chased the Danites, but were threatened with violence and had to leave the idols to the tribe of Dan to set up in their new capital.

In the above note, ephod and teraphim are treated as images. Normally an ephod is a priestly vestment, that of the high priest being elaborate and heavy (Exodus 39), while other priests and Levites wore simple linen 'surplices' (1 Samuel 2:18; 22:18). The ephod made by Gideon (Judges 8:24-27) was a heavy metal object, capable of being worshipped, and Micah's is likely to have been similar, though of less intrinsic value.

It is possible that Hosea 3:4 refers to this type of ephod. One may suppose that the image was modelled stiffly like the high priest's elaborate garment, and had roughly the shape of a man. An object of worship need not be carved or cast to be exactly like a man or a woman, as witness the standing stones which represented Baal. In the muddled days of the Judges (Judges 17:6) Micah may well have treated his images as symbolizing Jehovah (17:3). (For teraphim, see **Rachel**.)

An undue amount of space has been taken up with this first Micah, but his story illustrates important features in the religious life of Israel. There are other important features in this second character:

2. A prophet, Micaiah, the son of Imlah, who foretold the death of King Ahab. His story in 1 Kings 22 must not be read superficially. Ahab enlisted the help of Jehoshaphat of Judah in his attempt to recapture Ramoth-Gilead from Syria. Jehoshaphat insisted on having a message from the Lord, and Ahab supplied this through some 400 prophets, who were evidently replacements for the prophets of Baal that Elijah had executed on Carmel (1 Kings 18:40). Speaking in the name of Jehovah, they unanimously declared that Ahab would be successful at Ramoth-Gilead. Jehosaphat was sceptical, and asked for an independent prophet.

Ahab, who badly needed Jehoshaphat's help, reluctantly produced Micaiah, who was unpopular at court because his messages were always critical of Ahab. The messenger who brought Micaiah warned him to back the other prophets, and he obligingly repeated exactly what the others had said, but evidently in so sarcastic a voice that even Ahab knew he was mocking him, and challenged him to speak the truth.

Micaiah replied with the vision that God had given him. He had seen the nation leaderless. Then he had seen God declaring it as his will that Ahab should fall at Ramoth-Gilead, and selecting a spirit to lead him to go. The spirit who was selected was one who could use the prophetic state of trance, or lessened conscious awareness, to inspire the court prophets who had probably prostituted such gifts as they had in order to keep their place in court. Micaiah's exposure moved the leader of the prophets to hit him in the face and ask sarcastically how the lying spirit from the Lord managed to move from him to Micaiah. Ahab intervened and had Micaiah locked up, as the prophet called on the people to witness that the Lord had declared that Ahab would not return in peace from the battle. Ahab was indeed killed, but we are not told what happened to Micaiah.

Some readers of this chapter have found a moral difficulty over God's deliberate deception of Ahab through sending an evil spirit to inspire the 400 prophets. In fact, the incident is one of the clearest in the Bible for indicating how God's providence and man's free will are bound up together. The time had come for the long-delayed death of Ahab, who had done such damage to God's cause. Ahab's heart was set on reconquering Ramoth-Gilead. His tame prophets, inspired by an evil spirit, back him in the name of God. But God gave him a genuine warning through a true prophet, Micaiah, and Ahab recognized that Micaiah's message was worth more than that of the others (1 Kings 22:15-16). Yet he went on his way to the end that God had predestinated for him and that he had predestinated for himself, and he did it after due warning.

Another lesson from the story is that one must not identify psychism with divine inspiration. These prophets undoubtedly had psychic gifts, but their desire to please Ahab and Jezebel, even though they were not prophets of Baal, led them to open up the area of these gifts to evil spirits that impersonated the Spirit of God.

3. Micah, some of whose prophecies remain in written form in the Bible, was the contemporary of Isaiah in the second part of the 8th century BC. We gather that he was a countryman, and that, whereas Isaiah moved in court circles, he saw things from the point of view of the oppressed. Yet both prophets testify to the same abuses that marred the political and social life of the day. It is worth reading Micah 2 and 3 alongside of Isaiah 2-5, especially chapter 5.

It is interesting that Micah calls attention to himself by using the famous slogan of his predecessor, Micaiah the son of Imlah (Micah 1:2; 1 Kings 22:28). He shows that Judah and Israel were as bad as each other, and punches home his message with a series of puns on the names of towns which naturally cannot be kept in English (Micah 1:10-12). One might try the effect with British names, e.g. 'In Blackburn, burn yourselves black; in Bath drown yourselves; in Wales take up wailing; in the Isle of Wight let your faces turn white with fear.'

In view of the above note on false prophets, one observes Micah's words about them in Micah 3:5-8, and may compare verse 8 with Jeremiah 23:22, and 1 Kings 22:9 (of Micaiah).

In Micah 4:1-4 there is a passage identical with Isaiah 2:1-4. There is no reason why one prophet should not quote from another, and thus give a double witness to God's message. It is likely that Micah is the original, since Isaiah 2:5 appears to be an exhortation based on what Micah says will be true when Micah 4:1-4 is fulfilled. There has been a major fulfilment during the whole of the Christian (Messianic) era, when the word of God first went forth from Jerusalem, and continues to go forth from citizens of the heavenly Jerusalem (Galatians 4:26; Hebrews 12:22). Peace is the Christian ideal, but alas is still a long way off, and maybe must await the Second Coming of the Messiah.

Jerusalem's subjection is followed by the coming of the Messiah of the line of David, whose rule is destined to be worldwide (Micah 4:6-5:4). Meanwhile, Judah will not lose her destiny by being swamped by the Assyrian invaders (5:5-6). Israel and Judah (and we may well include the new Israel of Galatians 6:16) will be used of God among the nations (Micah 5:7-9), as we now know with the all-conquering power of the gospel (compare Acts 15:16-17 with the original in Amos 9:11-12). But we must ourselves be clean, and especially must see God's requirements for all of our social life (Amos 5:10–6:16, especially 6:8). Persecution may come and we may have to wait, but at all times we are to cast ourselves upon the God of the covenant (Micah 7:1-20).

MICHAL. Similar to **Michael**, *Who is like God?*
Saul's younger daughter. David should have been given the elder sister Merab as the promised reward for killing Goliath, but she was eventually married off elsewhere. Michal was in love with David, and since Saul had simply promised 'his daughter' as a reward he could keep his word by offering Michal, though he laid down appalling conditions which he hoped would result in David's death at the hands of the Philistines (1 Samuel 18:17-29). Michal was a good wife to David, and saved his life when Saul sent men to arrest him. She not only lowered David out of the

window, but delayed pursuit by putting a teraphim image in the bed, with a pillow of goat's hair to make a wig, and giving out that her husband was ill (1 Samuel 19:11-17). (See **Rachel**).

For some reason she did not join David in exile, and Saul had his revenge by giving her in marriage to a man named Palti (1 Samuel 25:44). After Saul's death, David demanded her return as the price of opening negotiations with Abner, much to the distress of her new husband who was obviously very much in love with her (2 Samuel 3:13-16). But by this time Michal was soured, and when she saw David leaping unashamedly in front of the ark on its entry into Jerusalem, wearing only a short kilt, she charged him with deliberate indecency. If the criticism of his apparent behaviour was in any sense justified, it was purely accidental as David was caught up in his enthusiasm for demonstrating 'Long live God!' (6:21-22). But he had no further relations with Michal (6:23). (See also **Merab**)

MIRIAM. Meaning uncertain. The Hebrew equivalent of Mary.
Sister of Moses and Aaron. Since Aaron was only three years older than Moses (Exodus 7:7), and Miriam was old enough to deal with the princess when Moses was a baby, she must have been the big sister of the family (2:1-10). After the miraculous crossing of the Red Sea, she was seized with the spirit of prophecy (15:20), and led the women in celebration. It may be that the quotation in verse 21 indicates that she composed the whole song of triumph in chapter 15.

Big unmarried sister and big brother objected when Moses married a foreign woman (Numbers 12), perhaps after Zipporah had died, and as often happens they added criticism to criticism and ended up by claiming that their inspiration was as good as that of Moses. God intervened and showed them that Moses had a far fuller knowledge of God's will than they had. The cloud of God's presence melted away, and Miriam, who must have been the leader, was left a leper. In answer to Moses' prayer we presume she was healed, after being secluded outside the camp for seven days, but it is possible that she remained a leper of the type mentioned in Leviticus 13:12-13. She eventually died in Kadesh, before either of her brothers (Numbers 20:1), but was of sufficient importance to be mentioned with them as a God-sent deliverer in Micah 6:4.

MOAB
See **Lot**.

MORDECAI.
Presumably the first part of his name is formed from the Babylonian god Marduk. We do not know his Hebrew name. The hero of the book of Esther, who with Esther's help averted a massacre of the Jews in the Persian empire, and became grand vizier after the execution of the anti-Jewish Haman. Since he lived in the reign of Xerxes (485-465 BC) it is obvious that it was his great-grandfather, Kish, who was taken captive in 597 BC, and not Mordecai himself (Esther 2:5-6).

There is a case for identifying him with Matakas, whom the Greek historian Ctesias says was the most influential of the eunuchs. Mordecai was apparently a eunuch since he has no wife or family (Esther 2:7) and has access to the women's quarters (2:11). Matakas helped Xerxes to destroy a pagan shrine, which as a Jew he would have been delighted to do. A Persian inscription also mentions a certain Marduka as a privy counsellor or court accountant early in the reign of Xerxes. Certainly Mordecai, though presumably for the time a fallen favourite, is more than just a Jew of the city, since he is able to push Esther forward (2:5-11), and Haman, the grand vizier, who would have executed anyone on sight, hesitates when Mordecai refuses to bow to him (3:1-6).

It is perfectly possible that Mordecai recorded the events of the book of Esther (Esther 9:20), and his omission of the name of God from the book was due to his writing for inclusion in the Persian annals (10:2; 6:1). (See **Esther** for another account of the book; also **Vashti**)

MOSES

Many pages have been written to prove that his name is Egyptian and as many to prove it is Hebrew. Perhaps we can have the best of both worlds in the light of Exodus 2:10.

Princess to Moses' mother, Jochebed, masquerading as nurse: 'What shall we call this little Hebrew baby that I pulled out of the water?'

Jochebed: 'In our language the word for 'pull out' is *mashah*, and this is like your Egyptian word *mosheh*.'

Princess: 'Why, of course, that means *Son,* and as I'm adopting him we'll call him that.'

So Mosheh became his name, although we know him by the Greek form of it. The story of how Jochebed put Moses in a watertight basket in the reeds of the Nile is one of the best known in the Bible. There is no need to discredit it because a similar story is told of a King Sargon many centuries earlier. If Jochebed and her husband Amram knew how Sargon was rescued and raised to high honour, they would trust that God would work with equal power.

The life of Moses falls into three periods of forty years each. During the first, he was brought up at the court of Pharaoh. This was an honour coveted by rulers of civilized countries who sent their sons to have one of the best educations of the day. During this time Moses 'was instructed in all the wisdom of the Egyptians' (Acts 7:22), and we can see how God prepared him to be the penman of his people. In fact, it may have been during this time that he first edited the old writings of the nation, translating the proto-Hebrew where necessary, and thus compiling the book of Genesis.

Since these writings came from different people, it is not surprising that there are differing styles, and sometimes Moses blends together records of the same event from the hands of more than one person, as in the records of the flood, and perhaps from the records of more than one brother who told of how they had taken and sold Joseph. Moses found no contradiction in the records, nor need we. At the end of this period Moses fell foul of

Pharaoh through intervening in a quarrel and killing an Egyptian who was beating an Israelite, and escaped into Midian (Exodus 2:11-15).

It is amazing how easily Moses slipped off the luxuries of the court and for forty years took up the life of a shepherd (Exodus 2:16–3:1, compare Hebrews 11:24-27). He married Zipporah, daughter of Jethro, or Reuel (see **Jethro, Hobab**). She bore him two sons (Exodus 2:22; 1 Chronicles 23:15). During this period Moses became familiar with desert life, which again stood him in good stead later. At the end of it God spoke to him from a bush which burned without being burnt up. Probably this was a symbol of God's undying covenant, since immediately God declared that he was communicating with Moses as he had done with Abraham, Isaac and Jacob (Exodus 3:1-6).

He commissioned Moses to bring Israel out of Egypt into Canaan via the mountain of Sinai, or Horeb, where Moses was then standing. He then reminded Moses of one of the names by which he had been known, Jehovah or Yahweh, although this name had not formed the basis of a covenant, nor had it been so well known. Later, when Moses produced his final edition of Genesis, he sometimes put this name into the stories, but made it clear that God Almighty was the original covenant title (Genesis 17:1; 28:3; 35:11; 43:14; 49:25). This is pointed out in Exodus 6:3-4. Moses also used the general term for God, especially when dealing with peoples outside of the chosen descendants of Abraham.

Now God indicates that his covenant will be renewed with the title Jehovah or Yahweh at the centre. Actually, Yahweh comes nearest to the meaning of the word, which in 3:14 is expounded as I AM, the name itself meaning HE IS, the deepest possible title for the one source of all existence. In this book we have used the old familiar transliteration, Jehovah. Because the Jews from about 300 BC regarded the sacred name, written without vowels as YHWH, as too sacred to pronounce, they substituted a more general word, *Adonai,* my lord, in reading. The vowels, written under the consonants in later times, were transferred from Adonai to Yhwh, and eventually in about the twelfth century AD produced the Name Jehovah. Fortunately in most English translations of the Bible the name is rendered by LORD in capitals.

Moses, with all his wisdom, felt totally inadequate for the task of challenging Pharaoh, so he was given two simple signs to perform (Exodus 4:1-9). When he still complained of not having the ability to argue his people's case, God gave him his brother Aaron to be his spokesman (4:10-17). So Moses went, but he had forgotten one thing. He was to be the spokesman of the covenant, and the covenant included on man's side the acceptance of circumcision as an essential and not an optional extra. In trying to understand the brief story of Moses at the inn (4:24-26), we have to build up a background into which it fits.

We surmise that Moses, like Abraham, had to wait until old age before he had his two sons, since the implication here is that they were still young. Evidently one had been circumcised, presumably the elder, but Zipporah thoroughly disliked the messy operation done with a flint knife, and had insisted on keeping the second son uncircumcised. Moses had agreed, and had thus broken the covenant, and must bear the responsibility for his son being cut off from God's chosen people (Genesis 17:14). How could he now become the messenger of the covenant?

So God brought him and Zipporah to their senses by a sudden illness which could quickly have carried Moses off. Zipporah had the insight to know what God was saying by this illness; maybe she and Moses had been discussing this very thing during the journey, and she had refused to give way. But now she circumcises her son with her own hand, and places the evidence at Moses' feet — the place of submission — with the bitter words that marrying him has stained her hands with the blood of the son she bore him. But her submission to the will of God saved her husband's life, for Moses was not indispensable, and God had Aaron as his second string (Exodus 4:27-31).

After their first thrill, the people of Israel turned against the two brothers, since their interview with Pharaoh only resulted in tougher treatment (Exodus 4:29–5:22). Moses was in the depths of despair and reminded God of his own commonsense in being reluctant to undertake the mission (5:22-23). God then reiterated his promise, and again spoke of the eternal title of Jehovah, to be made the centre of a fresh covenant in a way unknown before. But still the people remained unconvinced, as was not surprising in their state of physical and mental depression (6:1-9).

Now God intervened in a drastic way to secure their release. Pharaoh had an iron will or hard heart to keep them as slaves, but he and the country were rocked by a series of disasters. Each one of them individually could be given natural explanations by Egyptian scientists, but the fact was that they came in rapid succession, and each began at the moment when Moses and Aaron took action after giving due warning of God's intentions (Exodus 7:1–10:29). Finally, after the plague on all firstborn males, in which the Israelites were passed over through the blood of the lamb, Pharaoh hurried them out of the land and the Egyptians paid them to go (11:1–12:41).

Almost immediately Pharaoh changed his mind, but the force that he sent in pursuit was first miraculously checked, and was finally swamped as the cavalry and chariots tried to follow the Israelites across the causeway of a reedy inlet from the Mediterranean. The Hebrew words are now generally translated Reed Sea. A violent gale, possibly coupled with seismic disturbances, had temporarily parted the waters (Exodus 14:21-31). The references in verses 22 and 29 and the poetry in 15:8 do not justify the old pictures of enormous waves frozen into immobility and towering on each side of the marching columns. The waters on each side of the causeway saved the people from being outflanked, and thus acted like a wall.

There is still uncertainty over the exact place of crossing and over the exact route taken by the Israelites on their way to Sinai. But after several miracles of provision, in spite of near revolution when things went wrong, they arrived at Sinai where God spoke to the people in a way that they would understand, through fire and earthquake on the mountain. It would be hard to keep the people from following the easily manipulated gods and goddesses of the Canaanites. So God showed that he was the God of power over his creation, but he was also concerned with the inner power of the moral law. Thus he summoned Moses to come up into the fierceness of the mountain scene and receive the Law (Exodus 19:1-25).

Here we may take the types of Law which God revealed on this occasion and later. At the forefront he gave the Ten Commandments that have formed a marvellous overall summary, capable of application and extension (Matthew 5:27-30, etc.) right up to the present day (Exodus 20:1-17). Next came some practical applications for the nation as it was, and as it would be settled in Palestine. These were in part edited versions of the old laws of civilized behaviour that had existed in the nation since Abraham and his family brought them from Babylonia (Exodus 21:1–23:33). To these laws the people pledged assent, and their leaders were given a startling vision of the glory of God at a sacred meal on the mountain (24:3-11).

Next, Moses was given a detailed plan of the ark of the covenant, the tabernacle of worship, and the conduct of the worship by Aaron and his sons (Exodus 25:1–30:38). The significance of this is that God is approachable but cannot be approached in a casual way. From time to time during his leadership Moses received other detailed instructions about worship and behaviour particularly for the priests, and this was naturally given in formal terms like the rubrics in the Anglican Book of Common Prayer. The formal language does not denote another author than Moses.

When Moses came down from the mountain he found that Aaron had weakly allowed an astounding outbreak of idolatry and sex around a golden calf. He dealt with this drastically (see **Aaron, Levi**). Then he interceded for mercy in a prayer that is unequalled in its terms, unless one can count Paul's words in Romans 9:3 as also expressing a prayer (Exodus 32:30-34). After a fresh vision of God on the mountain, Moses was given a further set of laws, which reinforced the duty towards God that had been expressed in the first laws, since this was the side that had been broken when the people made the golden calf (33:17–34:28).

During his long time in the mountain, the face of Moses had been astoundingly transformed, and reflected some of the divine glory that had surrounded him; so much so, that he had to veil his face when he mixed with the people, although he unveiled when he went into his tent to speak to God in the stillness (Exodus 34:29-35; note the application in 2 Corinthians 3:7-18).

Moses used his own tent as the place of meeting before the tabernacle was made, (see Exodus 33:7-11). The close of Exodus describes the making and erection of the tabernacle. Hebrews 8-10 sets out what can be learnt from it, and how its principles are to be applied in our own approach to God through our Lord Jesus Christ.

One can only mention a few incidents during the wanderings, which were extended for forty years after the refusal of the people to go into the land (see **Caleb**). For one rebellion see **Abiram**, **Koran**. The incident of water from the rock, which was the cause of both Moses and Aaron being refused the right to enter the Promised Land, is recorded in Numbers 20:2-13. At first reading it seems astounding that such a small error of judgment could have had such dire results. Hence one must read more carefully. Moses and Aaron had had a long experience of God, and thus they had a very great responsibility to obey God and not take liberties of their own.

On a previous occasion Moses had been told to strike a rock with his rod, and God had opened it up to produce a stream of fresh water. On this second occasion God told Moses and Aaron merely to speak to the rock, and water would flow. But the two men of God were tempted to show themselves off as the injured subjects of the people's grumbling. 'Hear now, you rebels; shall we bring forth water for you out of this rock?'

Moses then smote the rock twice, and the water streamed out. God's words of blame were that they had not sanctified him in the eyes of the people, a thing that is sadly possible for any

Christian leader who unguardedly puts himself in place of God. A further significant point, which Moses and Aaron could not have known, is that the living water was a parable picture of the life that flows from Christ (John 7:37). In 1 Corinthians 10:4 Paul says that the rock was Christ, and speaks of the rock as following the Israelites, meaning that the supply of water was still miraculously available on the second occasion, at the end of the wanderings as at the beginning.

In the light of Paul's equation of the rock with Christ, we may say that Jesus Christ was smitten once on the cross, and thereafter he is available when we call upon him. To attempt to smite him twice would be to try to offer him in sacrifice again. Thus Moses and Aaron, in setting themselves up as dispensers of the water through their use of the rod, were not only putting God in second place — for which they were deprived of their privilege — but spoilt one of God's blueprints of salvation.

Before Moses died, he summarized and expanded the laws of God under the inspiration of God. Many of the laws already given were for the guidance of the priests and other authorities. In Deuteronomy we have a more popular exposition, which Moses wrote down (Deuteronomy 31:24), and left for the Levites to use as a textbook for teaching the people (31:9-13). (See **Josiah**).

Finally, after a poem concerning the character and prospects of Israel, Moses blessed the tribes individually (32 and 33). Then on Mount Pisgah, overlooking Jericho, God took him out of his long life and buried his body in a place unknown (34:1-8). But what was denied to Moses in life in the body was granted to him in spirit, when he appeared in the Promised Land at the transfiguration (Matthew 17:3).

In Deuteronomy 18:18 God promises to raise up a prophet like Moses. The writer of the appendix to Deuteronomy has a note that by his day no prophet like Moses had been raised up. He rightly sees that there was a special prophetic experience that Moses had, a face to face experience which involved immediate access to God. This is borne out by Numbers 12:6-8; Exodus 33:8-11. On no occasion do we find Moses having to wait for an answer, as did other prophets (Jeremiah 42:4-7). In this way, our Lord Jesus Christ resembled Moses, and Deuteronomy 18:18 is quoted of him in Acts 3:22 and 7:37. Jesus had immediate access to his father and instantaneously knew his will (John 8:28; 12:49).

There is no reason at all why Moses should not have edited and written the Pentateuch, the first five books of the Old Testament. The stories in Genesis were naturally handed down to him in differing styles. The remainder of the writings show no greater differences than what one would expect from the subject matter. It would be natural for Moses to write on the skins of sacrificed animals, and these would be stitched together, often grouping subjects together. It is interesting that the official copy of the Law in every Jewish synagogue is on parchment (from skin) and not on paper. (For date of the Exodus, etc, see **Pharaoh**)

NAAMAN. *Pleasant*
A tough Syrian general, who in private life showed a very human side to his character. All that we know of him is contained in 2 Kings 5. He and his wife were remarkably kind to their slaves, and this stood him in good stead when he developed an incurable leprosy. An Israelite maid, a great admirer of Elisha, maintained that her master could be cured if he went to the prophet. At the moment, after a series of campaigns which Naaman had doubtless conducted, Israel was licking her wounds, and the king of Syria sent a strong letter along with Naaman demanding that the king of Israel should cure his general.

The king of Israel decided that this was an excuse for a fresh quarrel, but Elisha stepped in and declared that he would treat the patient, 'that he may know that there is a prophet in Israel' (2 Kings 5:8). (This is one sentence in the Bible where the public reader has to make up his mind which of the main words to emphasize; each one makes a different sense, i.e. 'he ... know ... is ... prophet ... Israel'. Try it and see.)

His cure was the simple one of dipping seven times into the

river Jordan. Naaman's rage was appeased by his servants, who understood that their master was reasonable at heart, and eventually he agreed with them that he might as well have a try. He was instantaneously healed. His reaction was to attempt to load Elisha with gifts, and declare his devotion to Jehovah. When Elisha refused the gifts, Naaman asked permission to take back enough earth to construct a small altar in his house.

Then this great man faced the fact that from time to time he had to accompany the king in his worship in the temple of Rimmon. Could the Lord understand? Elisha simply told him to go in peace, which was a meaningful answer. Elisha's servant, Gehazi, imposed upon Naaman's generosity with the sort of lie that would move a generous man, and received Naaman's leprosy as an additional gift. (See **Gehazi**.)

NABAL. *Fool*
A rich sheep farmer whose greed made him despised by his wife and servants. When his wife saved his life by paying David and his men legitimate protection money, his rage brought on a fatal stroke (1 Samuel 25). (See **Abigail**).

NABOTH. *Eminence*
An old-fashioned Israelite who owned a vineyard next door to the royal palace of Ahab and Jezebel. Ahab decided to go in for vegetables, and naturally thought it would be easy to do a deal or make an exchange with Naboth. Naboth, however, stood up for his rights as an Israelite property owner (Leviticus 25:23), and Ahab recognized this. But he went off his food and sulked in bed until Jezebel took a hand, and with Ahab's tacit agreement arranged for Naboth to be put on trial and stoned to death on the testimony of two hired witnesses that he had cursed God and the king. But when Ahab set foot in the vineyard he met Elijah, and soon learnt that there were worse things in store for himself and his wife than looking over the garden fence at someone else's desirable plot (1 Kings 21).

NADAB. *Generous*
1. Eldest son of Aaron, who with his brother Abihu died when they experimented with some fancy form of worship (Leviticus 10:1-7). Since the chapter immediately afterwards warns against drinking before leading the worship, it is likely that both brothers were under the influence of drink at the time.

2. Another Nadab succeeded his father, Jeroboam I, on the throne of Israel (c. 915 BC), but was assassinated after two years (1 Kings 15:25-28).

NAHASH
A king of Ammon, whose brutal terms for the surrender of Jabesh-Gilead first brought Saul into prominence (1 Samuel 11). He may be the same man who was on good terms with David and whose son, Hanun, insulted David's ambassadors, though this would mean that he had a long reign (2 Samuel 10).

Another Nahash creates a problem, or solves one. In 2 Samuel 17:25 he is said to have been the father of Abigail and Zeruiah. But these were David's sisters, according to 1 Chronicles 2:13-16, and David's father was Jesse. The way in which the two sisters are mentioned in 1 Chronicles 2:16 could imply that they were not the daughters of Jesse, and thus we conclude that Jesse married the widow of Nahash, who had borne two daughters, who thus were David's step-sisters. A problem that this may solve is that in reading the story of David we gather, rightly or wrongly, that the three sons of Zeruiah – Joab, Abishai and Asahel – were about the same age as David, although they were his nephews.

NAHUM. *Compassionate*
We know nothing of this prophet except that he came from the unidentified town of Elkosh (Nahum 1:1). His book was written after the fall of No-amon, or Thebes, in Egypt in 663 BC (3:8), and before the fall of Nineveh in 612 BC. The book is primarily concerned with the fall of Nineveh, the capital of the brutal Assyrian empire. The descriptive chapters speak for themselves,

but amid the welter of destruction there stands out the verse which has cheered so many Christians (Nahum 1:7). The permanent value of the book is that it shows God's hatred of nations who attain and hold power by brutality, so sadly the book is not out of date.

NAOMI. *My delight*
During the time of the Judges, Naomi and her husband Elimelech took their two sons Mahlon and Chilion into Moab to escape the famine in their locality. In the next ten years her husband died, followed by her two sons who left Moabite wives behind them. Naomi determined to return to her home town of Bethlehem, and one of her daughters-in-law, Ruth, went back with her. Naomi had a warm welcome from her old friends, and in spite of her bitter experiences set about building up a new life for Ruth and herself. There was a field that had belonged to her husband, and this now was hers. She used this field and the law of inheritance to bring about a happy marriage for Ruth with a kinsman of her late husband named Boaz. (See **Ruth**.)

NAPHTALI. *Wrestler*
Second son of Rachel's maid Bilhah, by Jacob (Genesis 30:7, 8). His name reflects the mad competition for children between Leah and Rachel. Rachel thought she had won when this child was born. Nothing more is said of him, but his father spoke of him as a hind let loose with comely fawns (49:21). This may mean that he was more of a roamer than his brothers, but could also refer to the crags and peaks of the Naphtali tribe's territory in Galilee, associated with deer and gazelles.

NATHAN. *He (God) had given*
In reading the history, we find that God raised up one or more prophets to act as immediate guides for the reigning king. They were there to be consulted on the will of God, or if they were not consulted they might be given a direct message from God to pass on to the king. Nathan and Gad were two important court

prophets during David's reign. When David wished to build a temple in Jerusalem, Nathan, speaking as an enthusiast, backed him. But that night God spoke to Nathan as a prophet and told him that David was not to build it(2 Samuel 7).

It is important to note that prophecy was different from wise advice, and always came directly from God if it was genuine. (For false prophecy see **Micah**.) The next appearance of Nathan is to rebuke David over Bathsheba, enforcing his words with a telling parable (2 Samuel 12). He and Gad had a gift for music, and helped David in arranging the singing and orchestration in the worship in the tabernacle, which was afterwards carried on in the temple (2 Chronicles 29:25).

At the end of David's reign, Nathan took the initiative in thwarting Adonijah's attempt to seize the throne, and he was one of the three who crowned Solomon king (1 Kings 1). We have no further knowledge of him, except that he, Samuel and Gad chronicled David's reign (1 Chronicles 29:29-30), and he shared with Ahijah the chronicles of part of Solomon's reign (2 Chronicles 9:29). It seems that the court prophets frequently acted as scribes of contemporary events, and the compilers of books of Kings and Chronicles used their records.

The Jews describe the historical books of Joshua, Judges, Samuel and Kings as the Former Prophets. Thus the pronouncements that a king did that which was right in the sight of the Lord, or the reverse, are God's contemporary verdicts through the prophets, even when we may have only a brief description retained by the compiler of the history as it has come down to us.

Naturally there was not room to reproduce all the contemporary records, any more than there was to include all the events of Christ's earthly ministry (John 21:25). One might add that the priestly compiler of Chronicles had additional temple records to draw on. The prophets were less concerned with the details that interested the priests, but both kept true records.

NATHANAEL[NT]. *Gift of God*

A native of Cana, who is mentioned by name only in John 1:45-51; 21:2. It is possible that he is the same as **Bartholomew**, for reasons given under that heading. When he came to Jesus, Jesus startled him by showing that he had known his movements and the Scripture he had been studying (i.e. Jacob's ladder), and elicited a confession of his Messiahship. Jesus described him as a genuine man of God (1:45-51).

NEBUCHADNEZZAR, or **Nebuchadrezzar**

Both Hebrew renderings occur in Scripture, with the second and less familiar being the closer to the original, which probably means, *Nebo protects the rights of succession*. The other version may come by way of an Aramaic variant.

Nebuchadnezzar, king of Babylon 605-562 BC, is mentioned in the Bible more frequently than any other foreign ruler. While still crown prince, he campaigned successfully in Palestine, defeated the Egyptians at Carchemish (606 BC), and took hostages, including Daniel, from Jehoiakim of Judah (Jeremiah 46:2; Daniel 1:1-2). While still in the south, Nebuchadnezzar heard of his father's death, and with a small force took the short cut across the desert regions to Babylon to make sure of the succession. The prisoners would have followed by the normal route of the Fertile Crescent to the north.

After a few years Jehoiakim rebelled, and was killed in the subsequent Babylonian punitive attack. His son Jehoiachin was taken captive to Babylon, with Ezekiel and others (2 Kings 24:1-17). Nebuchadnezzar put Zedekiah on the throne, but eventually he also rebelled, and his broken pledge of loyalty to Babylon was one of the reasons why Jeremiah kept urging submission when Nebuchadnezzar again invaded the country (Jeremiah 27). The city fell and was destroyed in 587 BC, and many of the people were taken into exile.

Nebuchadnezzar's relations with Daniel are mentioned under **Daniel** and **Abed-nego**. We lack contemporary records of the period of his madness (Daniel 4), but a writer, Megasthenes (about 300 BC), says that Nebuchadnezzar on the roof of his palace was suddenly possessed by a spirit, and after foretelling the end of the Babylonian empire he disappeared. This could be a variant of the actual event that Daniel describes in chapter 4. As the king was boasting of the wonderful city that he had built, he was suddenly seized with the rare hallucinatory illness of boanthropy, in which he behaved like an ox, even trying to eat grass. His ministers did their best to hush things up, probably on the advice of Daniel who knew that he would return to sanity again, and they put him in seclusion, probably in a private park.

The period of 'seven times' (Daniel 4:32) is unlikely to have been seven years, but even if it was a potential seven years it could be terminated as soon as the king admitted in his heart of hearts that the true God was greater than he, as verse 32 makes clear. He was certainly afflicted for six months to a year (perhaps seven months) (verse 33), while the beast, or shadow, side of his personality was dominant, and while in the depths of his mind he was coming to terms with God and himself.

As suddenly as he had collapsed, he returned to full sanity, and immediately glorified God, using expressions that he had heard from Daniel, drawn from Psalm 145:13 and Isaiah 40:22-26; 43:13 (Daniel 4:34-36). In general, it sounds from Daniel as though he was a sensible and thoughtful ruler when one came to know him, though terrifying when he was crossed.

Humanly speaking, he had much to boast about, making Babylon one of the seven wonders of the world. He constructed the so-called Hanging Gardens that rose up in a mound from the level ground, to please his wife who missed her native hills. If you are ever in Berlin, give yourself a thrill by visiting the Pergamon Museum and walking the processional way to the reconstructed Ishtar Gate, with a wall of the original coloured tiles depicting great lions.

NEBUZARADAN. *Nebo has given seed*
Nebuchadnezzar's general in the final capture of Jerusalem in 587 BC. He had the responsibility of destroying the city and of

selecting prisoners to go to Babylon. Naturally, he chose the more important men and women (2 Kings 25:8-21). He had special orders to spare Jeremiah's life, and to allow him either to remain or go to Babylon (Jeremiah 39:11–40:6).

NECO
See **Pharaoh**.

NEHEMIAH. *Jehovah has comforted*
When the first return of the Jews took place in 536 BC, Nehemiah's grandparents had evidently decided not to go back, and in 445 BC we find him cupbearer to the Persian king, Artaxerxes I (Nehemiah 1 and 2). This was clearly an important office. News came to him that Jerusalem was in a bad state, with its walls and gates thrown down. While this could refer to the original destruction in 587 BC, it makes more sense if there had been an abortive attempt to rebuild the walls, and a fresh destruction, probably that recorded in Ezra 4:7-23, which is dated in the reign of Artaxerxes. Nehemiah prayed hard, and God opened up the way for him to go back himself and do the reconstruction that was so badly needed if Jerusalem was to maintain its separate identity as Jehovah's city. The king detected his sadness, asked him the reason, and appointed him as governor of Jerusalem and the neighbouring area, with a grant for necessary materials for the wall and other things in the city. If Ezra 4:7-23 refers to this period, the king had left open the possibility of changing his mind (verse 21).

Nehemiah was at once exposed to the hostility of local governors and officials who disliked the thought of Judah once more becoming independent, but he managed to outwit their threats and plots. By rallying all the available help he completed the walls and gates in the incredible time of fifty-two days (Nehemiah 6:15), which suggests that much of the preliminary material had already been dug out of the old ruins and put in place, even though the enemy had pulled it down again.

When the wall was built, Nehemiah set about building

houses and encouraging the Jews to move in from the country. Up till now they had been reluctant to collect in an undefended centre (Nehemiah 7:4-5; 11:1-2). Then everyone came together for a solemn dedication and renewal of the covenant with God. Ezra, the expert in the Law, was invited to come back, probably from Persia, to read and expound the law of Moses with the help of the Levites, and all pledged themselves to keep it (chapters 8-10). Finally, to dedicate the walls, Ezra and Nehemiah led processions round the city (Nehemiah 12:27-43).

Nehemiah returned to Artaxerxes at least once (Nehemiah 13:6). Probably he went back earlier too, since twelve years is a long time for his first absence in the light of Nehemiah 2:6. During his last absence his enemies seized the opportunity of infiltrating into the city, and on his return Nehemiah reacted violently against Tobiah, who had been given a bed-sit in the temple, and against the starving out of the Levites (Nehemiah 13:4-14). Then there was the attraction of the street market on the Sabbath (13:15-22), and the fresh outbreak of marriage with foreigners, whose children gave the show away with their appalling dialects (13:23-27).

Even the grandson of the high priest was involved with the daughter of Nehemiah's chief opponent San-ballat, and it must have been worth seeing when, as Nehemiah says, 'I chased him from me' (Nehemiah 13:28), though even more spectacular was the treatment of some of the others who were unfortunate enough to be caught by the indignant governor, who beat them and plucked out their hair (verse 25). It may seem to us a lot of fuss about a small thing, but Nehemiah dreaded to see the nation sliding down to destruction again through involvement with the degrading foreign religions. (See **Tobiah**, **Sanballat**)

Nehemiah was a sincere man of God, as we can see from the brief prayers that he includes in his memoirs which form a large part of the book that bears his name (e.g. Nehemiah 1:4-11; 2:4; 4:9; 5:19; 6:9; 13:31). He was also extremely clear-headed and practical in meeting the opposition to his work. Unlike many governors, he refused to tax the people for his own needs, so he must have had considerable money of his own which he used for his own support (5:14-19). His position at court and the fact that he had no wife or family suggest that he was a eunuch.

NICODEMUS[NT]

One cannot guess why a prominent member of the Sanhedrin bore the Greek name of *Conqueror of the people*. He appears in John's Gospel as a fair-minded Pharisee, who in standing up in the council for fair treatment for Jesus was jeered at by the opposition for not knowing the Scriptures (John 7:45-52). Jesus said the same thing to him rather more gently when he came by night to discuss the real issues of his claims, and had these summed up as new birth through the Spirit of God (John 3).

Nicodemus had at first tried to be facetious about what new birth would involve, but soon expressed the longing of his heart by asking, 'How can these things be?' It is likely that he became a secret follower of Jesus and joined another secret follower, Joseph of Arimathea, in preparing the body of Jesus for burial (John 19:38-42).

There is a fictional book dating from about AD 350 variously called *The Gospel of Nicodemus* or *The Acts of Pilate*. It describes how Joseph and Nicodemus were persecuted after the resurrection, but two men, who had been raised from the dead, described to the Sanhedrin what they had seen in Hades when Jesus died. Nicodemus and Joseph reported everything to Pilate, who caused the evidence to be written in the acts of council.

NICOLAUS[NT] or Nicolas

Strangely enough, his name has the same meaning as Nicodemus (*Conqueror of the people*), but with a different Greek word for *people*. A native of Antioch who had become a Jewish proselyte and then a Christian believer. At this stage in the church's life, he must have previously become a full Jew and accepted circumcision, since uncircumcised Gentiles were not yet found in the church. He was chosen as one of the seven 'deacons' who especially looked after the material needs of Christian widows

(Acts 6:1-6). There is no evidence that he founded the sect of Nicolaitans (Revelation 2:6,15), but readers have naturally jumped at the similarity of name.

NIMROD
We think too easily of the leaders of the ancient world as complete pagans. Nimrod is a corrective, since although he founded the cities of Babylon, Erech, Accad, Nineveh and others, he was specially remembered as 'a mighty hunter before Jehovah' (Genesis 10:8-12). Several ancient cities commemorate his name, such as Burs Nimrud near Babylon, and Micah 5:6 describes Assyria as the land of Nimrod. Suggested identifications with Sargon of Agade (c. 2300 BC) or the hero Gilgamesh (date unknown), are no more than guesses. As with other intriguing names of old, traditions have clustered round Nimrod, one of the happiest being that he inherited the suit of skins that God made for Adam, and when he put it on he became a mighty hunter.

NOAH. *Rest* or *Relief*
So called by his father **Lamech** who was glad to have a son to take on the heavy work in the fields (Genesis 5:29). Noah was a good man who lived close to God in his daily life (6:9), and tried to exert an influence on others (2 Peter 2:5). When God was about to blot out the degenerate human race with a flood, he told Noah to build an ark large enough for his family and for representatives of the animals.

Noah took God at his word (Hebrews 11:7) and in this ark he survived the flood, and afterwards offered a sacrifice of thanksgiving to God, during which God chose the rainbow as a pledged sign that the flood would not be repeated (Genesis 6:11–9:17). Unfortunately, later Noah experimented with wine making, and his son Ham found him lying dead drunk and naked in his tent. Ham evidently made some unpleasant remarks to his brothers, who then went in and covered their father with their faces turned away. (See **Ham, Japheth, Shem**.)

The scientific understanding of the flood itself is full of difficulty. Traditions of a great flood exist in all parts of the world, but the problem is to judge the extent of it. Taken at its face value the Bible seems to describe a worldwide flood, caused not only by a deluge of rain, but by upheavals that sent waters from the ocean pouring over the land (Genesis 7:11).

Suggestions as to how these could have been caused include violent seismic disturbances which altered the contours under the sea; an alteration in the earth's axis which might melt some of the enormous ice caps at the poles; or the near approach of a large heavenly body, perhaps the size of the moon, which piled up the waters around the equator and then, as it burst, released them.

It has been pointed out that the plateau of Iran, which now is a desert area with salt in the soil, was fertile and inhabited before about 7000 BC. Also the annual sedimentary layers in Lake Ragunda in Sweden, which mark out the annual amount of glacier melting, indicate an abnormal amount of melting about 7000 BC. It has been argued that the universal flood was responsible for the fossils, which have commonly been regarded as very old, but this idea has not been taken seriously by geologists.

An objection to a universal flood in Bible times is the preservation of the cave paintings in Europe. After being opened up for the public, the condensation of the breath of visitors caused deterioration of the pictures at the Lascaux caves in south west France (see also **Jubal**), and they are now closed to the public, although a replica cave with reproductions of the paintings has been constructed nearby. How much more would the originals have been affected by a flood. The pictures are estimated to be 17,300 years old.

In default of further evidence, which may well be forthcoming, we must consider the other interpretation of the Bible story, namely that the flood was localized, though sufficiently widespread to clean up the pollution of degraded mankind. This means that the story is told from the point of view of the observations of Noah and his family, who had no knowledge of what was happening outside the area of the Middle East. We naturally assume that the drift from Eden led to the colonization of the whole area round the Euphrates and Tigris.

The human race here had steadily deteriorated, and Genesis 6:1-4 may even indicate that they had attracted materializations of evil spirit beings. Indeed Jude 6 and 7 compares the fall of angelic beings with the immorality of Sodom. This area could easily be flooded. Indeed, archaeology has shown mud deposits in various parts that must have been laid down by local floods, although these deposits are not all of the same date. They are detectable in towns, where the mud interrupts the layers of buildings, but a general flood over the whole area at a much earlier date would not yield the same clear evidence. One cannot say how far the waters rose, but they floated the ark into the mountain area of Ararat, though we are not obliged to imagine it perched on the top, as in some old pictures.

This theory means that there were men and women in other parts of the world who were not destroyed, and one would assume that they had maintained moral standards, or, if one moves into speculations about pre-Adamites, that they had not yet been shown God's standards directly as the Adamites had. Thus their morals were primitive, but not sinful. (See **Adam**)

We must at least conclude that the flood was very extensive, since otherwise there would have been no point in building an enormous ark rather than simply migrating to another area. The ark was about 450 feet [137 metres] long, 75 [23] broad, and 45 [14] deep, and these are seaworthy proportions, unlike the ark in the Babylonian story of Gilgamesh which is in the form of a cube and consequently would have been bowled over and over. If the flood was not worldwide, the animals would have been limited to those in the area that was to be inundated. Some have thought that only domestic animals were to be taken in, which would have made housing and feeding comparatively easy, since none would be solely carnivorous. Otherwise there could have been some equivalent of induced hibernation.

Like all writers on the flood, we have felt bound to introduce speculations, some perhaps extreme. The main thing is to keep an open mind, and it may well be that some important piece of evidence will turn up at any time. Rumoured sightings of the ark embedded in the ice on Ararat have sent out more than one expedition in recent years. One 'authentic' story, centring round a Russian airman, was completely phoney, but who knows?

OBADIAH. *Servant of Jehovah*
Several bear this name, but two are important.

1. Ahab's right-hand man, who dared to stand up to Jezebel, and rescued 100 prophets of Jehovah, concealing them in two large caves (1 Kings 18:3-4). After some three years of drought, Ahab sent Obadiah on a tour of investigation to list any sources of water that remained. Ahab himself undertook a similar tour using another route (18:5-6). It was during this tour that Obadiah met Elijah who sent him to bring Ahab. Obadiah had joined Ahab in searching for Elijah for a long time, and was afraid that he would once more vanish into thin air if he left him, but eventually he agreed to find Ahab. The sequel was the challenge on Mount Carmel, which Obadiah undoubtedly watched with satisfaction. (See **Elijah**)

2. Obadiah the prophet, who attacked the Edomites for their treachery at the capture of Jerusalem. The reference is almost certainly to the capture by the Babylonians in 587 BC. The Edomites not only took advantage of the opportunity to loot (Obadiah 13), but caught the fugitives and handed them back to the enemy (Obadiah 14). Obadiah's story is confirmed by Psalm 137:7; Ezekiel 25:12-14, and the association of the trapping of King Zedekiah with a denunciation of Edom in Lamentations 4:19-21 suggests that the trapping of the fugitives in Obadiah 14 included the capture of the king.

Obadiah refers to the mountains and crags of Edom, which formed fine natural defences (Obadiah 3 and 4), and also to Edom as a centre of wisdom (Obadiah 8). (See **Job**). His prophecy of the subjugation of Edom by Judah was fulfilled finally in 109 BC when John Hyrcanus compelled all the Edomites to be circumcised, and absorbed them into Judah. The Herods were Idumeans, or Edomites.

OBED-EDOM. *Servant of Edom*
We easily forget that there were a number of foreign converts in Israel, including even Philistines, like Ittai, and Hittites like Uriah. Obed-edom came from Goliath's home town of Gath, as did Ittai and the men he brought with him. After David's first abortive attempt to bring the ark of the covenant into Jerusalem (see **Uzzah**), he sent the ark of the covenant to the house of Obed-edom where it stayed for three months (2 Samuel 6:10-11). Obed-edom must have guarded the ark of the covenant reverently, and so had a very different reward from that of the Philistines, including Gittites, who captured it from Eli and treated it with contempt (1 Samuel 5).

Another Obed-edom was a Levitical gatekeeper in Jerusalem (1 Chronicles 15:18). The Chronicler distinguishes him from the former (13:13-14). Perhaps both of them, or their parents, had been taken as slaves in Edomite raids, and rescued by Saul in one of his counter raids (1 Samuel 14:47). Hence their name, or nickname. Saul employed a particularly nasty Edomite as his chief herdsman (21:7). (See **Doeg**).

ODED. Perhaps, *He has restored*
A prophet of the northern kingdom who organized a demonstration that secured the release of prisoners that King Pekah had taken from Jericho (2 Chronicles 28:5-15).

OG
King of Bashan, defeated and killed by the Israelites on their way to the Promised Land (Numbers 21:31-35). He was a man of immense size (Deuteronomy 3:11), and consequently the Israelite success in conquering him was long remembered (e.g. 1 Kings 4:19; Nehemiah 9:22; Psalm 135:11; 136:20). Some modern commentators, and the NEB, have turned him out of his famous

bedstead of iron, some 13½ feet [4.1 metres] long (Deuteronomy 3:11), and made this a sarcophagus of black basalt. According to 3:11 it was put on display at Rabbah, an Ammonite city, but since it is no longer on view we shall never know which it was.

OMRI. Meaning uncertain
Omri came to the throne of Israel through a revolution. He was on a campaign in command of the army when news came that the man in joint command of the chariots, Zimri, had assassinated King Elah during an orgy of drinking. The army preferred Omri as king, and supported him in an attack on Tirzah, where Zimri was. Under pressure, Zimri committed suicide by burning down the palace over his head. But Omri still had a rival, Tibni, who had considerable popular support, but eventually Omri emerged on top and became king (886-874 BC).

The Bible merely records that Omri built and fortified Samaria, which now became the capital (1 Kings 16:24), and that he had to give up certain cities to Syria and allow Syrian traders to set up stalls in Samaria (20:34). But he made Moab pay heavily as acknowledgment of defeat, as we learn from Mesha's famous inscription (see Mesha). Some suggest that he deliberately gained the support of Tyre and Sidon by arranging the marriage of his son Ahab to Jezebel, but the Bible rather suggests that the choice was Ahab's own (16:31). His name became a byword for wrongdoing (Micah 6:16). His palace in Samaria has been excavated by archaeologists.

ONAN. *Strong*
Second son of Judah by a Canaanite girl, Shua. His elder brother, Er, died childless, leaving a widow, Tamar. It was then Onan's duty to take Tamar, and any child would count as Er's. This was the levirate custom or law (e.g. Deuteronomy 25:5-10). Onan professed to fulfil his obligation, but in fact refused to consummate the marriage. As with Ananias and Sapphira in Acts 5, his deception before God was followed by his death (Genesis 38:6-10). His action cannot be used as an argument against the use of

birth control methods within marriage, although medically and psychologically his particular method of withdrawal is not without problems. Nor was his sin, as has often been maintained, masturbation.

ONESIMUS^{NT}. *Profitable*

A runaway slave who forms the subject of Paul's letter to his former master, Philemon. Paul makes a play on his name in Philemon verses 11 and 20. Onesimus had been converted through Paul from prison in Rome (Philemon verses 10, 15, 16), and had devoted himself to Paul's service. As a runaway he was liable to punishment, but agreed to return to his master with a personal note from Paul who had been responsible for Philemon's conversion also (verse 19). Presumably Onesimus carried the letter to the Colossians as well (Colossians 4:9).

We sometimes wonder why the Christian church did not insist on the abolition of slavery from the beginning. The answer is that slavery, like war, was so much part and parcel of civic life that it could only be eradicated by the yeast-in-the-dough method spoken of by Jesus Christ in Matthew 13:33. Reformers sometimes forget that the attempted sudden disruption of a pattern of life may create more chaos than it cures.

The Bible is the story of God working slowly but surely. The Christian gospel sowed the seeds which would ultimately destroy the system of slavery. Meanwhile the slave was accepted as a brother in Christ (Philemon 15-16), and no longer as a chattel. Relationships between master and man were better than those between management and employees in many firms today (Ephesians 6:5-9; Colossians 3:22–4:1; 1 Timothy 6:1-2; Galatians 3:28). The Christian principle of love and brotherhood hits at the very basis of slavery with its inequality and self-interest.

ONESIPHORUS^{NT}. *Bringer of profit*

In spite of his name, he has brought little profit into theological debate. Paul's reference to him and his household in 2 Timothy

1:15-18; 4:19 is the sole possible support for prayers for the dead in the New Testament. The way in which Onesiphorus and his household are separated suggests that he is dead; yet Paul prays that he may find mercy from the Lord on the day of judgment. There is no doubt that this could be the interpretation, but since it would be the only case in Scripture, and would appear to run counter to the New Testament teaching of justification by faith, we should certainly see what other interpretation is possible.

The context in fact shows one that is far more likely. Onesiphorus is linked with people who had turned away from Paul, and so presumably from the Christian faith. His fall even led him to desert his family. But, remembering what a fine Christian he had shown himself to be, Paul prays for his return to the faith (compare 1 Timothy 1:20; 1 Corinthians 5:5).

OREB. *Raven*
After Gideon had routed the army of Midian, he called on the Ephraimites to intercept the Midianite retreat over the fords of Jordan. This they did, and killed the two leaders, Oreb and Zeeb. The occasion was long remembered, and is referred to in Psalm 83:11.

ORNAN
See **Araunah**.

ORPAH. Perhaps, *Stubborn*
A Moabite girl, sister of Ruth. She and Ruth married Naomi's two sons, Mahlon and Chilion. When they were both widowed they contemplated returning to Bethlehem with Naomi. Naomi urged them both to go back to their own people and Orpah reluctantly agreed, while Ruth went on to Bethlehem (Ruth 1:3-14). There is no need to blame Orpah. Home ties are strong, and she had probably never seen the land of Israel.

OSNAPPAR
See **Ashurbanipal**.

OTHNIEL. *God is power*
Nephew of Caleb (Judges 1:13; 1 Chronicles 4:13). For his marriage with Caleb's daughter, see **Caleb**. He became the first judge over Israel, and broke the hold of the unidentified Cushan-rishathaim (Judges 3:7-11).

PALTI, Phalti, Paltiel, Phaltiel. *God delivers*
When David became an outlaw, Saul was spiteful enough to take his wife Michal, Saul's younger daughter, and marry her to a man named Palti from Gallim in Benjamin (1 Samuel 25:44). After Saul's death, David demanded her back as the price of opening up negotiations with Abner. Palti, who was clearly very much in love with her, made what protest he could, but had to give way to David's prior right, although in the end the remarriage turned out unhappily (2 Samuel 3:12-16, see **Michal**).

PASHHUR. Meaning uncertain
Jeremiah had two unpleasant encounters with men of this name.

One, a priest, who put him in the stocks to stop him preaching the coming ruin of Jerusalem (Jeremiah 20:1-6). Jeremiah nicknamed him with a slogan that he used more than once, namely *Terror on every side*. This would be Pashur's experience when Jerusalem was taken.

Another Pashhur joined the gang who left Jeremiah to die in a drainage pit (Jeremiah 38; see **Ebed-melech**).

PAUL[NT]
Since this name means *Little*, and he was originally called Saul (Acts 13:9), it is possible that Paul's new name became attached to him because of his size. He himself suggests that his appearance was far from imposing (2 Corinthians 10:10). In a book called *The Acts of Paul and Thecla*, which may contain early material, Paul is described as 'bald, bow-legged, strongly built but small in size, with eyebrows that met and a fairly large nose'. But he certainly had an iron constitution to stand all the experiences that he lists in 11:21-29. There is no evidence that he

was an epileptic as is sometimes stated, but it sounds as though he suffered from eye trouble (Galatians 4:13-15; 6:11; perhaps Acts 23:1-5).

Paul was born at Tarsus with a father who was already a Roman citizen, a valuable asset, whether given or earned (Acts 22:28). He was brought up as a completely orthodox Pharisee (Acts 23:6; Philippians 3:5), was trained by the great Gamaliel (Acts 22:3), and may have been a member of the Sanhedrin council (Acts 26:10). Since all Jews learned a trade, Paul was a tentmaker (Acts 18:3), and during his later travels he kept himself by this means (1 Corinthians 9:6). Since members of the Sanhedrin were expected to be married, some think that 7:8 indicates that Paul was a widower and not a bachelor (compare verse 40).

We first meet him as a leader of the persecutions of the Christians after the death of Stephen, at which he was present (Acts 7:58–8:3). On his way to arrest the Christians in Damascus he was suddenly stopped by a blinding light and heard the voice of Jesus speaking to him, asking him why he was persecuting him in the person of his followers. The story of Paul's conversion on this occasion is important enough to be related three times in the Acts (9:1-9; 22:6-11; 26:12-18). Putting the three accounts together, we gather that his companions saw the bright light and heard the sound of the voice from heaven, but did not hear the words as Paul did. One may compare their experience with that of the bystanders when God's voice spoke of Jesus. Some heard words, others heard thunder (John 12:28-29).

Paul was blind for three days until a disciple, Ananias, came and laid his hands on him (Acts 9:10-19). Almost at once he began to preach, naturally starting with the Jews in Damascus (9:20-22), and reserving until later the special charge to preach to the Gentiles also (9:15; 26:17-18). From this time onwards there are one or two uncertainties about chronology, but probably after a short time in Damascus Paul retired by himself into Arabia to let God speak to him more fully, and then returned to Damascus for further preaching (Galatians 1:17).

Three years after his conversion he escaped death by being lowered over the city wall after dark (Acts 9:23-29; 2 Corinthians 11:32). At Jerusalem Paul was suspect, until Barnabas took his side (Acts 9:26-27), and gave him the chance of discussion with Peter, and James the Lord's brother (Galatians 1:18-20). He also preached Jesus Christ in the synagogues, but in a very short time he was again in danger of his life (Acts 9:28-29). While in the temple praying, he had a vision of Jesus Christ, who told him now to leave the city and prepare for work among the Gentiles (22:17-21). The other Christians agreed, and Paul went back home for a time to Tarsus (9:30).

We do not know how long Paul remained there before Barnabas fetched him to Antioch to help in a flourishing work among the Gentiles (Acts 11:20-26). The stay in Antioch concluded with Paul and Barnabas taking money for famine relief to Jerusalem (11:27-30). Then came the First Missionary Journey about AD 46 when Barnabas and Paul, at first with Mark, visited Barnabas's home island of Cyprus, and from there travelled through the south-eastern part of the bulge that is Asia Minor, after Mark had gone home (Acts 13:13, see **Mark**). Luke's account in Acts 13 and 14 records an encounter with a magician (Acts 13:1-12, see **Elymas**), a sermon to the Jews in Antioch of Pisidia (13:13-41), followed a week later by another sermon to a crammed house, and then a work among the Gentiles, until persecution drove them to Iconium (13:42-52).

From now onwards the Gentile mission developed so far as Jewish opposition allowed. A miracle at Lystra led to the apostles being hailed as visitors from Olympus, the dignified Barnabas being acclaimed as King Zeus or Jupiter, while Paul who did most of the talking was identified with the messenger of the gods, Hermes or Mercury. But this did not prevent the same people joining the Jews in stoning Paul almost to death (Acts 14:1-20). The journey ended by a return over the ground they had previously covered until they reached Antioch and reported their experiences to the church there (14:21-28).

The status of converted uncircumcised Gentiles now boiled

up. It was undeniable that the Old Testament spoke of Gentiles being received into Judaism, but it was possible to argue that unless they became circumcised Jews, or even if they did so, they were no more than second-class citizens. The gospel that Paul and Barnabas preached went far beyond this, and Paul does not hesitate to speak of it as something new; the Gentiles in Christ were on an absolute equality with Jewish believers (Ephesians 3:4-6).

A representative council met at Jerusalem to discuss this, with James in the chair, and after hearing evidence from Peter, Paul and Barnabas, the council, guided by the Holy Spirit, wrote a circular letter to the churches, which is best understood as referring to mixed communities of converted Jews and Gentiles, such as existed in most Gentile towns. The Jews should accept the Gentiles, but the Gentiles should give up some of the things that belonged to their past and that would unduly shock the Jews. For example, 'kosher' foods should be served at communal meals, and they should be particularly careful over proper sex relations (Acts 15:19-20,29). Judas Barsabbas (otherwise unknown) and Silas were officially commissioned to join Paul and Barnabas in carrying and interpreting the letter (15:22-32).

Although some refer Galatians 2 to this occasion, others refer it to the earlier occasion of Acts 11:29-30 when Paul and Barnabas brought money for famine relief. It is obvious that there was a strong minority group in Jerusalem who would not accept Gentile Christians as full members (Acts 15:5), and Paul needed to clear up some points personally with James, Peter and John (Galatians 2:9). The main thing that emerged was a recognition that the latter were called especially to the Jews, while Paul and Barnabas had a special ministry to the Gentiles (Galatians 2:9). One may suggest that the call of God was reinforced by the ability of Paul and Barnabas to speak fluent Greek, while the Jerusalem apostles were still very much tied to Aramaic. (But see **Peter**)

The Second Missionary Journey began in AD 49 or 50. Paul and Barnabas disagreed over taking Mark again, and sadly separated (see **Barnabas, Mark**). Paul's companion this time was Silas, and they broke into the route of the previous journey by travelling overland from the east. At Lystra they picked up a young man, Timothy, of mixed parentage, and since he was half-Jewish Paul felt it right to circumcise him so as not to set up barriers between Christians and the unconverted Jews with whom he tried to mix at first in each town (Acts 15:36–16:5). Much ink has been spilt over discussing the general route that Paul and Barnabas took through Phrygia and Galatia, but commentators or no commentators, they arrived safely at Troas on the north coast opposite Greece (Acts 16:6-8).

Here occurred something for which we can be specially thankful; the meeting with Luke, as the switch to the first person plural indicates. Indeed Luke may have been the man of Macedonia whom Paul saw in a vision asking him to cross over into Europe (Acts 16:9-10). Their first experiences in Europe at Philippi were both encouraging and frightening, resulting in imprisonment, scourging, and release with full apologies (16:11-40).

After being hounded by the Jews from Thessalonica and Beroea, Paul went on alone to Athens (Acts 17:1-15) where he delivered his famous address on the Areopagus hill, starting on common ground with Greek thinkers who had no time for idolatry, and explaining that the so-called Unknown God had made himself known in Jesus Christ. But he did not tone down the gospel, and ended by speaking of Christ as risen from the dead and coming to judge the world.

It is important to notice that to Paul and his hearers resurrection meant the resurrection of the body, and not merely survival of the spirit or soul which is what Socrates and other enlightened thinkers accepted as likely, and as some try to equate with resurrection today. Paul knew that the concept of resurrection would be dismissed out of hand by most of his hearers, but he preached it as God's truth (Acts 17:16-34).

He moved on to Corinth and joined Aquila and Priscilla, fellow Christians and fellow tentmakers (Acts 18:1-4). Silas and

Timothy joined him, and their report of the church in Thessalonica led Paul to write 1 Thessalonians, and after further news 2 Thessalonians. He may also have written Galatians about this time, although some date this letter even before the Council of Jerusalem in Acts 15.

In addition to the description of Paul's activities in Corinth for some eighteen months among Jews and Gentiles (Acts 18:5-17), we have some idea of the composition of the church from reading 1 Corinthians. Its members were predominantly, though not entirely, from the simpler members of society (1 Corinthians 1:26) who seem to have been treated shabbily by the few rich men in the church (1 Corinthians 11:17-22). Eventually Paul returned to Caesarea and Antioch via Ephesus. He had kept up the Jewish custom of letting his hair grow uncut to show that he was keeping some vow. There is no hint of what the vow was for which he had his hair cut at Cenchreae (Acts 18:18).

For the Third Missionary Journey Paul took the overland route again, but this time ended up at Ephesus, presumably staying again with Aquila and Priscilla who had moved from Corinth. At Ephesus there was a group of followers of John the Baptist who were still looking for the Messiah and who consequently were without the gift of the Holy Spirit. Aquila and Priscilla had already won over Apollos, and Paul was able to win about twelve others (Acts 18:24–19:7). Then followed a most effective work among pagans, especially in meeting the challenges of occult forces (19:8-20). During this period Paul received a letter from Corinth (now lost) which he answered point by point. It is important to read 1 Corinthians with this in mind, picking out the quotations from what the Corinthians had written.

After a riot in Ephesus, stirred up by idol makers with vested interests (Acts 19:23-41, see **Demetrius**), Paul paid a further visit to Greece via Macedonia (19:21-22–20:1, 2). It is possible that he had paid a brief visit to Corinth directly from Ephesus (2 Corinthians 12:14). Meanwhile he was worried because he had received no communication from Titus whom he had sent to deal with some of the problems in the Corinthian church. To his immense relief Titus met him in Macedonia and brought him good news of the response to the strong words that Paul had addressed to them. This was the occasion of his writing 2 Corinthians from Macedonia, preparatory to his further visit in person (2 Corinthians 7:5-16). From Corinth Paul wrote the letter to the Romans to prepare the church for his projected visit. This letter, having Jews and the Old Testament especially in mind as well as Gentiles, contains a marvellous exposition of justification by faith.

But before fulfilling his dream of visiting Rome, Paul deliberately walked into trouble in Jerusalem (Acts 21:11-13), returning there via Troas and Miletus, where he had a solemn farewell talk with the elders of Ephesus (20:3–21:16). At Jerusalem there was still a tense situation between Christians and Jews, and the Jews were specially sensitive to any violation of the temple by Gentile converts. Paul agreed to show that he was not one to offend legitimate Jewish practices, and was willing to pay the temple expenses of four men who were going there to be released from a vow.

If this vow was that of a Nazirite (Numbers 6), it would involve a sacrifice, and all such sacrifices were done away through Christ's sacrifice on the cross. Since the Bible does not commend Paul for his action, we are entitled to criticize him if we wish. But it is very difficult for us to picture ourselves in the transition period in Jerusalem, when Jewish Christians were only gradually being disentangled from Judaism. The situation was not helped by reports about Paul which suggested that he was a wildcat revolutionary among the Gentiles (Acts 21:21-22).

Paul had already indicated to the Corinthians that he was prepared to go a long way to win Jews (1 Corinthians 9:20), and on this occasion, rightly or wrongly, he believed that he ought to make things easier for the Jerusalem church. But it was the old story; when people have it in for someone, nothing he can do is right; and busybodies from Asia raised a riot against Paul on an entirely false charge (Acts 21:27-29). He was dragged from the temple, and only rescued from a violent death through the intervention of the tribune, who despairing of finding out what all the trouble was about allowed Paul to address the crowd. Paul told the story of his conversion, but could not resist adding his commission to go to the Gentiles (21:30–22:21). This of course was as much as the Jews allowed him to say, but the tribune determined on a quieter investigation before the Jewish council next day.

Here Paul played the Pharisees off against the Sadducees, which he afterwards admitted was wrong (Acts 23:1-10; 24:20-21). The tribune had to save him from being lynched by the council, and spirited him away to Felix the governor in Caesarea – after hearing from Paul's nephew that over forty Jews had sworn not to eat or drink until they had killed Paul. Naturally, they did not starve when Paul escaped them, since there were ways of buying themselves out of an oath. Meanwhile Paul was given the assurance in a vision that he would be called to witness in Rome (23:11).

For the separate trials at Caesarea, see **Felix**, **Festus**, **Agrippa**. Paul was kept in prison for over two years (Acts 24:27), but eventually he appealed to go to Rome for trial before Caesar, as he was entitled to do (25:11-12). Luke gives a vivid description of the voyage to Rome and the total loss of the boat on the shores of Malta (Acts 27 and 28). In Rome he was placed under house arrest (28:16,30), constantly under guard and probably fettered to some extent to prevent any attempt at escape (Colossians 4:18). The traditional view is that the so-called Prison Epistles (Ephesians, Philippians, Colossians, Philemon) were written during this period, though a more recent view places them during the two-year imprisonment in Caesarea, or even during an unrecorded imprisonment in Ephesus.

It is tantalizing that Luke ends his record in Acts without telling us of Paul's trial after at least two years of waiting. It may be that he completed his book before the trial had taken place. We therefore have to put two and two together from allusions in the Pastoral Epistles (1 and 2 Timothy, Titus). These letters are quite different in scope from the general epistles, and correspond somewhat to the instructions to the priests in the Pentateuch. This would account for their more formal style and presentation.

We gather that Paul was acquitted, and travelled again to Asia Minor and Macedonia, and thence presumably to Athens and Corinth (1 Timothy 1:3). He and Titus visited Crete, and Paul left Titus there to establish the local churches with their overseers (Titus 1:5-9). Meanwhile, if he carried out his intentions, Paul would have wintered in Nicopolis on the west coast of Greece (Titus 3:12).

We cannot say how long Paul spent at liberty before being rearrested, but 2 Timothy is the last letter that we have from him, and this time he seems to be in more rigorous imprisonment in Rome (2 Timothy 1:16-17; 2:9). Already his case had been heard once, and many of his friends had deserted him (4:9-18), and he believed that the next hearing would be the end for him (4:6-8). Meanwhile he was feeling the cold, and asked Timothy to bring his cloak from Troas, and also some books and scrolls.

There have been speculative sermons preached on 'especially the parchments' (2 Timothy 4:13), but beyond the fact that the Greek word describes expensive vellum rather than papyrus we have no idea what they could be. Some have suggested they were certificates of Paul's Roman citizenship, but he would have been as unlikely to leave these behind as a motorist to leave his driving licence when being summoned to court. According to tradition, Paul was beheaded on the orders of Nero about AD 67 on the road to Rome's port of Ostia.

For the period between the imprisonments this is the most we can gather from the Bible. But very early Christian writings (e.g. Clement of Rome before AD 100) say that Paul preached to the limit of the west, which must at least mean Spain, to which Paul earlier had declared his intention of going (Romans 15:28). From the time of Theodoret (AD 435) there have been statements that Paul went as far as Britain, and, even earlier, Eusebius (c. AD 320) wrote that the apostles had gone as far as the Britannic isles. Whether this is so or not, it is fairly certain that Paul in prison had a definite link with people from Britain (see **Pudens**).

PAULUS[NT]
Sergius Paulus, the Roman proconsul of Cyprus, was the first recorded convert on the First Missionary Journey of Paul and Barnabas. It is probably no more than coincidence that this is the place in the story that Luke changes over from using the original name Saul for the apostle (Acts 13:9). It is most unlikely that Saul would have changed his name as a kind of compliment to the proconsul, though there is no reason why in saying, 'Saul who is also called Paul', Luke should not have meant, 'Saul also, like the proconsul, had the name of Paul.' For resistance to Paul's preaching, see **Elymas**.

PEKAHIAH. *Jehovah has opened*
Son of Mehahem, king of Israel, whose two-year reign began 742 BC. He was assassinated by one of his generals, Pekah, with a group of Gileadites (2 Kings 15:23-26).

PEKAH. *Opening*
Murderer of Pekahiah about 740 BC. In order to resist the invasions by Assyria, he and Rezin of Syria tried to force Ahaz of Judah to join them, and this formed the subject of Isaiah's words in 7:1-9. They did considerable damage to Judah (2 Kings 15:37; 2 Chronicles 28:5-15), but could not prevent Assyria from devastating a large extent of northern territory and transporting a number of the inhabitants (2 Kings 15:29). Eventually Pekah was himself assassinated by a rebel named Hoshea, who was the last king of the northern kingdom (15:30).

PELATIAH. *Jehovah has delivered*
A leader or maybe a prince of the royal family, whom Ezekiel saw in a vision with others, perhaps worshipping the sun, as they faced east (Ezekiel 11:1, compare 8:16). As leaders they gave bad counsels (see **Ja-azaniah**). Ezekiel is given a message for them,

but since he had only been transported in spirit from Babylonia to see what was going on in Jerusalem (8:2-3), it is unlikely that the people heard what he had to say, nor would they have cared if they had. But at the end of the message Pelatiah dropped dead, and this was probably an actual occurrence (11:13).

PELEG. *Division*
Son of Eber, ancestor of the Hebrews (Genesis 10:25). One of those fascinating and mysterious descriptions of Scripture is attached to his name, and indeed accounts for it: 'in his days the earth was divided'. There are three main interpretations of this remark. **1.** The scattering of the nations after the tower of Babel in Genesis 11:1-9. **2.** The digging of irrigation channels which divided up cultivatable land. **3.** A fresh splitting up of land masses.

PEREZ. *Breach*
One of the twin sons of Judah by Tamar, who forced his way out in front of his brother Zerah after the latter had made an abortive attempt. The midwife used a similar method to that in modern maternity hospitals and tied a thread round Zerah's wrist for identification as the elder (Genesis 38:27-30).

PETER[NT]
An unusual example of a man with four names, each apparently used regularly:

1. Symeon (Acts 15:14; 2 Peter 1:1 in original Greek). This was his Jewish name.

2. Simon. Used fairly frequently in narrative (e.g. Mark 1:16) and address (e.g. Matthew 16:17; Luke 22:31). A Greek name, reasonably common, and obviously resembling Symeon in sound.

3. Peter, a nickname given by Jesus (Mark 3:16) but the name by which he is most commonly known. It means *rock,* and Jesus plays on the meaning in Matthew 16:18.

4. Cephas. The Aramaic equivalent of Peter (John 1:42), used

in 1 Corinthians 1:12; 3:22; 9:5; 15:5; Galatians 2:9.

Peter was the son of a man named John (John 1:42) or Jonah (Bar-Jonah means Son of Jonah, Matthew 16:17). He was a native of Bethsaida, on the north coast of the Sea of Galilee (John 1:44), but had evidently married a girl from Capernaum, a few miles to the west, since we read that his wife's mother lived there. Perhaps he and Andrew had moved into the house, if Peter's father-in-law had died. (Mark 1:29-31).

We do not know how long before his call Peter first met Jesus (John 1:41-42), but when the challenge came to follow Jesus absolutely, he left his work as a fisherman and obeyed (Mark 1:16-18). It is important to notice that 'following Jesus' did not have the same meaning then as now. In the Gospels it meant leaving home and travelling in the company of the Master up and down the country. The ordinary reader, and even the preacher, does not realize this, and hence gives a false interpretation of Luke 9:49 where the man who was casting out demons was a true believer but he had not left his home to travel with the others. There was no question of his being a member of another 'denomination' or being unsound in his views.

Peter is named first in the list of the Twelve (Mark 3:16, etc.), and shared several unique occasions with James and John, i.e. the raising of Jairus' daughter (Mark 5:37), the transfiguration (Mark 9:2), and the agony in Gethsemane (Mark 14:33). He was strong in asserting his loyalty (John 6:66-69; Mark 14:27-31), and had an acute perception of Jesus as being the Son of God in a unique sense. When he made what is called the Great Confession (Matthew 16:16), Jesus answered in words that have been the subject of considerable discussion.

Undoubtedly there is a play on Peter's name, but Jesus does not actually say that he will build his church on Peter. Indeed he says, 'You are *Petros,* and on this *petra* I will build my church.' In other words, he varies the two words slightly, and whatever words he may have used in the Aramaic in which he spoke, Matthew believed that his Greek translation made a proper distinction between them. Having said this, we are still faced with the precise interpretation, and perhaps the simplest is to paraphrase as follows: 'You, Peter, have lived up to the name I gave you, and this outcrop of your firm personality, this confession of yours, is the foundation on which I shall build my church.'

The remainder of the sentence in the KJV, ('the gates of hell shall not prevail against it') has been almost universally misused in prayer and quotation because of the ambiguity of the word 'hell', and the Miltonian concept of Satan in hell. The word here is 'Hades', the sphere of the departed, and has nothing to do directly with Satan. Thus the RSV translates, 'the powers of death shall not prevail against it', although there is no reason to alter the literal translation of 'gates'. The meaning is that the church will never be blotted out through the death of all its members.

When we come to Mathew 16:19 it may be felt that we should have laid more stress on Peter's prerogatives in verse 18. Peter with his confession is certainly given a special commission here of bringing together God's effective action on earth with his total will in heaven. It is obvious that we must see what indication there is of this in Peter's behaviour in the Acts, and it is significant that Peter uses the keys on three occasions, opening up each sphere mentioned in Acts 1:8.

1. He is the spokesman who interprets the Jewish Christian Pentecost to his fellow Jews (Acts 2).

2. He opens the door of full membership to the Samaritan Christians (Acts 8). Here God held back the experience of Pentecost until the Jewish Christians had worked out that the Samaritan believers were to be accepted as full members of the church. Peter and John then went as their emissaries, and laid their hands on them as a token of acceptance. The Samaritan Pentecost followed.

3. The full acceptance of Gentile believers was a more drastic step altogether, as we can see from the resistance that followed in the church (e.g. Acts 15). Peter was guided once more to use the keys, but with Cornelius and his household God sent the Gentile Pentecost while Peter was preaching, but before he had taken

any action (chapter 10). Thus no one could say afterwards that Peter had produced some result to justify his own behaviour (11:17).

Two further points must be added once one has embarked on interpreting these verses in connection with Peter.

A. There is no suggestion that Peter is here given a status and function to be handed on to a line of successors. He himself exercised a special power of the keys, but a similar promise in a more general context is given to the other disciples in Matthew 18:18, following on a discussion on church discipline, where binding and loosing has a special significance (e.g. 1 Corinthians 5:3-5). It is also worth noticing that Matthew 18:19-20 speak of effective prayer, which is also a means of binding and loosing for all Christians.

B. From another aspect, the church is built on the foundation of the apostles and prophets, not on Peter alone, but here again Christ Jesus is the chief cornerstone (Ephesians 2:21). And it is certainly significant that Peter himself emphasizes that the church is built on Christ as the cornerstone and with Christ as the top stone (1 Peter 2:4-7).

Immediately after this confession, Peter is rebuked for trying to turn Jesus from the way of the cross (Matthew 16:21-23). In other parts of the Gospel story we find Peter anxious to consult the Lord on different points, e.g. the payment of the temple tax (17:24-27), the limits of forgiveness (18:21), the name of the betrayer (John 13:24). With John he arranged for the final Passover meal (Luke 22:8), and at this meal he at first refused to allow Jesus to wash his feet, but then with the same impulse as he showed at his call (Luke 5:8) he asked to be made clean all over (John 13:1-11). He rejected Christ's warnings that he would deny him (13:38).

With James and John he slept the sleep of exhaustion in Gethsemane when told to pray against the hour of trial, and the Lord singled him out for rebuke, since he would be the one to undergo the special test of confession or denial (Mark 14:37-38). This is an illustration of the meaning of the sentences in the

Lord's Prayer, 'Lead us not into temptation (trial), but (if trial comes) deliver us from evil' (NB: Mark 14:38).

Peter was certainly brave enough to attack the high priest's servant with a sword (John 18:10) and to follow Jesus into the high priest's courtyard, where he was admitted through John's influence (18:15-16), but under pressure he denied three times that he was a follower of Jesus. It is interesting that while Matthew, Luke and John are content with the main fact that the cock would crow after the three denials (Matthew 26:34; Luke 22:34; John 13:38), Mark's version, which is likely to reproduce Peter's own record (see **Mark**) goes into fuller detail, and confesses that he even had an additional warning of a preliminary crowing (Mark 14:30, 66-72). It is clear from the accounts that, as we should expect in an excited crowd, Peter was challenged by more than three people, especially on the second and third occasions.

The text, 'The Lord turned and looked upon Peter' (Luke 22:61) has moved preachers and artists as it moved Peter himself. The effect on him was withdrawal from the whole scene in bitter self-reproach. We do not know whether he was present at the crucifixion, unless this is included in 1 Peter 5:1, but he was humble enough to go back to John's Jerusalem house where he and John were the first to receive news of the empty tomb from Mary Magdalene (John 20:1-10). They both ran to the tomb. John was the faster runner, but Peter was the more practical, and while John had merely looked into the tomb Peter went right inside.

Both of them realized from the position of the grave clothes and the head turban that the body of Jesus had not been taken out of them and removed, but had risen and left them intact. It is perfectly clear that everyone in the early church believed on the testimony of witnesses that the body of Jesus had been restored to life miraculously, although it was a new order of life. Nobody believed that resurrection was simply the survival of the spirit or soul. The risen Lord appeared to Peter personally before meeting the rest of the disciples (1 Corinthians 15:5).

Although the immediate appearances of the Lord were in Jerusalem, the disciples had been told from the beginning that they were to return to Galilee to meet him there (Mark 16:7). For the time being Peter went back to his former work of fishing (John 21), but during much of the period of forty days between the resurrection and ascension Jesus appeared in Galilee, and one assumes that he taught them there in quiet surroundings before sending them back to wait in Jerusalem for the coming of the Holy Spirit (Matthew 28:16-20; Acts 1:3-4). The Gospel writers keep the description of this period to a minimum. They use their space for the evidence of the empty tomb, knowing that Christ's fresh teachings, based on his cross and resurrection, (e.g. Luke 24:44-47), emerge in the history and preaching of the Christian church.

Peter was again commissioned after the meal by the lake, but the English translations cannot adequately reproduce the two words for 'love' in the Greek here. Twice Jesus asks, 'Do you love me?', and Peter, with his old self-confidence shattered, replies, 'You know that I am fond of you.' The third time Jesus uses Peter's weaker word, 'Are you fond of me?', and this is what upsets Peter, that the Lord should have to ask for his assurance even on this; but he still dares not use the stronger word (John 21:15-17). But this time, instead of speaking of denial, Jesus speaks of the martyr's death that Peter would suffer (John 21:18-19).

In the story in Acts we have seen how Peter opened the doors, but in the day-to-day life of the church he was used to work miracles (Acts 3:1-9; 5:12-16; 9:32-43). He was put in prison with others and miraculously released (5:17-21), and was similarly released when he was arrested by Herod (12:1-17). He is not mentioned in Acts after the Council in chapter 15 where he stood up for the equality of the Gentile converts.

We gather from Galatians 2:11-14 that on one occasion Peter hedged over this through fear of falling out with the Jewish orientated group. But more importantly he, James and John agreed that God had called them to preach specially to Jews, while Paul and Barnabas went to the Gentiles (2:7-10). Elsewhere in this book (**John, Paul**) we have speculated that one reason for this was that Peter, James and John were not fluent Greek speakers, as were Paul and Barnabas. One must add, however, that there was a considerable Greek influence in Galilee, so Peter and John could have been bilingual, though with more fluency in Aramaic, in spite of Peter's strong north country accent (Matthew 26:73; Luke 22:59). We do not know how much Latin he picked up when he went to Rome.

It is impossible to say how far Peter travelled with the gospel, but it looks as though he visited Corinth, where presumably he concentrated chiefly on the Jews, whose converts claimed to be Peter's men rather than Paul's (1 Corinthians 1:12). His wife normally accompanied him (9:5). Since his first epistle is addressed to Christians in Asia Minor (1 Peter 1:1), we presume that he travelled extensively there. Finally we cannot doubt the uniform early tradition that Peter went to Rome, and that it is Rome that is denoted by the description 'Babylon' in 1 Peter 5:13. Mark is closely associated with him, according to this verse, and there is little doubt that Mark's Gospel is basically from Peter (see **Mark**).

Since Paul does not mention Peter in any of his letters from Rome, we must assume that he went there at the end of Paul's first imprisonment, and was absent again when Paul wrote 2 Timothy. There is no alternative tradition to that which makes him, like Paul, a martyr in Rome during the persecution by Nero, say, soon after AD 64. Out of the various apocryphal stories concerning Peter, the best known are Peter's meeting with the risen Christ when he was running away from Rome, and the tradition that he asked to be crucified head downwards so as not to seem to be dying the identical death that Jesus died.

Two letters of Peter's have survived. The differing styles of Greek could be due to the scribe that he used. The first letter is both doctrinal and practical, with useful quotations from the Old Testament. Peter points out that the Messianic prophecies had puzzled their authors as to the time of their fulfilment (1 Peter

1:10-12), a fact worth remembering when we are tempted to find always a contemporary fulfilment for those prophecies that are definitely Messianic.

The authenticity of the second epistle has been disputed, largely because there is no external claim for it until about AD 250. The more awkward Greek is easily accounted for by a different scribe, or more probably by Peter himself doing his best, as someone has said, with the aid of a dictionary. Certainly the writer claims to have been an eyewitness of the transfiguration (2 Peter 1:16-18), to have written a previous letter (3:1), and probably alludes to Christ's words about his (Peter's) death as recorded in John 21:18-19 (2 Peter 1:14). These allusions are not claimed as conclusive, but play their part. It is interesting that Peter ranks Paul's writings with 'the other scriptures' (2 Peter 3:16), which must mean the inspired writings of our Old Testament. For other points in this letter, see **Jude**.

PHARAOH

(A common spelling mistakes is to put the O before the A.) This is the title of the royal line in Egypt, and the Old Testament is often content to use the title by itself, as we might say 'The King' or 'The Emperor' without attaching any proper name.

Since there is still uncertainty about Abraham's date, we cannot tell who was the ruling unnamed Pharaoh when Abraham visited Egypt (Genesis 12). Between about 1700 and 1570 BC Egypt was under the rule of invaders from the Palestine area, known as the Hyksos, and Joseph as a Hebrew could well have been easily accepted in Egypt during this period.

But the problems of further identifications arise from uncertainty over the date of the Exodus. Taking 1 Kings 6:1 at its face value, the Exodus took place 480 years before the building of Solomon's temple, i.e. in about 1440 BC. This would mean that the birth of Moses was in the time of Thutmose I (1539-1514) and the persecuting Pharaoh of the Exodus was Amenhotep II (1449-1423). Because of certain apparent archaeological evidence, an alternative date has been suggested of about 1290, or even later.

If so, the birth of Moses would have been in the reign of Amenhotep IV, the king who changed his name to Ikhnaton, and whose wife, Nefertiti (variously spelt) is the most attractive feature of the Egyptian room in any museum, the original bust being in the Dahlem Museum in Berlin. It would be nice to think that baby Moses sat on her lap, though that is no argument for his having done so! Amenhotep's date was 1377-1360 BC. Moses would then have known the famous Tutankhamun, before escaping to Midian in the reign of Harmhab, and returning to rescue the Israelites in the reign of Ramses II (1301-1234 BC).

Any attempt to summarize the intricate archaeological arguments for the date would only be misleading. There is, however, a further point which may be relevant. Were the Israelites in Egypt for 400 years, as is commonly thought? None of the genealogies suggests a period of more than about 160 years, and although one can allow for gaps in any genealogy it would be curious if there are gaps in all the references. Thus Moses' mother was the daughter of Levi (Exodus 6:18-20; Numbers 26:59), and Zerah, born before the entry into Egypt (Genesis 46:12) was great-grandfather of Achan, who was alive forty years after the Exodus (Joshua 7:1).

The statement in Exodus 12:40 that the Israelites dwelt in Egypt 430 years may be modified in the light of the reading in the Septuagint and the Samaritan versions, which add, 'and in the land of Canaan', i.e. including the period from the time of Abraham. In fact Paul follows this dating from Abraham in Galatians 3:17, and so do other Jewish writers. Similarly, Genesis 15:13 may refer to the whole time from Abraham onwards when he and his descendants did not own any land in Canaan or elsewhere.

There is one further problem that is relevant, and that is the numbers who came out of Egypt at the Exodus. It has been calculated that by taking the Bible numbers as they stand, the total of men, women and children would be something like two million. Instead of laughing at the idea of such an impossibly large number, some modern scholars have had a fresh look at the

Hebrew words involved. The early Hebrew words were written with consonants, or virtual consonants, only, and the reader supplied the vowels. Obviously a set of consonants might have a different meaning if other vowels were supplied. Thus in English PTR might be POTTER, PATTER, or PETER. Normally the reader would already have been taught the Scripture passage orally, and the written version would be there either to prompt him or for him to copy out to make yet another edition. In much later times small vowel signs were put under the letters, and obviously this fixed the words.

The point of all this is that the letters forming the word *thousand* not only have the variant and obvious translation of *clan* or *group*, but also with other vowels can be rendered *chief* or *warrior*, the latter denoting full men at arms as distinct from the rag tag and bobtail called up to fight as best they could. It seems likely that at some point in the transmission of the text the reckoning of able-bodied fighting men, or of military units, or of families, has been mistakenly turned into thousands.

This is true of some other large numbers in the Old Testament as well as of the Exodus. The deciphering of the possible originals in Numbers 1 is somewhat technical, but working from the reinterpreted totals given here it has been calculated that the whole Israelite nation on the march was about 27,000.

After this digression on the difficulty of identifying the Pharaohs mentioned in Exodus, we have the tantalizing mention of a certain Mered, of the tribe of Judah, who married a daughter of Pharaoh. She took the name of Bithiah, *Daughter of Jehovah* (1 Chronicles 4:17). How we should love to know the story behind the headlines! And how did the new wife Bithia get on with 'his Jewish wife' (verse 18), who is not even given a name?

Solomon (see entry) c. 970-930 BC married the daughter of Pharaoh who had captured Gezer (north-west of Jerusalem) and given it to Solomon as a dowry (1 Kings 3:1; 9:16, 24; 11:1). Solomon's father-in-law may have been the Pharaoh Siamun, who certainly raided as far as Philistia. It may have been the same Pharaoh who received young Hadad after Joab's massacre of the Edomites (11:14-22), and married him to his sister-in-law. Hadad later returned to harass Solomon.

Shishak (or Sheshonk) (c. 945-924 BC) is named as the Pharaoh who sheltered Jeroboam when he had to run from Solomon (1 Kings 11:40), and who later invaded Judah and took some of the temple treasures as tribute from King Rehoboam (14:25, 26; 2 Chronicles 12:1-12). Archaeological evidence shows that Shishak went north into Israel as well.

In rebelling against Assyria, King Hoshea of Israel tried to get help from So of Egypt (2 Kings 17:4). This would have been about 725 BC, and the name So might perhaps be an abbreviation of Osorkon IV (c. 727-716 BC), although he might not be a Pharaoh at all, but some monarch who ruled under Pharaoh.

Tirhakah (Taharka) was a Pharaoh of the Libyan dynasty (690-664 BC), whose invasion of southern Palestine caused the king of Assyria to send a further threatening letter to Hezekiah (2 Kings 19:9). If this was in 701 BC, Tirhakah is called king by anticipation, since he was then only the commander of the Egyptian forces. But the letter may belong to a later date. (See **Hezekiah**, **Sennacherib**.)

Neco (Necho) (c. 610-595 BC) attacked Assyria, but killed **Josiah** of Judah at Megiddo when he intervened. He then put Jehoiakim on the throne of Judah and taxed the land heavily, taking the people's choice, Jehoahaz, to Egypt (2 Kings 23:29-35). He was eventually defeated by the Babylonians at Carchemish in 605 BC (Jeremiah 46:2).

In Neco's reign, Africa was circumnavigated for the first time in recorded history. Herodotus relates the story, but says he does not believe it because the sailors said that 'in sailing round Libya they had the sun on their right hand' — one of the finest proofs of the accuracy of an old seadog's story, since in the southern hemisphere the sun goes round by the north, and in rounding the Cape from the Indian Ocean it would be on their right.

The unnamed Pharaoh of Jeremiah 37:5-11; Ezekiel 17:11-21; 29:2-3, and perhaps Jeremiah 47:1, is Hophra (c. 589-570 BC), who made an abortive attempt to drive away the Babylonian forces in Palestine.

Several prophecies speak of the subjugation of Egypt (e.g. Isaiah 19; Jeremiah 46; Ezekiel 29-32; see also Jeremiah 46). Nebuchadnezzar invaded Egypt in 568 BC, though we have no records surviving to give the extent of his conquests. It is worth noting that Isaiah 19:19-24 speaks of a revival of true religion in Egypt. Egypt, and especially Alexandria, became a powerful centre of Judaism and later of Christianity. King Ptolemy Philadelphus of Egypt (285-246 BC) commissioned the translation of the Hebrew Bible into Greek, and thus was the founding father of the translation which gradually grew into the Septuagint (with the letter g pronounced more as a j), commonly denoted LXX.

PHILEMON[NT]. *Loving*
A Christian at Colossae whose runaway slave had ended up in Rome as one of Paul's converts and helpers. Paul writes to Philemon and returns the slave to him (see **Onesimus**). Probably Philemon's wife and son are the two addressed as Apphia and Archippus in verse 1.

PHILETUS[NT]
See **Hymenaeus**.

PHILIP[NT]. *Horse-lover*
1. Philip the Apostle. One of the small group who were impressed by Jesus before he began his full ministry. He was a native of Bethsaida, and was probably a disciple of John the Baptist. He introduced his friend Nathanael to Jesus (John 1:43-46), and later a group of Gentiles (12:20-26); it is unlikely that the story means that Jesus refused to see them. Philip was staggered at the idea of buying enough food for the crowd in the wilderness (6:5-7), and was slightly exasperated by the way in which Jesus spoke about knowing the Father (14:8-11). He is last mentioned in the list of the Eleven in Acts 1:13, but traditionally he worked extensively in Asia Minor, and was buried with his daughters in

Hieropolis.

2. Philip the Evangelist. Early Christian writers sometimes confused the apostle Philip with Philip the Evangelist who had been born a Gentile but had become fully a Jew by circumcision, and who was one of the Seven chosen to look after the day-to-day running of the material side of the church's welfare, especially among the Hellenist converts like himself (Acts 6:1-6).

Soon afterwards, Philip the Evangelist opened up work among the Samaritans, preaching and working miracles of healing and exorcism, and Simon Magus declared himself a convert (8:5-13). Because the acceptance of Samaritans was such a momentous step, God waited for official welcome for them by the central church leaders before pouring out the Samaritan Pentecost (8:14-24). (See **Peter**.)

Philip was next sent to meet and win an Ethiopian minister on his way back to the royal court, and this man probably became the founder of the ancient Ethiopian church (Acts 8:26-38). We read that 'the Spirit of the Lord caught up Philip', and, although this may signify a miraculous transportation, it could also mean that he was energized and guided by the Spirit as Elijah was when he ran before Ahab (Acts 8:39-40; 1 Kings 18:46). Paul and Luke stayed in his house in Caesarea, and it is mentioned that he had four unmarried daughters with the gift of prophecy (Acts 21:8-9).

3. Tetrarch of Iturea and Trachonitis (Luke 3:1). (See **Herod 4**.)

4. Son of Herod the Great and Mariamne, daughter of Simon the high priest. Lived as a private citizen. Mentioned only because his wife Herodias left him in order to marry Herod Antipas (Matthew 14:3). (See **Herod 3**)

PHINEHAS. Meaning uncertain
1. Grandson of Aaron, who succeeded Eleazar as high priest (Exodus 6:25; Joshua 24:33). He killed an Israelite and a Midianite woman at a time of wholesale lapse into the sexual excesses of Baal worship (Numbers 25). Soon afterwards he took

part in a campaign against Midian (Numbers 31). The drastic measures of extermination were almost certainly due to the fact that the promiscuous sex of Midianite worship had left most of the adult population plagued with syphilis, and the Israelites with their clean living were particularly vulnerable. Similarly, syphilis, probably brought by sailors from America, devastated Europe in the early 1500s.

Phinehas was in charge of the committee of investigation into an enormous altar that was set up near the Jordan by the tribes that settled on the eastern side outside the Promised Land. The committee was reassured that the altar was no more than a memorial of their link with their fellow Israelites, and they had no intention of making offerings there instead of at the tabernacle. The committee reported back accordingly. The last mention of Phinehas is when he consulted God about the punitive expedition against Benjamin (Judges 20:28).

2. One of Eli's two sons (1 Samuel 2-4, see **Hophni**). The report of the capture of the ark of the covenant and the death of her husband induced premature labour in his wife, and she died in giving birth. But before her death she named her child Ichabod, *The glory has departed,* having more concern for the loss of the ark than for the loss of her husband, who had been more interested in the girls in the tabernacle than in her (2:22; 4:20-22).

POTIPHAR. Probably, *Given by Re, the sun god*
A captain under Pharaoh who bought Joseph from the Midianites. He found Joseph so reliable that he made him steward of his household. His wife tried to seduce Joseph, and when he refused her she charged him with assault, and Potiphar committed him to prison (Genesis 39).

This story is often compared with the Egyptian *Story of the Two Brothers,* the parallel being an unsuccessful attempt at seduction. But the situation has been repeated again and again down the years, and it would be no bad thing if we had more Josephs and less Judahs today. (See **Judah**.)

PRISCILLA^{NT}, Prisca.
See **Aquila**, her husband.

PUBLIUS^{NT}
Called 'the chief man' (literally 'the first') of Malta. Probably a native of the island or a Roman whose family had been settled there for some time. He entertained Paul and Luke after their shipwreck, and presumably the centurion, and did so gladly and not grudgingly, all the more so when Paul cured his father of dysentery (Acts 28:7-10).

PUDENS^{NT}. *Modest*
Of all the people who have a single mention in Paul's letters, Pudens is one of the most interesting to British readers. He is linked with Linus and Claudia (2 Timothy 4:21). We know that Gladys, the daughter of Caradoc (Caractacus) was adopted by the emperor Claudius and renamed Claudia. The Roman poet Martial celebrates in a poem the marriage of Claudia from Britain to Pudens.

In a second poem he celebrates the birth of her daughter Pudentiana, and this time he calls her husband 'Sanctus' or 'Holy', which probably shows that he had now become a Christian (Martial iv.13 and xi.53). Pudens may have first met Claudia when he was stationed in Chichester, where an inscription records his dedication of a temple to Neptune and Minerva. It has been reasonably supposed that their house in Rome became a meeting place for Christians and was on the site of the church still called St Pudentiana. Clement of Rome, before AD 100 says that Linus was the brother (one text says *son*) of Claudia.

QUIRINIUS^{NT}
Governor of Syria when the census was taken which sent Joseph and Mary to Bethlehem (Luke 2:2). We know that he was governor in AD 6-9, and that he supervised a census on that later occasion (Acts 5:37), but this is too late, since the birth of Jesus

Christ is likely to have been about 7 BC. Since a census was normally held every fourteen years, the date of the earlier census would be right, but the difficulty is that Saturninus was governor of Syria 9-7 BC and Varus 7-4 BC.

We know that Quirinius carried out successful campaigns against rebellious highlanders in Asia Minor during the period 12-2 BC, and he may well for a time have had a joint governorship in Syria, as Josephus says a certain Volumnius had with Saturninus. If so, he would have been the emperor's competent commissioner for carrying out the tricky business of the census, which certainly could provoke riots (Acts 5:37). There is an inscription which mentions someone who governed Syria twice, but although this has been claimed as Quirinius, the actual name is too mutilated to read.

Luke 2:2 may be translated as the NEB margin, 'This was the first registration carried out while Quirinius was governor of Syria', implying that there was a second one while he was governor.

RABMAG, Rabsaris, Rabshakeh

Admittedly these names raise a smile, but they are titles of Assyrian and Babylonian officers. The exact significance is not clear in each case, but *Rab* means 'Chief or 'Head'. (See 2 Kings 18:17; 19:4-8; Jeremiah 39:3.)

RACHEL. *Ewe*

The wife whom Jacob loved best. Mother of Joseph and Benjamin. For the story of her life see **Jacob, Leah, Laban**. The fascinating piece of history that belongs to Rachel alone is her outwitting of her father when Jacob and his household were on the run from him (Genesis 31). Like Shylock, Laban's priorities seem to have been, 'My ducats, and my daughter!' (31:30). He was concerned over the loss of his household gods (Hebrew *teraphim),* to which Rachel had helped herself on leaving home (31:19,32,34). These 'gods' were probably the size of an average doll, and were certainly small enough to be concealed in the camel's saddle without even Jacob knowing they were there (31:32,34).

There is no reason to think that Rachel wanted them for worship. Contemporary Mesopotamian records show that household images often went with the inheritance, and there is little doubt that Rachel was helping to establish any future claim that her husband might make on Laban's estate. At least she had scored off her brothers who had turned against her husband (Genesis 31:1-2).

Connection with the inheritance suggests that the origin of the name, *teraphim,* may be in the root found in *rephaim,* translated by RSV 'the shades' in such passages as Psalm 88:10; Proverbs 2:18; Isaiah 14:9; 26:19. We distinguish these from the early giants, also called Rephaim, in e.g. Genesis 14:5; Deuteronomy 2:11.

Originally they may have been doll-like figures representing ancestors, but certainly they were used by some people as idols to be worshipped (e.g. Judges 17:5; 18:14-31; 1 Samuel 15:23, where RSV has 'idolatry'; Hosea 3:4) or consulted in divination (Ezekiel 21:21; Zechariah 10:2). When David's wife Michal put teraphim in David's bed to make Saul's messenger think he was ill, like Rachel she may have tried to secure her father's inheritance by taking them with her on her marriage, being rather smarter than her elder sister Merab (1 Samuel 18:19). The story as it stands gives the impression that these teraphim were much larger than Rachel's, but Michal may have relied on the goat's hair to look like David's head, and added the teraphim for luck.

Without claiming any connection, we may compare the old Chinese ancestral tablets. They preserved the names of the family forebears, and the head of the family was responsible for making offerings to the tablets as though the ancestors were still present in them. Normally Christian converts burned the tablets when they were baptized, but presumably some retained them, feeling that the value of preserving the family tree was more important than the risk of idolatry. But the danger of relapse was a very real one, as it certainly was with the teraphim.

We have referred to the teraphim as 'they' and 'them' because the ending -*im* is plural, but some of the Bible references make more sense if they apply to a single image. Occasionally popular usage overrides correct etymology. Thus, nowadays it would be pedantic to say 'a die' as the singular of 'dice', and it is usual to speak of 'a dice'. So it is likely that 'teraphim', starting as a group name, eventually became used of the individual image that incorporated the ancestors. (See also **Micah**.)

RAHAB

In its literal meaning of *Pride*, the name is used as a description of Egypt, especially as the proud beast crushed at the crossing of the Sea (Psalm 87:4; 89:10; Isaiah 51:9-10; 30:7).

But this has no connection with the prostitute of Jericho who sheltered the Israelite spies, and allowed them to escape out of her window on the city wall (Joshua 2). She declared her faith in Jehovah, and was given a guarantee that if she tied a scarlet cord in her window, she and all she brought into her home would be spared when the city was destroyed. She acted on this, and she and her relatives became members of Israel (Joshua 6:17,22-25). The New Testament quotes her as an example of the proper blend of faith (Hebrews 11:31) and works (James 2:25, where the distinction in the section is between what God sees as justifying faith and what others see demonstrated as living faith, NB: 'You see' in verses 22 and 24).

There is no doubt that Rahab was a true convert, and her former life, that she renounced, did not stand in the way of an honourable marriage with Salmon (compare 1 Corinthians 6:9-11), and she became an ancestress of Jesus Christ himself (Matthew 1:5). There would be no point in mentioning the name of Salmon's wife unless she was the famous Rahab. The rabbinic tradition that she married Joshua is unlikely to be true. If she had married the leader of the nation, this would certainly have been mentioned.

REBEKAH. Perhaps a *cord*
Grand-niece of Abraham (Genesis 22:20-23) and sister of Laban (24:28). Genesis 24 is a long and pleasant account of how she came to be Isaac's bride. For some years she and Isaac were without a child, but in answer to sustained prayer Rebekah conceived and found that she was to have twins. God told her before they were born that the elder (Esau) would be the servant of the younger (Jacob/Israel) (25:21-26).

Rebekah clearly favoured Jacob, and inexcusably tried to override God's memory when the time came for Isaac to bless the two boys (Genesis 27) (See **Esau, Jacob**). Jacob had to run from Esau's revenge, and Rebekah made the genuine excuse that he ought to find a wife from her own people and not follow Esau's example of marrying unpleasant Canaanite girls (Genesis 26:34-35; 27:46).

It is usually said that Rebekah did not see Jacob again. This may well be true, but it is an argument from silence, based on the fact that she is not mentioned when Jacob goes back to see his father on his return (35:27-29).

RECHAB. *Horseman*
1. Rechab and his brother Baanah murdered Ishbosheth and brought his head to David, hoping for a reward. David had them executed for what he described as the cold-blooded murder of a good man (2 Samuel 4:5-12).

2. An unknown person whose son, Jonadab, named a puritan order after him, calling them Rechabites (Jeremiah 35). (See **Jonadab**.)

REHOBOAM. *May the people grow larger*
It would be interesting to know why out of Solomon's 700 wives the son of an Ammonitess should be his successor (1 Kings 14:21). It sounds as though he was in with a group of young revolutionaries who hoped to ride to power on his shoulders, and he chose to be a dictator with them rather than a servant of the people such as the older counsellors wanted (1 Kings 12). This led

to the revolution of the northern tribes under Jeroboam, and to the continuing split between Judah and Israel. A prophet stopped Rehoboam from retaliation (12:21-24), but he had the humiliation of seeing Jeroboam fortifying his kingdom, and setting up golden calves as alternatives to the temple (12:25-33).

Rehoboam himself had no more regard for the exclusive worship of Jehovah than his father had (1 Kings 14:21-24), even though, doubtless for political reasons, he welcomed the Levites who came as refugees from the north (2 Chronicles 11:13-17). In spite of his own attempts at fortifying his cities, he was invaded by Egypt and had to pay heavy tribute from the temple treasures (1 Kings 14:25-28). Among his many wives, his favourite was Absalom's daughter Maacah, whose son Abijah succeeded him (2 Chronicles 11:18-23).

REHUM. Perhaps, *Beloved*
An official under Artaxerxes who wrote and protested to the king about the Jewish attempts at rebuilding the city and its walls (Ezra 4:7-24). His title, the commander (RSV), has been rendered also *Lord of report,* i.e. postmaster, and he could have been specially authorized to send reports to the king, which he dictated to Shimshai his scribe.

REUBEN.
See, a son!
Jacob's eldest, Leah being his mother (Genesis 29:32). As a boy he brought his mother some mandrakes, plants of the nightshade family with a forked root often resembling the human body, believed to be love charms or aphrodisiacs. Leah bought Jacob for the night by passing these on to Rachel, but they did not do Rachel any good and she remained childless (30:14-17). When Reuben was grown up, he had an affair with Rachel's maid who had already borne sons to Jacob (35:22).

The good side of his character came out when he suggested putting Joseph in a deep pit, when his brothers wished to kill him. He went off for a short time, and then came back intending to release Joseph, but in the meantime Judah had persuaded the others to sell him as a slave (Genesis 37:12-30; 42:22). Later Reuben offered his two sons as hostages to his father when Joseph demanded that Benjamin should be brought to Egypt (42:37). When Jacob came to bless his sons he remembered Reuben's incest, and saw this as a mark of the instability of his character, unworthy of the firstborn (49:3-4). His descendants occupied territory on the east of Jordan.

REUEL. *God is (my) friend*
Father-in-law of Moses. (See **Jethro, Hobab.**)

REZIN
The last king of Damascus (Syria), who persuaded Pekah of Israel to join him in rebelling against Assyria. The two of them invaded Judah in 735 BC to force Ahaz to join them. Ahaz in turn appealed to Assyria, and Tiglath-Pileser came in and captured Damascus (2 Kings 16:5-9; Isaiah 7). (See Ahaz, **Pekah.**)

RIZPAH. *Live coal*
A tragic figure, who became the centre of one of the most puzzling stories in the Old Testament. She was first taken as Saul's concubine, and bore him at least two sons (2 Samuel 21:8). After Saul's death Abner took her, possibly to strengthen any future claim he might make to the throne (3:6-11). (See for a similar case Abishag, 1 Kings 2:13-25). The protest by Saul's son Ishbosheth led to Abner's negotiations to turn the kingdom over to David.

The only other mention of Rizpah is when there was a three-year famine (2 Samuel 21:1-14). David was told by God, presumably through Nathan or Gad the court prophets, that the famine was due to Saul's murder of a number of Gibeonites, and we must accept this as the true cause. Although the record stands at the end of David's reign, it is in an appendix that includes earlier events, and hence it may be early while Saul's act was still comparatively fresh. This is made even more likely by the fact that this was the occasion when David collected the bones of Saul and Jonathan and interred them (21:12-14).

Today we often consider that we have outgrown the morality of the Old Testament, but one thing that we have overlooked is the priority that God gives to the sacredness of covenants and agreements, whether national or individual (e.g. Psalm 24:4). In this instance, the lives of the Gibeonites were secured by a firm national agreement (Joshua 9). On some occasion towards the end of his life, Saul had violated this treaty by murdering a number of them (2 Samuel 21:2).

God called attention to the crime by sending the three-year famine. He left it to David to find a solution, which virtually had to be in terms that would be accepted by the Gibeonites as adequate compensation. They might have chosen money payment, but since they had lost their relatives they claimed the right, which was legitimate according to their beliefs, to see seven of Saul's sons put to death, either directly by hanging or by being exhibited on poles after death. They were not offered as a sacrifice to God, and although the famine ceased when the Gibeonites were satisfied, we assume that God would have brought it to an end if they had made lesser demands.

Rizpah suffered through losing her two sons at the hands of the Gibeonites, and we have the sad picture of the mother watching over the hanging bodies night and day to keep away scavenging birds and beasts. The whole story reads like a true account, including the small detail of Rizpah sitting on the rock on a sackcloth rug. One must either dismiss the whole thing as coincidence and the prophet as mistaken, or accept the Bible warning that God is concerned over broken faith, although he was not responsible for the penalty that the Gibeonites fixed.

RUFUS[NT]. *Red,* perhaps with red hair
Evidently well-known in the early church, since Mark mentions that Simon of Cyrene, who carried the cross, was 'the father of Alexander and Rufus' (Mark 15:21). He may well be the Rufus, 'eminent in the Lord', who is greeted by Paul in Romans 16:13,

together with his mother, who had mothered Paul also. Rufus must often have heard his father tell the story of what happened on the morning of the crucifixion.

RUTH. *Friend*
One of the really beautiful characters of the Old Testament. The open-mindedness of the Bible is shown in the space it gives to the story of a Moabite girl, making no secret of her being an ancestress of the great hero-King David, and so of Jesus Christ. There were many more converts from non-Israelites than we commonly realize. (See e.g. **Ittai**, **Uriah**.)

Ruth married Mahlon (Ruth 1:1-5; 4:10), son of Naomi and Elimelech who had come to Moab to escape a famine in Judah. Eventually Elimelech, Mahlon and his brother Chilion who had married another Moabite girl, Orpah, all died, and Naomi determined to return to their home town of Bethlehem. Orpah decided to stay in Moab, but Ruth returned with her mother-in-law.

They arrived in Bethlehem in April or May, and Ruth went out to glean in the barley harvest. By chance, she found herself in the fields of a near relative of Elimelech named Boaz, and she caught his attention, not only by her good looks but because of her reputation in standing by Naomi (Ruth 2). She continued to glean in his fields for the rest of the barley harvest, and for the wheat harvest that followed a week of two later.

Naomi saw how the land lay, and was additionally encouraged by knowing that Boaz was a kinsman, though not the nearest. When the time came for winnowing the barley, Naomi told Ruth to go to the threshing floor and at the end of the day to lie down at the foot of Boaz' bed in the straw when he had gone to sleep. In the night Boaz woke up and felt her at his feet, and surprisingly she asked him for marriage (Ruth 3:9, compare Ezekiel 16:8). This was not as bad as it sounds, since Ruth was actually invoking the levirate law by which a man had to take his brother's widow if she was childless, and give her children to be brought up in her husband's name (Deuteronomy 25:5-10;

Matthew 22:23-33). Evidently the law was extended to other kinsmen beside brothers.

There is no doubt that Ruth preferred Boaz to the nearer kinsman, who was apparently a married man (Ruth 4:6), and Boaz had already had his eye on her sufficiently closely to know that she had not been running after the lads of the village (3:10). He promised to act in the morning, and meanwhile he did not take advantage of Ruth, but let her continue sleeping at his feet on condition that she left before it was light, so as not to cause any tongues to wag (3:1-18).

In the morning, Boaz summoned witnesses to the court, which was normally held in the space inside the city gates. He then challenged the nearest relative to exercise his option on Elimelech's field that Naomi was about to sell. The relative was delighted, until he heard that Ruth went with the land, whereupon he backed down with the words, '... lest I impair my own inheritance' (Ruth 4:6). Since no one knows exactly what this means, one suspects that he visualized the break-up of his family life if he introduced another woman.

In Deuteronomy 25:7-10 the law prescribed a strange ceremony where the next of kin refused to take the widow. She was to pull off his sandal and spit in his face. This law had evidently been adapted to a case where the next of kin knew that another kinsman was willing to take his place, and now the first man took off his sandal himself and gave it to Boaz, thus signifying that he was handing on the responsibility to him with goodwill on both sides (Ruth 4:1-12). So the bachelor Boaz took Ruth and the land, and we conclude lived happily ever after, with mother-in-law as baby-sitter when Obed was born to carry on the line to David (4:13-22).

One can be thankful that God has given us a clean romantic love story to counterbalance the unsatisfying exploits of Solomon in the Bible and Casanova in secular history.

SALOME[NT]. *Peace*
1. Mentioned twice by name, as present at the crucifixion and on

the visit to the tomb on Easter morning (Mark 15:40; 16:1). The former reference includes her among women who ministered to Jesus and his disciples during their time in Galilee. Some have attempted a little legitimate detective work on her identity. Thus Matthew, in his parallel reference in Matthew 27:56 replaces Mark's Salome with 'the mother of the sons of Zebedee'. This description suggests that her husband was now dead. The next clue is John 19:25, where John lists the women at the cross as follows: 'Standing by the cross of Jesus were his mother, and his mother's sister, Mary the wife of Clopas, and Mary Magdalene.'

Mary Magdalene appears in both lists, but the question arises: who is 'his mother's sister'? It is unlikely that 'Mary the wife of Clopas' is intended to refer to her, since this would mean that there were two girls named Mary in the same family. John deliberately hides his own identity in his Gospel, and never names himself when we know he was present (e.g. John 19:26-27). Thus it is reasonable to identify 'his mother's sister' with Salome, whom we know from Mark was present at the cross. Thus we have the equation, Salome = the sister of the virgin Mary = the mother of James and John, making James and John the cousins of Jesus, and accounting for their mother's assumption that they might be candidates for the chief places in the Kingdom (Matthew 20:20-21).

2. Most Christians and non-Christians know the other Salome as the girl who danced the dance of the seven veils and obtained the head of John the Baptist as a reward. But it comes as a surprise to find that her name does not occur in the Bible, where she is simply called 'the daughter of Herodias', while the dance of the seven veils belongs only to the stage and cabaret (Matthew 14:1-12; Mark 6:14-28). It is Josephus, the Jewish historian, who tells us that the girl was called Salome, the daughter of Herodias by her former husband. Herod Antipas had persuaded Herodias to leave his half-brother Philip, and this is the reason why John the Baptist denounced him and incurred her anger which ultimately brought about his death. Later, Salome married Philip the Tetrarch, but when he died childless she married Aristobulus, another descendant of Herod the Great, and by him had three boys. (See **Herod.**)

SAMSON. *Little sun*
The playboy of the Old Testament, whose exploits are recorded in Judges 13-16. When from time to time today we read of the moral collapse of a Christian who has been used of God, we are puzzled how to assess his previous Christian work and his relationship to God. In Samson, God has given us the unadorned story of a man who was filled with the Spirit on occasions, but whose moral life tended to be siphoned off into self indulgence.

He was chosen of God to have the restrictions of a Nazirite from the day of his birth. During the pre-natal period his mother also had to observe the Nazirite restrictive diet (Judges 13:1-14). The law of the Nazirite (probably meaning *Separate*) is given in Numbers 6, and while some took the vow for a period only, it seems from Judges 13 that it could be for life.

At first Samson was conscious of the atmosphere of his home, and had an experience of the Spirit of God (Judges 13:24-25). It was obvious that he was beginning to kick over the traces of his upbringing when he went courting a Philistine girl. His tribe of Dan at that time adjoined Philistine territory, and the Philistines in fact were strong enough to dominate the Danites (13:1). We may assume that there was some measure of revival among the Israelites, since in the book of Judges this preceded each deliverance. This time God used Samson's love life to bring him out as a deliverer (14:1-4). Samson took father and mother to see the girl in Timnah, and on the way tested his Spirit-given strength by killing a lion with his bare hands.

While he went on to Timnah and then back home, the creatures of the countryside got busy on the lion and left no more than its bones and leathery skin. A swarm of bees, looking for a hollow in which to start their new colony, found a ready-made hive in the lion. When Samson passed by again and went to see his former conquest, he found the lion had become a honey pot. There are some commentators who quote Aristotle and Virgil who believed that to obtain a swarm of bees you left a carcass in the open, and eventually bees emerged from it. They couldn't tell bees from bluebottles. But there is no trace of this armchair non-science in early days, and even Samson could tell the difference between maggots and honey.

Samson went on to the wedding, and used the honey from the lion as the basis of a riddle for the thirty young Philistines who came to support him. He wagered sixty sets of clothes as a prize. Some of us learnt the riddle when we were first learning to read, and studied the picture of the lion and 'Out of the strong came forth sweetness' on the golden syrup tin on the kitchen table. But Samson's friends got the answer by bullyboy threats to his wife, and Samson took his revenge and paid the wager by killing thirty men of Ashkelon and bringing back their clothes; or maybe he stripped them of any things of value and traded these in to buy thirty pairs of best clothes. He went back home in a temper without his wife (Judges 14:5-20).

Her father married her to Samson's best man, and when Samson came back to make up the quarrel with a handsome present he found she had gone, and was not pleased to be offered her younger sister in exchange. He promptly burnt down the local corn and olive orchards by tying torches to the tails of foxes and letting them loose.

One may query the number of 300 foxes, and suppose that a copyist, in his excitement over the story, changed this figure from an original thirty, which would not be very different in the Hebrew. The Philistines retaliated by setting fire to the home of the girl and her father, and burning them alive, after which Samson took his revenge on them, killing a large number in unarmed combat.

The struggle continued, including a Houdini escape by Samson, and his slaughter of a large number of Philistines with the jawbone of an ass, followed by an unexpected appearance of a spring to quench his thirst (Judges 15:9-20). Philistine women had a fatal fascination for Samson, and he was trapped in Gaza when he visited a prostitute there. The Philistines knew he was in the city and began by watching the gate. But thinking they could afford to catch him when the gates were opened in the morning, they relaxed their watch.

At midnight Samson pulled the gates of the city to pieces and went off with the doors that were part of the gates. Most commentaries interpret Judges 16:3 as meaning that Samson carried the doors to Hebron, a distance of 38 miles [61 km], which is rather a long way for a practical joke. The Hebrew could quite well be translated, 'the hill that looks across to Hebron'. This would make far better sense. The Mayor of Gaza confirmed that there is such a hill, and writes in a letter to the author, 'I am glad to inform you that it is possible to see the Hebron mountains from hills close to Gaza, especially from Muntar Hill [Ali el-Muntar].'

By now, Samson was the Number One enemy of the Philistines, but every time they met him he was too strong for them. Finally they caught him through another Philistine girl, Delilah, and this time the VIPs themselves intervened and offered her a bribe if she could find out the secret of her lover's superhuman strength. It seems incredible that Samson did not see through Delilah's crude attempts to find out his secret, and one wonders whether by now he had drifted so far that he doubted the significance of his Nazirite vow, and imagined that he was strong enough in himself to deal with anything. So he abandoned such dedication to God as still remained, and let his hair be cut, with the result that he suddenly found himself as weak as any normal man. The Philistines put his eyes out, and set him to turn the millstone in Gaza gaol.

The story may suggest that Samson turned back to God as his hair grew once more. The end came when the Philistines promoted a festival in honour of their god Dagon, who to their mind had at last triumphed over Jehovah. They gathered in a central building which had wooden pillars on stone pedestals supporting deep balconies crowded with sightseers. Their captive stood between two of the pillars, and as they jeered at him he leaned heavily on the main supports and collapsed the crowded balconies on to the spectators below, dying himself in the disaster. His final prayer is so self-centred (Judges 16:28), that one wonders whether it was God who restored his strength, or whether his work in the mill had restored his muscles sufficiently for this final effort.

His prayer is typical of the man. No doubt he was a fair enough judge (Judges 15:20) so long as he was advising others and not himself, and he certainly protected his people against Philistine oppression, though with little permanent result, since soon afterwards a large number of Danites had to migrate to the north (18:27-31). He is an example of a man who was used by God through one thing that he had to offer, his phenomenal strength, but he would not have understood the hymn,

'Take *my life* and let it be
    Consecrated, Lord, to Thee'.

SAMUEL. *Name of God*

The Hebrew writer, of course, knew the meaning of the name, but his mother gave the name a special significance by linking it with a word meaning *ask* (1 Samuel 1:20), as one might say, 'I call him Neil in memory of my *kneeling* in prayer for him.'

Samuel's father Elkanah was a Levite, descended from Korah, (1 Chronicles 6:33-37). Most of the Levites were settled up and down the country among the tribes, and Samuel's parents had their home in the hill country of Ephraim (1 Samuel 1:1). His mother, Hannah, conceived him in answer to special prayer, and as soon as he was old enough she dedicated him to the service of God under Eli in the simple temple that housed the ark of the covenant in Shiloh, and saw him only once a year when the family came to worship (1 Samuel 1:9-28; 2:18-20).

Eli's sons, who were the effective priests as he grew old, were thoroughly immoral men (see **Hophni, Phinehas**), and Samuel became the centre of spiritual life in Shiloh, especially when God spoke to him as a prophet. The story of his call (1 Samuel 3) shows that prophets truly heard God's word as a voice, as indeed we should gather from other passages in the Bible (NB: 3:1,21).

After Israel's defeat by the Philistines, and the destruction of Shiloh (1 Samuel 4:1-22; Jeremiah 7:12, confirmed by archaeology), and the return of the ark to Kiriath-jearim (1 Samuel 6:1–7:2), Samuel may well have returned home, until after some years he rallied the Israelites back to God and set out to rid them of Philistine domination. He gathered an army together at Mizpah in Benjamin, and symbolically pleaded their frailty before God by pouring water out on the ground to vanish into the soil (1 Samuel 7:6, compare 2 Samuel 14:14). In the battle that followed, and during further campaigns, the Philistine hold was broken for the time being (1 Samuel 7:7-14).

Samuel, the last of those the Bible calls judges, was perhaps the most conscientious of all, travelling round the country in circuit like a modern judge, and returning to his home in Ramah. Since there was now no central place of worship, Samuel built an altar there (1 Samuel 7:15-17). He was, like Eli, disappointed in his sons whom he hoped would succeed him. They were too ready to take money (8:1-3). This led the people to ask for a king, and although the law had made provision for a king one day (Deuteronomy 17:14-20), it was for God to choose the time, and not for the people to force his hand (1 Samuel 8:4-9). Samuel vividly described the hard ways of an oriental monarchy, but the people refused to listen (8:10-22).

The three steps in the election of Saul can best be treated under **Saul** himself, but we must note the position of Samuel in 1 Samuel 9, since casual reading might suggest that he is treated as a fairly insignificant local seer. In fact, Saul and his servant find themselves near a town where there is a seer who has the reputation of being able to find lost property, and who consequently might tell them where to find their lost donkeys. *This* seer lives in the town, but the seer whom they meet is a visitor who has just arrived (1 Samuel 9:12), who is in fact Samuel on his circuit and who tells them that *he* is the seer they need to see. The writer accounts for the confusion by explaining that *seer* and *prophet* were interchangeable terms (verse 9).

When Saul was finally accepted as king by the whole country,

Samuel spoke strongly to the people, promising them that in spite of everything God would continue to bless them if they and their king obeyed him – but not otherwise. He ended by calling on the Lord to send thunder and rain from a clear sky as a sign, and assured the people of his own prayers for the future (1 Samuel 12:16-25).

Although Saul now took over the government of the country, Samuel remained as God's chosen adviser. Saul became restive, and when on one occasion he was told to wait up to seven days for Samuel to come and offer sacrifice before battle, and Samuel was late, he decided to perform the sacrifice himself. Since Samuel then rebuked Saul, it sounds as though he did actually arrive at the very end of the seventh day, when Saul had given him up (1 Samuel 13:1-15).

Saul's next act of disobedience strikes us as strange, and some have taken his side against Samuel. God told Samuel to send Saul to attack Amalek and to destroy its king, Agag, and all of its possessions. Saul conducted a successful campaign, but brought back Agag and any flocks and herds that were worthwhile. There is no suggestion that he was moved by humanitarian motives, and Samuel treated his conduct as a straight act of disobedience to God, for which God would reject him as king. Samuel executed Agag with his own hands. As a comment on this chapter, we note that Amalek was always liable to boil over into an attack on Israel after the unprovoked attempt to wipe Israel out on their way to the Promised Land (1 Samuel 15:2; Exodus 17:8-15; Deuteronomy 25:17-19; Judges 6:33; 7:12), and perhaps God knew that a fresh attack was imminent. Agag himself was no angel (1 Samuel 15:33).

All down the ages we find God working within human frames of reference, but moving towards the goal that will transform them. This is true of such things as war, slavery and marriage. (See **Onesimus**). When war was still accepted as normal, God spoke to men through war, but showed that war was not the true answer. Thus he barred David as a man of war from building the temple (1 Chronicles 22:8), and included peace in nearly every prophecy of the work of the future Messiah.

Although Saul really cared only for his own prestige (1 Samuel 15:30-31), Samuel was concerned over his collapse (16:1). But he was called by God to anoint a successor, and was guided to David (16:1-13). After this, Samuel fades into the background, but he was probably responsible for organizing groups of prophets into community centres. We may assume that these centres were something like the Celtic monasteries, with individual huts, and that they were called Naioth, or Dwellings.

The Naioth centre where Samuel and David took refuge from Saul for a time is said to be 'in Ramah', and thus is unlikely to have been the name of a separate town (1 Samuel 19:18-24). Commentators often speak of these groups of prophets as though they were little more than dancing dervishes.

They may often have flung their bodies about under the prophetic impulse, but there is never any hint that their prophecies were of less worth than those of Samuel or the written prophets, though they may have been more tied to minor events in the contemporary scene, and less worth recording for posterity. (See also **Saul** in 19:24.)

Samuel was buried in his town of Ramah amid national mourning for a great man (1 Samuel 28:3). Saul's last act of disobedience was to apply to a medium to bring back Samuel from the dead on the day before his final battle with the Philistines. Interpreters differ over whether the spirit that appeared was really Samuel, but the story reads as though God permitted Samuel's return on this occasion, and the medium realized that this was a type of spirit that she had not encountered before. So, far from being glad to remake contact with the world of the living, Samuel is disturbed at being recalled (28:15). But God gives him once more the gift of prophecy to declare that Saul will join him next day (1 Samuel 28:1-25; 1 Chronicles 10:13-14).

SANBALLAT. A Babylonian name, *The moon-god Sin has given life*

The chief opponent of Nehemiah, probably because Nehemiah was given the post Sanballat wanted. His native town was Beth-horon, about 20 miles [32 km] north-west of Jerusalem (Nehemiah 2:19). He tried organized ridicule and terrorism to stop the building of the walls of Jerusalem (4:1-9), and when the walls were finished he mounted a plot to draw Nehemiah to one of the villages under pretence of a conference (6:1-4). Next he sent a letter accusing Nehemiah of organizing a rebellion which would set him on the throne, and cleverly left the letter unsealed so that the postman could show it to others on the way (6:5-9). Finally he tried to discredit Nehemiah by suggesting he should take sanctuary in the temple to save himself from assassination (6:10-14).

The grandson of Eliashib the high priest actually married Sanballat's daughter. Nehemiah adds in his dramatic way, 'therefore I chased him from me' (Nehemiah 13:28). This may or may not have been the end of the affair, since the Jewish historian Josephus says that Sanballat built the Samaritan temple on Mount Gerizim for his son-in-law Manasseh, brother of Jaddua the high priest. Josephus dates this about 330 BC, whereas the incident in Nehemiah would have been about 100 years earlier. We do not know when the rival temple was built, and it may be that Josephus confused Sanballat's date, unless there was a repetition of the incident with a second Sanballat.

There is a letter from a Jewish colony in Egypt in 407 BC which speaks of Sanballat as governor of Samaria, although his two sons, Delaiah and Shelemiah, were clearly acting for him. The names of his sons, which incorporate the Jehovah ending, show that Sanballat must have had some respect for Jehovah, whether or not he worshipped him exclusively.

SARAH. *Princess*
Called Sarai (meaning unknown) until Genesis 17:15. The wife and half-sister of Abraham (20:12), already married to him when he came into Canaan from Mesopotamia (11 ;27–32). She was evidently extremely beautiful, and Abraham was afraid that in

his travels she would be taken by some powerful ruler, and he himself would be murdered. So he found a way round by regularly insisting that she was his sister — which she was — and not his wife (20:12-13). As a result he lost her for a time to Pharaoh, and was roundly rebuked by the king in consequence (12:10-19), and suffered the same humiliation later at the hands of Abimelech of Gerar (20:1-18).

Sarah clearly kept her looks in spite of her age, but she and Abraham were without a child when she was apparently beyond childbearing. She followed a standard practice of the day and gave Hagar her maid to Abraham to bear him a child, Ishmael (Genesis 16, see **Hagar**), but God twice promised that she herself would become a mother (17:15-19; 18:9-15). The second occasion was one of the rare pre-incarnation appearances of God, probably here the Second Person of the Trinity, accompanied by two angels. This appears from the story in chapter 18. Three visitors appeared at Abraham's tent, two of them went on to Sodom (18:16; 19:1) while Abraham remained in conversation with the Lord (18:22). Sarah overheard the promise of a child to be born in the spring and treated it as a joke (18:9-15), but in due course Isaac was born, apparently in Gerar (chapter 21).

Sarah died in Hebron at the age of 127 and was buried in a cave called Machpelah, purchased from a Hittite. This later was the tomb of Abraham (Genesis 25:9), Isaac and Rebekah, Jacob and Leah (49:29-32). The traditional site is now incorporated in a mosque.

SARGON. *Established as king*
A powerful king of Assyria, (722-705 BC) but mentioned only once by name in the Old Testament, when he is conducting a campaign against Ashdod in 712 BC (Isaiah 20). He was the unnamed king of Assyria who finally captured Samaria in 721 BC at the end of a siege that had been begun by Shalmaneser V (2 Kings 17:5-6). He deported a large number of Israelites into Mesopotamia (but see **Shalmaneser**).

SAUL[NT]. *Asked (of God)*
The Apostle – see **Paul**.

SAUL. *Asked (of God)*
The King.
An extraordinary man to be chosen as the first king of Israel. We can only suppose that with all his ups and downs, spiritual and physical, he was the best man available. When God selected him in response to popular demand he made it clear that this was a second best, and that it was not yet his purpose to change an *ad hoc* form of government under Spirit-guided men into a monarchy (1 Samuel 8).

There were three steps in Saul's coronation. They are not alternatives or contradictory, but each depends on the one that has gone before. Saul and his servant go to look for his father's lost asses. They decide to consult a small-time local seer with a gift for finding lost property, but when they enter the town they are surprised instead to find Samuel who has just come on one of his circuit visits (1 Samuel 9:6,12, see **Samuel**), and who is commissioned by God to anoint Saul as king (9:15-10:1). Saul is renewed in his inner man (10:9).

On his way home, Saul was told he would meet a small group of worshippers, and also a larger group of prophets returning from worship and singing under the inspiration of the Spirit. Saul himself would be caught up by the charismatic gift. This indeed came to pass, to the bewilderment of friends who had known him before, and who were amused that he should be mixed up with a group of nonentities of unknown parentage (10:1-13).

The second step to the throne was the public drawing of lots for the kingship under Samuel's direction (1 Samuel 10:17-27). Saul knew that God had already chosen him and anointed him at the hands of Samuel, but was doubtful about his ability for the task. Hence he went off and hid, believing that God would indeed guide the outcome of the lot. When he was dragged out from his hiding place he was approved by popular acclamation, but was not crowned, since there was a minority group who objected to him.

The third step followed the siege of Jabesh-Gilead by the Ammonites. The proposed terms of surrender included the gouging out of the right eyes of everyone in the city, but the inhabitants were given seven days of truce to try to find someone to help them. Nahash of Ammon did not rate their chances highly. Because Saul had been chosen king, the messengers from Jabesh naturally went first to him, and he rallied a force which swooped suddenly on the Ammonites and utterly routed them. This confirmed Saul's position absolutely, and now he was properly invested with the kingship (1 Samuel 11).

The opening verse of 1 Samuel 13 lacks the original figures which originally gave Saul's age and the length of his reign. All that we know is that Saul was a 'young man' when Samuel anointed him (1 Samuel 9:2) and that his grandson was five years old when Saul and Jonathan were killed (2 Samuel 4:4). It is difficult to justify the NEB guesses of 50 years old and a 22-year reign. Even if the second is correct, the former is far too old.

One must, however, assume that 1 Samuel 13 passes in silence over the early years of Saul's reign, since from verse 2 onwards his son Jonathan is an active combatant. The Israelites suffered through the Philistine monopoly of the iron and smithy trade, which restricted their use of weapons, but when Saul began to get to grips with the Philistines he met with considerable success, although he clashed with Samuel over the right to offer a sacrifice (chapter 13), and nearly lost Jonathan through imposing a ban on taking any food during one of the battles, a ban which Jonathan violated in ignorance, and for which Saul wished to put him to death if the people had allowed it (chapter 14).

Saul's next clash with Samuel came when he was commissioned to attack the Amalekites — which he did willingly — and not spare any who fell into his hands, nor bring back any spoil. Saul defied this second commission, not for any humanitarian reasons, for which one might have forgiven him, and he brought back King Agag, presumably as one king doing a kindness to another, and also such valuable spoil as he could manage. He began by lying to Samuel, but in return was told that without the principle of obedience to God's commands he could not continue as king. Saul then blamed the people for putting pressure on him (as Aaron did over the matter of the golden calf in Exodus 32:21-24) but anxious to keep up appearances after admitting he had done wrong he begged Samuel to join him in publicly worshipping God, and allowed Samuel to execute Agag. (For the moral problem, see **Samuel**.)

Soon after this, Samuel was sent to anoint David secretly as Saul's successor, although he did not declare in so many words what the significance of the anointing was to be; it might, for example, have signified that David was to be a prophet (1 Samuel 16:1-13). By a divine coincidence, David was summoned to play to Saul when the king had one of his attacks (16:14-23). These attacks are said to have been due to 'an evil spirit from the Lord' in place of the Spirit of the Lord who had equipped him for his work.

When a person's inner world has been opened up to direct Spirit influence, he may, if he is disobedient, find that evil spirit influence comes in through the same door. This is 'from God' inasmuch as it is one of the God-given laws of man's nature. On the other hand the term 'spirit' here may be a general term, and Saul may have been suffering from bouts of intense depression. We are not to suppose that music alone soothed him, but David was a composer of music and words that spoke of God and his ways, and undoubtedly he sang some of his psalms to bring Saul back to reality. Robert Browning grasped this in his marvellous poem, *Saul,* the longer version in his *Men and Women* being the one in which he works out the concept fully (1 Samuel 16:14-23).

Things began to work out badly after this, and the challenge of Goliath would have routed the Israelites if it had not been for David. It is puzzling why Saul took such trouble to learn the name of David's father (1 Samuel 17:55-58) not of David himself whom he already knew, but he had promised to make the victor's parents free from taxes (17:25), and it may be that somewhere at the back of his mind he connected David with Jesse (16:18), and rumours had got back to him of some suspicious anointing of one of Jesse's sons, which might be a threat to him as king.

From now onwards Saul used David against the Philistines, and jealousy made him put him in really dangerous positions, promising first his elder daughter and then his younger in return for the risks he was taking (1 Samuel 18. (See **Michal**). In one of his fits he nearly speared David, who had to run for his life and take refuge with Samuel (19:8-17). Samuel and David went to the community of prophets (see **Samuel**), and Saul's messengers, who came to arrest David, were all caught under the influence of the Spirit of God. Eventually Saul came himself, and he also had a similar experience to that which he had had earlier in his life (10:9-13), only this time there was little joy for him. In his humiliation and conviction he was led to symbolize his nakedness before God by stripping off his clothes, an obvious psychological action (19:18-24).

He had one further outburst when David refused to attend the official court dinner over the period of the new moon. Jonathan shielded David (1 Samuel 20), and from henceforth David was on the run as an outlaw, although twice Saul himself might easily have become the victim unsuspectingly if David had chosen to kill him (chapters 24 and 26). Saul was even mad enough to murder Ahimelech the high priest, and his eighty-five fellow priests, for innocently helping David (21:1-9; 22:6-19). (See **Ahimelech**, **Doeg**.)

Eventually Saul realized that he must meet a final challenge by the Philistines who had overrun the country as far as Gilboa in the north. Hitherto he had done his best to suppress mediums, but now, when God refused to answer him by the usual means, he turned to one of the surviving mediums at Endor, some ten miles [16 km] north of what was to be the battlefield (chapter 28). Although she is commonly called 'The witch of Endor', she was not a witch but an ordinary medium, one who was 'mistress of an *ob,* or a control spirit', as is the literal Hebrew of 28:7.

Mediums today generally have one spirit who acts as a control for communications that are alleged to come from the departed.

Saul wished to consult Samuel, and there is a difference of opinion as to whether the spirit who appeared was actually Samuel or whether it was an impersonating spirit. If it was Samuel himself, God allowed him to return as an exceptional case, and it looks as though the medium was frightened by a spirit of a different order from those she usually produced; moreover she left Saul while the spirit spoke (28:12-14, 21), a thing which does not happen in alleged materializations in séances today. Samuel, distressed at being contacted, spoke with the gift of prophecy once more, and told Saul that he and his sons would die in the battle (1 Samuel 28). In 1 Chronicles 10:13-14 it is said that Saul's approach to a medium, an act which is always condemned in Scripture, was the final act of unfaithfulness to God. (See Deuteronomy 18:9-13; Isaiah 8:19-20.)

In the battle on Mount Gilboa Saul received severe wounds, and after trying in vain to persuade his armour-bearer to put him to death to avoid capture he fell on his own sword and died. His sons also were killed in the battle (1 Samuel 31). When the Philistines found the bodies they beheaded Saul and nailed the bodies to the walls of one of the temples in Bethshan. They were not left long, since a force from Jabesh-gilead, the place that Saul had saved when he first became king, broke into the temple and removed the bodies (31:8-13). Perhaps to prevent the Philistines from exhuming the bodies they took the rare step of cremating them, probably the only case of deliberate cremation in the Old Testament, apart from criminals occasionally (2 Chronicles 34:5) and perhaps during a plague (Amos 6:10; though see margin).

An Amalekite looter came across the dead king and removed his crown and bracelet. He went straight to David, who was three days' journey to the south, reckoning that he would be well paid if he claimed to have killed Saul with his own hands, and could produce his crown and insignia to prove it. But he did not know David, and the looter's claim to have killed the Lord's anointed rebounded in the death sentence on himself (2 Samuel 1:1-16;

4:10). Archaeology has shown that Saul's 'palace' at Gibeah (1 Samuel 15:34, etc.) was comparatively small and simple, but strongly built.

SCEVA[NT]

One of the high priests whose seven sons practised as exorcists in Ephesus (Acts 19:13-17). Jesus himself accepted Jewish exorcism as a fact, without expressing approval of the methods used (Matthew 12:27). Christ's reference and the story in Acts show that these exorcists followed one of the standard methods of calling on more powerful spirits to expel the demon that was possessing a victim. In a sense this was a case of Satan driving out Satan, but Jewish and pagan exorcists did not claim to be glorifying God, as Christ did, nor did their methods make any inroads upon Satan's kingdom.

Naturally they were on the look-out for new techniques, and the miracles done through Paul in the name of Jesus Christ suggested to some of the exorcists, including the sons of Sceva, that Jesus must be a more powerful spirit than any they had yet manipulated. But the seven sons of Sceva suffered the sort of experience that any dabbler, or even practitioner, in magic and the occult may have, and were overwhelmed and beaten up by the victim of possession with the superhuman strength that the evil spirit gave him. The name of Jesus should never be used as a charm.

SENNACHERIB

King of Assyria 705-681 BC. He clashed with King Hezekiah on three occasions, as recorded in 2 Kings 18 and 19. The first tallies with Sennacherib's own account of an invasion in 701 BC (18:13-16). Both speak of the tribute of 30 talents of gold and 300 talents of silver. Scholars differ over the dating of the next two contacts in 18:17-19:8 and 19:9-36, and some think that all three are variants of the 701 BC campaign. But the conclusion of the third (19:35) hardly suggests the success with which Sennacherib terminated this campaign, since inscriptions say that he exacted tribute from Hezekiah. It is therefore reasonable to hold that these other two campaigns, with a short interval in between, took place later in Sennacherib's reign in a period for which no Assyrian records remain. This explains the reference to Tirhakah, who became king in 690 BC (19:9, see **Pharaoh**) and the mention of Sennacherib's murder in 19:37, as though it followed soon afterwards.

The sudden destruction of the Assyrian army (2 Kings 19:36) could have been due to bubonic plague. We know now that rats and mice are carriers of this plague (e.g. 1 Samuel 5:6; 6:4-5), and the Greek historian Herodotus repeats a story that on one of his expeditions against Egypt, Sennacherib had to retreat because mice ate the leather equipment and the bowstrings of his army. If there were so many mice, and perhaps rats, this makes the plague explanation very likely.

The Bible says that Sennacherib was killed by his two sons while worshipping in the temple of Nisroch (2 Kings 19:37). The Babylonian Chronicle says he was killed by his son (singular), and Sennacherib's grandson speaks of his grandfather having been crushed by images of the gods. It could be that his sons killed him by bribing men to push down the colossal images on top of their father while he was worshipping them.

SERAIAH. *Jehovah has prevailed*
Several men in the Old Testament have this name, but it is interesting that four are mentioned during the last days of Jerusalem. One was sent to arrest Jeremiah (Jeremiah 36:26). Another accompanied Zedekiah on a visit to Babylon, and was given a scroll by Jeremiah on the damnation of Babylon to read aloud before tying it to a stone and hurling it into the Euphrates as a symbol of Babylon's utter destruction (51:59-64). Modern translations have has spoilt many a good sermon based on the KJV, 'This Seraiah was a quiet prince' (51:59), by more correctly telling us he was quartermaster or staff officer. A third Seraiah was high priest when Jerusalem fell, and was put to death on Nebuchadnezzar's orders (52:24-27). He was the ancestor of

Ezra, either grandfather or great-grandfather (1 Chronicles 6:11-15; Ezra 7:1-5). The fourth was a leader who was loyal to Gedaliah who was appointed governor after the fall of Jerusalem (Jeremiah 40:8).

SETH. *Substitute*
The third son of Adam and Eve, accepted as a substitute for Abel (Genesis 4:25-26). We are not told when his sisters were born, but presumably he married one of them, which at this stage of Adamic history would not have been incest (5:3-4).

SHADRACH. Meaning unknown
One of Daniel's three friends taken captive to Babylon. His name was changed from Hananiah, *Jehovah is gracious.* For the exploits of these 'Three Musketeers', see **Abednego**.

SHALLUM. *Recompense*
Fifteen men in the Old Testament have this name. Two were kings, one reigning for one month only (c 745 BC) after assassinating Zechariah of Israel. He consequently fulfilled the prophecy that the dynasty of Jehu would last for four generations only, but himself was one out of many proofs that those who take the sword may in turn suffer the sword on their own necks, when he was assassinated by Menahem (2 Kings 15:10-15, compare Matthew 26:52; Revelation 13:10).

The other king is more usually known as Jehoahaz, but is called Shallum in Jeremiah 22:11; 1 Chronicles 3:15.

SHALMANESER. *The god Shulman is head*
Several kings of Assyria bore this name. Only one is named in the Old Testament, i.e. Shalmaneser V (727-722 BC), who exacted tribute from Hoshea, the last king of Israel (2 Kings 17:3). When Hoshea rebelled, he invaded Israel and besieged Samaria, although the final capture may have been due to Sargon. Sargon claims it in an inscription, but in any case the fall of the city took place at the very end of Shalmaneser's reign when things were

obviously chaotic (17:1-6; 18:9-12). It is probable that Shalman in Hosea 10:14 is Shalmaneser V, and that the town he destroyed, Beth-arbel, is Arbela in western Galilee. Others think the king here is a Moabite king named Salamanu. In Hosea 5:13; 10:6 (KJV) 'King Jareb' *Boss King,* may be Shalmaneser V.

An unexpected omission from the records is Shalmaneser III (859-824 BC), who tells us that he met a confederacy of Palestinian nations at Karkar, north of Damascus, in 853 BC. He says that Ahab supplied 2000 chariots and 10,000 troops. Shalmaneser withdrew after the battle, but in 841 BC he defeated Hazael of Damascus and also forced Jehu of Israel to pay tribute. This is depicted on the so-called Black Obelisk. He did not bequeath his obelisk to the British Museum, but that is where you will find it, with replicas in the USA.

SHAMGAR

The meaning of his name is uncertain, but it occurs in Mesopotamian records. He brought relief to southern Israel by killing 600 Philistines, not necessarily all at once, with a metal-tipped goad. At this time (say perhaps 1100 BC) the Philistines were not as well established in the country as they were in Samson's day. (Judges 3:31; 5:6).

SHAPHAN

His name is that of the animal which is variously translated. Thus we have 'coney' (KJV), 'badger' (RSV twice), 'rock badger' (RSV twice, JB once, and NEB), 'rock rabbit' (NEB margin and JB once), and the only one which zoologists accept, 'hyrax' (JB twice). Even JB dare not use the ugly sounding 'hyrax' in Psalm 104:18 and Proverbs 30:26[*], where in fact the creatures are in the plural, which would be even uglier. The rock hyrax is the size of a rabbit with short ears. Was Shaphan named 'Bunny' by his parents, or was it his nickname at school because he had a

---

[*] The NIV uses hyrax in the Psalm reference, and hyraxes in Proverbs. Other recent translations use a mix of the above.

rabbity face?

He was the reliable secretary of King Josiah, and acted as the go-between for the king and the high priest Hilkiah in ordering the repair of the temple, and bringing the book of the law to the king when this turned up unexpectedly. (See **Hilkiah, Josiah**). Shaphan read the book aloud to the king, and was one of the deputation who went to consult the prophetess Huldah (2 Kings 22). He does not appear again, except as the father of **Ahikam**, Elasah (Jeremiah 29:3), Gemariah (36:10,25), and grandfather of **Gedaliah**, together with one son, **Jaazaniah**, who was the only one to turn out as a baddy (Ezekiel 8:11).

SHEAR-JASHUB. *A remnant shall return*
Isaiah's son (Isaiah 7:3), named, like his second son (8:3), to enshrine some aspect of his message. From the time of his opening vision (6:13) Isaiah saw that the nation as a whole would go into exile, but a remnant, and only a remnant, would return.

SHEBA
The unnamed Queen of Sheba who visited Solomon (1 Kings 10) is thought nowadays to have been a Sabaean from South-western Arabia. The Arabs call her Belkis. The Sabaeans were wealthy traders (e.g. Isaiah 60:6; Jeremiah 6:20), and ancient records mention that their monarchs were often queens. Ethiopian tradition maintains that this queen, Makeda, or Woman of Fire, came from Ethiopia and that the child she bore to Solomon became the first emperor, Menelik, from whom the subsequent line of emperors descended. The two versions are not incompatible, since it is likely that there was close contact by sea between Ethiopia and Arabia, and the son might well have been adopted as emperor by Ethiopia when he was grown up.

SHEBNA. Perhaps, *Youthfulness*
An important official under King Hezekiah, being the court scribe who negotiated with the Rabshakeh, and tried to get him to talk in the diplomatic language of Aramaic, which the ordinary

people on the wall would find hard to follow (2 Kings 18:18-27). One assumes that he is also the man who holds the post of chamberlain in Isaiah 22:15-19. This man appears to have been a foreigner (implied in the first clause in verse 16) who had pushed himself forward by building an elaborate mausoleum for himself, and by driving around in all the new models (verses 16,18). Clearly he was taking advantage of his position (verse 18), and Isaiah declares that he will be demoted and ultimately taken into exile, giving place to Eliakim. (See **Eliakim**).

SHECHEM
Son of the ruler of the town of Shechem. He fell in love with Jacob's daughter Dinah, and after raping her wished to marry her. Jacob would have been willing, but Dinah's brothers, Simeon and Levi, tricked the Shechemite males into submitting to circumcision, and then massacred them while they were still incapacitated (Genesis 34).

SHEM. *Name,* perhaps with idea of *Reputation*
Eldest son of Noah (Genesis 5:32), saved in the ark, and ancestor of the Hebrews and others listed in 10:21-31. These peoples are not all synonymous with those to whom the term Semitic is applied by modern philologists. (See **Ham, Japheth**.)

SHEMAIAH. *Jehovah has heard*
A prophet who stopped Rehoboam campaigning against Jeroboam, on the ground of the fratricide that would be involved (1 Kings 12:21-24). Later he wrote a record of Rehoboam's reign (2 Chronicles 12:15).

Another Shemaiah, taken captive with Jehoiachin, did his best to stop Jeremiah prophesying (correctly) that the exile would be long. He also claimed the gift of prophecy, and declared that the exiles would soon return (Jeremiah 29:24-32; see the whole chapter for the significance).

SHEMER. *Guard*
Owner of the hill on which Samaria was built. He at least has the honour of giving his name to this famous city, but financially he received something under little money from the property developer Omri, king of Israel (1 Kings 16:24). David was much more generous when he bought the site for the future temple (2 Samuel 24:240). (See **Araunah**).

SHESHBAZZAR
The governor appointed by Cyrus to bring back such of the Jewish exiles as wished to return and to rebuild the temple in 538 BC. Although he used to be identified with Zerubbabel, this is ruled out by Ezra 5:15, where in a letter written in 520 BC Sheshbazzar is referred to as no longer alive, whereas Zerubbabel is now taking the lead in rebuilding the temple.

He is called 'the prince of Judah' (Ezra 1:8), which may well mean that he is of the royal family. Hence he has been identified with Shenazzar, a son of King Jehoiachin (1 Chronicles 3:18). His Babylonian name (meaning uncertain) may have been given as a compliment to **Evil-Merodach** who released **Jehoiachin** from prison (2 Kings 25:27-30).

In any event, he was not the moving spirit in the setting up of the altar and temple, but left this to Joshua and Zerubbabel, the latter also being of the royal family (Ezra 3). He is named in the letter of 520 BC as having laid the foundations of the temple (5:16), but this was because the letter is referring to the decree of Cyrus which the new king is asked to check. Only Sheshbazzar's name would appear in this as the one authorized to build the temple.

SHIMEI. *Jehovah has heard*
Out of some twenty men with this name, a significant one is the relative of King Saul who cursed David as he retired from Jerusalem before Absalom, and hurled stones for good measure. Abishai delightfully asked permission to go and 'take off his head', but David refused, holding that these curses were an

additional burden from God for him to bear (2 Samuel 16:5-13). When David was returning from his successful campaign, Shimei begged his forgiveness.

Once again Abishai wanted to kill him, but David promised on oath to spare his life (2 Samuel 19:18-23). Sadly enough, David never came to terms with himself so as to forgive him from his heart, and before he died he commissioned Solomon to do what he himself had sworn not to do (1 Kings 2:8-9). Solomon was not anxious to obey his father in this, but confined Shimei to Jerusalem, with the suspended sentence that if he left the city he would be executed. Shimei happily agreed, but after three years felt safe enough to go to Gath to extradite two runaway slaves, and Solomon had no hesitation in carrying out the death sentence (2:36-46).

SHISHAK
See **Pharaoh**.

SIHON
A very powerful Amorite king with wide stretching territory on the east of Jordan (Numbers 21:24; Judges 11:22). When he refused to allow the Israelites to pass peacefully through his lands, the Israelites met him in battle, killed him, and possessed his territory (Numbers 21:21-32).

SILAS[NT]
Probably an Aramaic variant of the name Saul, *Asked,* with Silvanus as the Latin equivalent. Silas and Silvanus in the New Testament are the same person, Silas in Acts, Silvanus in the Epistles. We do not know his native city, but like Paul he was a Roman citizen (Acts 16:37).

He first appears as one of the bearers of the letter from the Jerusalem council (15:22), and settled for a time in Antioch, where he exercised his gift of prophecy (15:30-32). When Paul and Barnabas dissolved their partnership because of Mark, Silas accompanied Paul on his second missionary journey through

Asia Minor (15:36-41).

At Philippi Silas shared Paul's imprisonment and release (Acts 16:11-40), and went with him into Macedonia, staying behind with Timothy in Beroea when Paul went to Athens and Corinth (17:15). They joined Paul again in Corinth (18:5) where they took part in preaching (2 Corinthians 1:19). When Paul wrote to the Thessalonians from Corinth, Silas joined him in greetings (1 Thessalonians 1:1; 2 Thessalonians 1:1). Peter mentions him as the secretary whom he used to write his letter (1 Peter 5:12).

SIMEON[OT/NT]. *Hearing*

1. [OT]One of the sons Leah bore to Jacob, and so named because she believed God had heard her desire to win her husband's affection (Genesis 29:33). He joined Levi in massacring the Shechemites in revenge for the treatment of their sister (34:25-31), and evidently the two of them were well known for other acts of violence (49:5-7). Simeon was kept as a hostage by Joseph in Egypt (42:24; 43:23). One of his wives was a Canaanite, and the descendants of her son Shaul were integrated into the tribe of Simeon (Genesis 46:10; Numbers 26:13) which was settled in the south (Joshua 19:1-9).

2. [NT]In the New Testament we find an elderly man named **Simeon**, who evidently had an occasional gift of prophetic awareness, a gift which had long been dormant in Israel but which was revived when the time of the Messiah came. He had been assured that before his death he would see the Messiah, and when Mary and Joseph brought Jesus as a baby to the temple Simeon was led to join them there. He recognized Jesus as the promised child, and he took him in his arms, gave thanks to God, and spoke the words of what is often called the Nunc Dimittis, which has been sung so often down the ages.

One notable thing is Simeon's realization that God's salvation was for Gentiles as well as Jews. But he also told Mary that this child would be the touchstone of life and death, and that she would suffer in seeing him suffer (Luke 2:25-35).

3. ᴺᵀAnother **Simeon** or Symeon is mentioned once only in Acts 13:1-2 as one of the prophets in Antioch who received God's orders for Paul and Barnabas to set out on their first missionary journey. He is nicknamed Niger, *Black,* so he was probably a black African; in fact some have identified him with Simon of Cyrene (Luke 23:26).

SIMONᴺᵀ
In the New Testament a variant of Simeon or Symeon (e.g. Acts 15:14), although as a Greek name it means *Snub-nosed.* It was the original name of **Peter**, and there are several others who bear the name.

1. Simon of Cyrene carried the cross of Jesus (Luke 23:26), and was the father of two sons well known in the church (see **Rufus**).

2. Simon, the cured leper entertained Jesus to supper in his home in Bethany (Matthew 26:6). (See **Martha** for the suggestion that she was his wife.)

3. Simon Magus assumed more importance later than he is given in Acts 8:9-24. He was a magician in Samaria who was converted, or professed to be converted, and was baptized. But he still looked with the professional eye of a former occultist on the miracles that Philip was used to perform, and then later on the demonstrations of the Holy Spirit that came through the laying on of the hands of Peter and John.

He offered to buy the 'trick' for his own use, and suffered a scathing denunciation from Peter. Whether or not he was a true Christian, his heart was in the wrong place, and he needed to seek the forgiveness of God. Simon accepted the rebuke, and asked for Peter's prayers.

From this time onwards we find Simon Magus spoken of as a heretic of a Gnostic type by early Christian writers. The statement in Acts 8:10 ('This man is that power of God which is called Great') certainly suggests that he had made semi-divine claims, and later he is said to have spoken of himself as the Father above all, and the prostitute with whom he was living as the original creative thought.

We cannot go into technicalities here, but the Simonians were said to hold his beliefs. More exciting (non-biblical) stories include the occasion when by his magic arts he was levitated in flight over Rome, only to be shot down by the prayers of Peter.

His name is commemorated in the Church of England. On appointment to a parish a clergyman was earlier obliged to declare that he had not obtained the parish through simony, or ecclesiastical bribery. Clergy are no longer required to make this declaration on ordination, although simony is still an offence (Acts 8:18).

SISERA
The general of Jabin, king of Hazor. He may have been a king himself, since the ruler of any considerable city could be termed a king, and attention is called to Sisera's home city Harosheth, probably close to Mount Carmel. In fact, in the story in Judges 4 and 5 of the oppression and deliverance, Sisera is the more prominent of the two. He and his army were defeated through Barak, who was driven on by Deborah. In the battle a heavy storm bogged down the Canaanite chariots (Judges 5:20, 21). Sisera himself escaped, and took refuge in what he believed to be a friendly camp, only to be killed while he slept. (For the moral problem, see **Jael**). It is curious to find that he lived with his mother, and that there is no mention either of his wife or of 'a maiden or two' for himself (Judges 5:28-30).

SO.
See **Pharaoh**.

SOLOMON. *Peaceable*
It seems extraordinary that God should have chosen such men as Saul and Solomon as kings, yet God did choose them both directly (1 Samuel 9 and 10; 1 Chronicles 22:7-10). One can only suppose that these were the best men available to rule, and anyone else would have developed even graver faults.

Solomon, born in wedlock to David and Bathsheba, was also named by the prophet Nathan 'Jedidiah', *Beloved of Jehovah* (2 Samuel 12:24-25). The book of Samuel does not mention him again, since this book is concerned with the rapid events of history, and Solomon played no active part in them until the death of his father. The book of Chronicles, on the other hand, is written by priests who were concerned with the ordinances of the temple, and 1 Chronicles 22-29 contains a great deal about David's introduction of Solomon to the temple that he was to build, and to forms of service which as king he would oversee.

In the end, it was only thanks to his mother that Solomon came to the throne (1 Kings 1), since his brother Adonijah took advantage of David's illness to have himself crowned king. Adonijah would have been a bad king in any case, given that he had been a thoroughly spoilt boy (1:6). Bathsheba intervened, and David commissioned Zadok the priest, Nathan the prophet and others to anoint Solomon. Adonijah's supporters rapidly faded away, but Solomon took the risk of sparing his life. It was indeed a risk, because Adonijah apparently planned to stake a claim to the throne by marrying the girl who had attended David in his last illness, and who might have been assumed to have been the most recent wife in his harem (see **Abishag**). This time Solomon put him to death (1:1-4; 2:13-25).

Saul's kingdom had been very much of an *ad hoc* affair. David had managed some organization, and Solomon went into competition with all the surrounding kingdoms, and was highly successful. But he faced the dangers that Christians today face when they enter the world of big business and the top people. There is no reason why Christians should not be there, but it is terribly easy for them to drop their standards.

Solomon was encouraged by a vision in which God offered him the choice of some gift, and Solomon asked for, and received, the wise ability to discern between good and evil in governing his people. God added the gift of riches as well (1 Kings 3:3-15). As often happens, one who guides others cannot always guide himself.

He proceeded to organize the country into taxation areas, and then began his great work of building the temple. In order that everyone should have a part in this, Solomon organized Israelite workers into three gangs of ten thousand, and sent them to bring timber and stone. Each gang worked for a month, and then had two months at home (1 Kings 5:13-18). He also had the help of builders from Tyre, and in particular Hiram, a man of mixed parentage whose father came from Tyre, was in charge of all the skilled metal work (7:13-47). At the dedication of the temple Solomon made a magnificent speech, in the course of which he made it clear that although the temple was a focus point for the presence of God on earth, God was higher than the highest heaven (8:13; 27-30).

The essential inner part of the temple was very similar to the tabernacle. The large altar of burnt offering was in the inner courtyard, but entrance into the temple proper was for the priests only. In the first section there were lamps, a table for the bread of the presence (KJV shewbread), and an altar of incense. At the far end the holy of holies contained the ark of the covenant of the covenant and the commandments. Aaron's rod and the pot of manna which were in the ark of the covenant in the tabernacle are not mentioned, and had probably been lost when the Philistines had the ark in their possession (1 Samuel 5). Entrance into the holy of holies was confined to the high priest, and he was allowed to go through the veil once a year only, on the Day of Atonement (Leviticus 16).

Full details of the tabernacle are in Exodus 36-39, and the items in the temple are found in 1 Kings 6-7 and 2 Chronicles 3-4. The Epistle to the Hebrews shows how the way of approach to God through the tabernacle and temple ritual is paralleled by the new approach through Jesus Christ and his atoning death. We may now all go through the veil at all times (Hebrews 10:20).

Solomon carried out other building also, including his own palace (1 Kings 7:1-12; 9:1-10,15-19). In spite of his heavy expenditure he became rich (10:14-27). His kingdom ran roughly from the northern Euphrates to the borders of Egypt, thus realizing the promise that had been made to Abraham (1 Kings 4:21; Genesis 15:18-20). This meant that he could control all the trade between Asia Minor and Egypt, both buying and selling for himself and taking a toll from through traffic (1 Kings 10:28-29). He joined the Phoenicians in extensive trading by sea, and opened up the port of Ezion-Geber (Elath) on the Gulf of Akabah (9:26-28; 10:22), where archaeologists have found extensive smelting works, and which dealt with imports and exports of copper and iron. It is only fair to say that some archaeologists disagree over the interpretation of the finds.

Solomon enslaved the Canaanites for workmen, but not the Israelites (1 Kings 9:20-22). The only time when the latter were drafted to work was in building the temple, so that all could have a hand in the house of God. But Israelites on a tribal basis were used as foremen-officers (9:23; 11:28). Unfortunately the upkeep of Solomon's entourage demanded taxes in kind (4:7-28), and this created the unrest which boiled over when Solomon's successor came to be appointed (12:1-15).

In setting himself up as the greatest monarch of the day, Solomon built up his reputation by collecting an enormous harem of 700 wives from various royal families, and 300 concubines (1 Kings 11:3). Beginning with an Egyptian princess (3:1), he found himself building pagan temples for his foreign wives to use, and thus wrecked the clear witness for Jehovah (11:1-13), and brought a troubled end to his reign (11:14-40). It is an extraordinary thing that with all these wives we hear of only one son, Rehoboam, and his mother was an Ammonitess (14:21).

One of Solomon's hobbies was natural history (1 Kings 4:33), though we need not accept the pleasant fable that he was a Dr. Doolittle before his time, able to converse with animals and birds, and entrusting the hoopoe with a letter to the Queen of Sheba. Anyone, however, who wishes to believe this is perfectly at liberty to translate 1 Kings 4:33 as 'he spoke to' rather than 'he spoke of'. Solomon has also been credited with magical powers and control of demons, and various magical textbooks and talismans were ascribed to him by Jewish practitioners of the occult in the Middle Ages. The plant known as Solomon's seal is said to have the symbol of the Star of David on its roots, and its white flowers were used as love potions.

Three books of the Bible are ascribed in whole or part to Solomon. The tradition that links his name with the collection and composition of many proverbs (1 Kings 4:32) need not be questioned. Other rulers, such as Ashurbanipal, have been great collectors of literature. Hence it is unreasonable to deny the nucleus of the book of Proverbs to him, while noting that the book itself says that it includes some proverbs from other sources (chapters 30 and 31).

A reader of the book of Proverbs may feel that the sayings are too good to be true, with the goodies always rewarded and the baddies punished. This, of course, is true of proverbs in general, and often a contradictory saying has to be produced to balance the scales, as, for example, 'Many hands make light work' and 'Too many cooks spoil the broth'.

The best way to look at the book of Proverbs is to see it as a blueprint for the ideal society, which can be effective only if it is one in which goodness is encouraged and prospers. Negatively, one cannot have a proper society if the advice in Proverbs is flouted. Meanwhile in an un-ideal society a good man may suffer and the wicked flourish, as Job, Ecclesiastes and some Psalms point out.

The Song of Solomon nowadays is often regarded as a set of love songs, but traditionally it represents a theme-story, which was not acted as a drama, but could be sung by a minstrel whose voice and gestures would denote the different speakers. There are, however, two main interpretations of what the theme is. The older view, by many still regarded as the orthodox one, is that Solomon is the bridegroom seeking a shepherdess bride, and this has always lent itself to a spiritualising interpretation of Christ making the church his bride, or Christ wooing the soul of the individual believer.

One difficulty of this view is that nowhere else is Solomon's love life held up to admiration rather than condemnation. Hence there is much to be said for the other view that Solomon is trying to entice a country girl into his harem, but in the end is noble enough to let her return to her shepherd lover. So the book is a tribute to true love, and has no need of spiritualizing. (For an extension of this interpretation, see **Abishag**).

The other book is Ecclesiastes, where Solomon is not named as the author although this is certainly implied (Ecclesiastes 1:1). The author adopts the title *Qoheleth*, difficult to translate but probably indicating one who addresses an assembly of people. There is nothing in the book which Solomon could not have written; even the criticisms of bosses (e.g. 4:1-2) and grief for the sufferings of the poor at their hands (e.g. 5:8), are things that governments are always having to admit, while being powerless to interfere as they would wish.

The type of Hebrew, however, belongs to a later date than the time of Solomon, unless as some modern scholars are now thinking the allegedly late factors derive from Phoenician grammar and syntax that would probably have been contemporary with Solomon. If the language is later, one may suppose that the contents, stemming from Solomon, were first handed down in oral form among groups of students of wisdom themes. When eventually they were written down, the scribe responsible used contemporary language forms as, for example, has been done with Chaucer and, of course, modern versions of the Bible.

The Apocrypha contains the book called the Wisdom of Solomon. It was probably written in Alexandria shortly before the time of Christ, and contains much of value; it may well include some of the thoughts of Solomon handed down by tradition.

SOSTHENES[NT]

When Crispus, the chief of the synagogue in Corinth, became a Christian (Acts 18:8), Sosthenes succeeded him (18:17). He was beaten up when Gallio dismissed charges made by the Jews against the Christians, apparently by the court officials and spectators in a burst of anti-Semitism. Since Sosthenes is not a common name, it is likely that it is he who, as Paul's brother in

Christ, sends greetings to the church in Corinth (1 Corinthians 1:1), in which case the synagogue lost its second leader to the Christians.

STEPHANAS[NT]. *Crown*
He and his household were the first to be baptized as a group in Greece (1 Corinthians 16:15), and they were some of the few to be baptized personally by Paul in Corinth (1:16). Stephanas himself crossed over to Ephesus to see Paul later, and probably brought a letter from the Corinthians and took back Paul's reply, i.e. 16:17-18.

STEPHEN[NT]. *Crown*
A Greek convert to Judaism who had accepted circumcision and other requirements for full proselytes. He was converted to Christ in Jerusalem, and was one of seven Hellenists chosen to supervise the distribution of the daily meals to needy widows, since there were complaints that Greek converts were not being properly catered for (Acts 6:1-6). Stephen made his mark as a preacher, and also was used by God for miracles of healing (6:8). His effective discussions with the Jews, especially from foreign countries, led to a charge of blasphemy which was heard before the Sanhedrin (6:8-15).

Stephen made a vigorous defence, pointing out how in the past God had intervened by sending effective leaders, even though the people often rejected them and their teaching, as now they had rejected God's Messiah.

Although the Sanhedrin had no official right to inflict the death sentence (John 18:31), there were occasions such as this when lynch law prevailed, and Stephen was stoned to death, with a vision of Jesus in heaven to strengthen him. The introduction of Saul (Paul) into the story here implies that this was the first step towards his conversion (Acts 7:54–8:1).

SYNTYCHE[NT]. *Fortunate*
When we suppose that everything in the early church was

marvellous, we are reminded that our problems were there also. Syntyche and Euodia were two Christian women in Philippi who were not on speaking terms (Philippians 4:2). There is no reason why we should not include here in our alphabet **Syzygus**, or **Synzygus** (4:3), whom RSV and NEB translate as 'yokefellow' and 'true comrade' respectively, but whom JB retains as a proper name. He is urged to bring these two women together, and yoke them together in Christ.

TABEEL
An official who joined in a letter of complaint to Artaxerxes concerning Jewish attempts to rebuild Jerusalem. He may well be the same as **Tobiah** (Ezra 4:7).

TABITHA[NT]
See **Dorcas**.

TAMAR. *Palm tree*
1. The main character of the unsavoury story of Genesis 38. Judah had married a Canaanite girl who gave him two sons, Er and Onan. Er married Tamar, who seems to have been a Canaanite also, and when he died Onan refused to complete the levirate marriage (Deut. 25:5-10; Matthew 22:23-33). Tamar, who knew Judah's weakness, disguised herself as a prostitute and induced the unsuspecting Judah into a sexual liaison, the result being twins, and an admission by Judah that he had wronged her in not giving her his third son. This was the only sense of guilt that Judah had, prostitution meaning nothing to him. Tamar joins Rahab as one of the two women with a dubious past in the genealogy of Jesus Christ (Matthew 1:3; Ruth 4:12).

2. Daughter of David, and sister of Absalom by his mother Maacah, daughter of Talmai king of Geshur. David's polygamy must have created stresses between the sons and daughters of the various mothers, and in this instance Amnon, son of Ahinoam a Jezreelitess, raped Tamar in what he would doubtless have sung about as 'Love, Love, Love,' but which he forgot and

turned against her as soon as sex was over. Tamar as a woman could not take it so lightly, nor could her brother Absalom who bided his time, and after two years murdered Amnon (2 Samuel 13).

TATTENAI
Supreme governor of the territory west of Jordan when the Jews began a fresh effort to rebuild the temple in 520 BC. He authorized a letter to King Darius to discover whether Cyrus had actually sanctioned the building (Ezra 5:6-17). The letter was a genuine request for information, and not, as often with letter-writers, a complaint (e.g. 4:11-16). Darius found the decree and told Tattenai to implement it with practical help for the temple (6:1-13).

TERTULLUS[NT]
A barrister with a Latin name, although he may have been a Jew. He opened the case for the prosecution against Paul before Felix (Acts 24:1-22). He began with a compliment to Felix, as also did Paul, but did not convince Felix, who in Luke's delightful summing up had 'a rather accurate knowledge of the Way'. (See **Felix**)

THADDAEUS[NT]
See **Judas**.

THEOPHILUS[NT]. *Lover of God*, or *Friend of God*
There is some question whether Theophilus, to whom Luke dedicates his Gospel and the Acts, is simply the Christian reader in general, or whether Theophilus is the baptismal name of some important person. The latter is the more usual view, and some think that the title 'Most Excellent' in Luke 1:3 indicates that he was a member of the Equestrian Order, say, a Knight. Suggested identifications with well-known Romans, such as Seneca, are no more than guesses.

THEUDAS^{NT}

A revolutionary mentioned by Gamaliel in Acts 5:36. Josephus says that there were many revolutionaries in the first part of the 1st century.

Another Theudas, a magician, led a minor demonstration about ten years after Gamaliel's speech.

THOMAS^{NT}

One of the Twelve (Matthew 10:3). His name means *Twin*, and this is translated into the Greek *Didymus* in John 11:16. John is the only writer to give any information about Thomas. He was a hard-headed extrovert, prepared to sacrifice his life in loyalty to Jesus (11:16), unable to grasp theological subtleties (14:5), and refusing to accept the word of anyone who said that Jesus had risen from the dead. His overwhelming acceptance when he saw Jesus for himself resulted in an extrovert no-nonsense declaration, 'My Lord and my God!', which even Jehovah's Witnesses cannot evade, since Jesus accepted his worship without any attempt to correct what would otherwise have been blasphemy.

The so-called Gospel of Thomas, discovered at Naj Hamadi in 1945, dates from about AD 140, and contains a number of sayings ascribed to Jesus, some of which may well be genuine.

TIBERIUS^{NT}

See **Caesar**.

TIBNI

When Omri claimed the throne of Israel in a military coup, Tibni defied him, with the support of some 50 per cent of the people, but without success (1 Kings 16:15-22).

TIDAL

Called King of *Goyim* (Nations), in Genesis 14:1. We know that several Hittite kings had the name Tudhalia, but this one has not been identified.

TIGLATH-PILESER

Also rendered into Hebrew as Tilgath-pilneser (1 Chronicles 5:6), was king of Assyria 745-727 BC, and is also known as Pul, both in Assyrian inscriptions and in the Bible. In 5:26 the RSV has corrected the KJV, which makes them two different people, by legitimately translating the KJV 'and' as 'even'. An inscription confirms his victory over Menahem and others in 743 BC (2 Kings 15:19), and his invasion of Syria and Israel in 733 BC (15:29; 16:7-9). Ahaz had appealed to him for help, and had to pay dearly in gold and silver (16:7-8).

TIMOTHY[NT]. *Honourer of God*

A child of mixed parentage, his father being a Greek (Acts 16:1). Whatever his father thought, Timothy was well taught in the Jewish scriptures by his mother and grandmother (2 Timothy 1:5; 3:15). His mother became a Christian presumably when Paul visited Lystra on his first missionary journey, and when Paul and Silas passed through Lystra on Paul's second journey Paul asked to have Timothy to accompany him, presumably in place of Mark (Acts 16:1-3). His father had refused to agree to his being circumcised as a baby, but inasmuch as he was of Jewish birth on his mother's side Paul decided to circumcise him so as not to cause unnecessary offence among the Jews whom he was trying to reach through the synagogues (contrast **Titus** in Galatians 2:3).

At some stage the choice of Timothy was confirmed through Christian prophets; indeed Paul himself may have received the direct word from God that came to prophets (1 Timothy 1:18). Timothy was commissioned by Christian elders, and on this occasion at least he also received a gift of prophecy (1 Timothy 4:14; 2 Timothy 1:6). In the days before the New Testament was written, it was important that some evangelists and teachers should have a 'Thus saith the Lord' message which interpreted the death, resurrection and ascension of Jesus Christ.

Timothy stayed with Paul and Silas as far as Beroea, where they remained for a time before joining Paul again in Corinth

(Acts 17:14, 15; 18:5). He was sent to Thessalonica to encourage the Christians there (1 Thessalonians 3:1-3), and joined Paul again in Corinth (Acts 18:5). Later he was with Paul in Ephesus, and was sent to Macedonia to prepare for yet another visit from Paul (19:22). He was among those who escorted Paul from Greece to Jerusalem (20:4-6), so may have been in Jerusalem when Paul was arrested. In the Prison Epistles, written probably during Paul's first imprisonment in Rome, but possibly during his imprisonment in Caesarea, Timothy was with Paul and is most warmly commended as a man of real integrity in Philippians 2:19-24.

If we take the traditional view of Paul's release after his trial in Rome, he commissioned Timothy to remain at Ephesus to deal with a speculative heresy (1 Timothy 1:3-7), and this epistle sets down guidelines for problems that tended to arise in the local churches. The second epistle is written during Paul's final imprisonment, and includes an urgent request for Timothy to come and bring some special books with him (2 Timothy 4:9, 13). The unnamed writer of the Epistle to the Hebrews refers to Timothy's release from prison (Hebrews 13:23), although we have no information as to the reason for his arrest.

Tradition says that he was bishop of Ephesus and was martyred when protesting against some unpleasant ceremony. Some have even regarded him as 'the angel of the church in Ephesus' (Revelation 2:1).

TIRHAKAH
See **Pharaoh**.

TITUS[NT]
It is curious that Titus is never mentioned in Acts, although the Epistles show that he was associated with Paul. Paul took him to Jerusalem some fourteen years after his own conversion. Unlike **Timothy**, he did not have even one Jewish parent, and so Paul refused to have him circumcised (Galatians 2:3-5), since he was determined to show that Christian Gentiles were saved through

Christ alone, and not through additional conformity to Jewish law. This is the theme of Galatians.

Titus was sent on a special mission to Corinth to help to settle the restless situation there, and Paul describes his own anxiety as he waited for him to return with good news (2 Corinthians 2:13; 7:6–8:23; 12:18).

After Paul's first imprisonment in Rome, Titus travelled with him again and was stationed for a time in Crete to set things in order in the church (Titus 1:5). Paul's letter instructs him especially in personal relationships, and concludes by inviting him to join him for the winter at Nicopolis, on the west coast of Greece opposite the toe of Italy (3:12).

Reasonably firm Christian tradition makes Titus bachelor bishop of Crete, and several churches on the island are named after him.

TOBIAH. *Jehovah is good.*
Probably the same man as **Tabeel**, *God is good*

In Ezra 4:7, in the reign of Artaxerxes before the coming of Ezra and Nehemiah, Tabeel joins in a letter demanding that the king should stop the building of the city of Jerusalem and its walls. In Nehemiah 2:10 he is called 'the servant, the Ammonite', which may mean that he was a freed slave, although he rose to be governor of Ammon.

Certainly the Tobiads were governors of Ammon for many generations after this date. He and others were anxious that Judah should be kept down, and Nehemiah records him as cracking a joke about the poor quality of the walls (Ezra 4:3), planning an attack on the city (4:7), hiring a prophet to get Nehemiah to take refuge in the temple for fear of an attempt on his life (Nehemiah 6:10-14), and being in constant communication with any who might form an anti-Nehemiah party (6:17-19).

It was awkward for Nehemiah that Tobiah had two marriage links with families in the city, for he himself had married a Jewish girl, and his son had married the daughter of one of the leading builders of the wall (Nehemiah 6:18; 3:4,30). So when

Nehemiah was away in Persia making his report to Artaxerxes, Tobiah was allowed, by permission of the high priest, to move into a bed-sit in the temple which had previously been used for storing vessels and offerings. On his return Nehemiah pitched Tobiah's goods out of the temple precincts, and had the priests fumigate the room (13:6-9).

TOLA
A very minor judge, who was such small fry after the glamorous Abimelech that nothing is said about anything he did (Judges 10:1-2).

TROPHIMUS[NT]
A Greek Christian from Ephesus who was a member of Paul's escort on his visit to Rome (Acts 20:4), and who was inadvertently the cause of the riot that resulted in Paul's arrest. The Jews had seen him in the city with Paul and assumed that he had brought him into the inner courts of the temple where no Gentile was allowed (Acts 21:27-29). After Paul's release from his first imprisonment in Rome, Trophimus travelled with him again, but became unwell and had to be left in Miletus, an indication that it is not God's purpose to heal every Christian – even when there is someone like Paul present who has a gift of healing (2 Timothy 4:20, compare Acts 19:11-12).

TUBAL-CAIN
One of the three remarkable sons of Lamech (Genesis 4:19-22). He discovered how to turn copper and iron into useful implements. Although there is little or no archaeological evidence of smelting being practised earlier than about 4200 BC, and iron considerably later, Tubal-cain could have discovered the possibilities of cold hammering native copper, and iron from meteorites, two thousand years earlier. Cold forged meteoric iron tools discovered in Iran date from the fifth millennium BC.

TYCHICUS[NT]. *Lucky*

An Asian, probably from Ephesus, who joined Paul's escort to Jerusalem (Acts 20:4), and evidently went with him to Rome. Paul found him to be a useful postman, and he almost certainly carried the Epistle to the Ephesians (Ephesians 6:21-22) and to the Colossians (Colossians 4:7-8), and possibly 2 Timothy (2 Timothy 4:12, where the tense, as in Ephesians and Colossians, can mean that he is sending him now with the letter). The only other reference to Tychicus is Titus 3:12, where Paul plans to send him to Titus in the near future.

TYRANNUS[NT]

What a revealing name for a schoolmaster, since its meaning is not hard to guess! Modern translations have deprived him of the school which he enjoyed in the days of the KJV (Acts 19:9), so there is no danger of our visualizing Paul as a member of his teaching staff when he held discussions there daily. Certainly the school was some kind of lecture hall, and since teachers like Tyrannus generally held their classes in the morning, Paul was able to use the premises later in the day.

UCAL

As Quince said of Bottom in *A Midsummer Night's Dream,* 'Bless thee! thou art translated', so one may say of poor Ucal, who with his friend Ithiel has been translated out of Proverbs 30:1 by NEB and some modern scholars. Since 'the Hebrew of this verse is obscure' (RSV margin), we may prefer to leave the three old men to end their days together in peace. (See **Ithiel** and **Agur.**)

URIAH. *Jehovah is light*
1. A Hittite convert who took a Jehovah name and gave himself unreservedly to the service of David (2 Samuel 23:39) and Israel. While he was away on active service, David took Bathsheba his wife (2 Samuel 11). He might have escaped detection, but Bathsheba found that she was going to have his child. David

panicked and fetched Uriah back so that he would spend a night or two with his wife, and would then assume that the child was his when it was born. Uriah was more scrupulous than David, and chose to spend the night on guard on the floor of the palace, and continue the hard life of those who were still campaigning. Even when David made him drunk, he stubbornly refused to spend the night at home.

So David sent him back to the field, carrying his own death sentence in a letter to Joab, the commander. Joab must make an attack on the city of Rabbah, and press as close as possible to the walls. Uriah must be in the front line. Then his supporters must withdraw quickly and leave Uriah alone, the target for the enemy attack. The result was as David hoped, and Uriah's wife was his for the taking. This was the great blot on David's life (1 Kings 15:6). In his moving psalm of confession (Psalm 51) David confesses to murder (verse 14), but knows that if he is to be forgiven this must be solely through the mercy of God, since the Law made no provision for animal sacrifice for this great sin (verses 16-17).

2. A prophet contemporary with Jeremiah, who like him spoke against the sins of the day, and had to go abroad to Egypt to escape the anger of King Jehoiakim. But the king managed to extradite him, executed him, and insulted his body after death (Jeremiah 26:20-23).

UZZAH. *Strength*

Uzzah and his brother were chosen to drive the cart carrying the ark of the covenant, which had been stored for many years in their father's house in Kiriath-jearim, also known as Baale-judah (2 Samuel 6). It is possible that they were Levites, but unlikely in view of what David says in 1 Chronicles 15:2. When the cart was near the city the oxen stumbled and Uzzah seized the ark. The story says that God smote him because he put forth his hand to the ark, and he died there.

It is hard to suppose that a well-meant attempt to steady the ark would have roused the anger of God. It may well be that if we had been standing in the crowd we should have seen Uzzah showing off, like Little Claus in Hans Andersen's story, with his 'Hurrah, my fine horses!' The climax came when the oxen stumbled and Uzzah seized the chance of demonstrating what a great man he was to be able to lay hands on the sacred ark, in a way that no Levite had been allowed to do. One hardly supposes that a stumble by the oxen would have done more than slightly tip the cart, and Uzzah need not have touched the ark at all.

UZZIAH. *Jehovah is my strength*

Also called Azariah. King of Judah (c. 767-740 BC), probably being co-regent with his father, Amaziah, from c. 790 BC. We learn more details of his reign from 2 Chronicles 26 than from 2 Kings 15:1-7. He was successful in a number of campaigns, and did much to improve and fortify Jerusalem. Unfortunately he decided to do what no king before him had done, and take the place of the priests in offering incense within the temple.

Resistance by the high priest only enraged Uzziah, and he forced his way in. God had decreed the pattern of worship in the tabernacle, as the Epistle to the Hebrews shows. Each aspect was a reflection of Jesus Christ's priestly work on the cross, leading to our approach to the full presence of God in and through him. Not even a king was entitled to destroy the blueprint, for the blueprint has to relate to the finished object. Uzziah was struck down with leprosy and spent the rest of his reign in comparative seclusion. Isaiah dates his call from the year of Uzziah's death (Isaiah 6:1). Uzziah in spite of his final lapse had been a good king, and it may be that, in the general depression at his passing, Isaiah is shown the King of kings enthroned, as was his right, in the temple.

VASHTI

The chief wife of Ahasuerus (Xerxes), who refused to exhibit herself at a drunken orgy, and was consequently demoted (Esther 1). Some four years later Esther was chosen to succeed her (2:16). It is objected that the name of Xerxes' queen was

Amestris, and that therefore the book of Esther is in error. In fact there is no Persian record of the name of Xerxes' wife, but two Greek writers say that she was called Amestris. When we remember that Akhashwerosh (Hebrew), Ahasuerus (English) and Xerxes (Greek) are all renderings of the Persian Khshayar-sha, we may well wonder whether Amestris (Greek) and Vashti (Hebrew) might not be the same person, especially when some scholars maintain that the name Vashti is equivalent to the god Mashti. There is not much difference between Mashti and Amestris.

What we know from the Greek historians, Herodotus and Ctesias, is that Amestris went with Xerxes on his expedition to Greece, which followed soon after the events of Esther 1. On the way back Amestris found that her husband was having an affair with his brother's wife and her daughter, and took her revenge by horribly mutilating the mother. This may well have moved Xerxes to carry out the threat of divorce that he made in Esther 1, and the choice of Esther coincided with his return from Greece.

Esther perhaps died soon after the close of the book in 473 BC, and when Xerxes was murdered in 465 BC we know that Amestris came back into power as queen mother, Artaxerxes I now being king. This was the Artaxerxes of Ezra and Nehemiah, and it could even be that Vashti/Amestris was 'the queen' of Nehemiah 2:6. Ctesias says she died as a very old woman.

Z. *Hebrew and Greek were far more lavish with their Z than the niggardly English. Those of us older folk, who as children were introduced to 'A was an Archer who shot at a frog ...' had to make do with 'Z was a Zany, a poor harmless fool', while the alternative 'A was an Apple Pie' sequence gave up in despair and lumped the last three letters of the alphabet together with ampersand in a rather feeble sequence. Today we can use Zebra and Zoo, but not much else. We are also sparing of Z within words, although publishers generally insist on being baptized rather than baptised, and occasionally we go to town with a double Z, as in 'Fizzy', and all continental with the explosive*

'Pizza'. Hebrew and Greek promoted Z to number 7 in the alphabet league. Before the discerning reader points out that in Greek it is number 6, I am counting the digamma. So, although we have reached our last letter, there are still some names to come.

ZACCHAEUS[NT]. From Hebrew meaning *Pure*
The chief taxman of Jericho, who followed the usual practice of the day in making quite a bit on the side, and was consequently classified as a sinner (Luke 19:7-8). Like a good press photographer he took up a position in a tree to see Jesus over the heads of the crowd. Jesus saw him and invited himself to dinner at his house, and during his visit Zacchaeus was soundly converted, and declared his intention to repay — and more — anything he had taken unjustly.

ZACHARIAH
See **Zechariah**.

ZADOK. *Righteous*
A priest descended from Aaron's son, Eleazar (1 Chronicles 6:4-8,50-53). He and Abiathar, descended from Aaron's youngest son Ithamar through Eli (see **Eli**), carried the ark of the covenant when David left the city in Absalom's rebellion (2 Samuel 15:24), but David sent them back, and deputed them to use their sons as spies (15:25-29). (See **Ahimaaz**).

When Adonijah attempted his coup to get the throne, backed by Abiathar, Zadok remained loyal to David and was commissioned to crown Solomon (1 Kings 1). As a result Zadok was appointed high priest, and his descendants remained true to Jehovah in spite of general apostasy (Ezekiel 44:15). The Zadokites retained the high priesthood until 171 BC. It is just possible that the name Sadducee is derived from Zadok.

ZEBEDEE[NT]
Father of James and John, who was with them in the boat when

they were called from their fishing (Matthew 4:21-22). His wife was probably **Salome**.

ZECHARIAH^{OT/NT} (**Zacharias**). *Jehovah has remembered*
Some thirty men have this name, including:

1. ^{OT}The last king of the line of Jehu, who reigned for six months before his assassination in 753 BC (2 Kings 15:8-12), which incidentally is the traditional date of the foundation of Rome!

2. ^{OT}The prophet who joined Haggai in 520 BC in urging the people to take up again the rebuilding of the temple in Jerusalem after neglecting it for a number of years, in spite of the commission of Cyrus some seventeen years before (Ezra 5:1-2). It may be that the two prophets returned about 520 BC, but it is more likely that they had been brought back as babies at the original return, and only received their call now.

The first six chapters of Zechariah's prophecies contain a series of visions that have to do with the rebuilding of the temple and the cleansing of the land from sin. If we say that these are 'types' of Christ, we are not saying anything unreal. Much that is true of building a temple of wood and stone to be the focus of God's presence on earth is true of the building of the spiritual/physical temple of the body of Christ, the focus of his presence on earth, as set out in Ephesians 3:20-22.

Thus Zechariah links priest (Joshua) and royal leader (Zerubbabel) as responsible for the building, Christ being the Priest/King (Zechariah 3:8-9; 4:9-10; 6:11-13). Indeed, Joshua is said to be the picture of the Messianic Branch of the line of David (Zechariah 6:12; Jeremiah 23:5). Both the foundation stone and the top stone are vital for the building (Zechariah 3:9; 4:7), and Jesus Christ is both (1 Peter 2:6-7; Ephesians 2:20), being the beginning and the ending (Hebrew 12:2). As priest and king the leaders are sustained by the oil of the Spirit (Zechariah 4:1-6; so Matthew 12:28; Hebrews 9:14; Ephesians 2:22). The temple is for those who have been made clean (Zechariah 3, where Joshua needs cleansing that Christ did not need; Zechariah 5:1-11;

Hebrews 10:19-22; Ephesians 2:1-6).

Zechariah 7 and 8 speak of the wages of sin and the blessings of righteousness, including the blessing of the knowledge of God that is spread through the people of God (Zechariah 8:20-23). Many commentators regard this as the end of the prophecies of Zechariah, and treat chapters 9-11 and 12-14 as additional pieces from other authors. One reason for this is the mention of Greece in 9:13. But if Zechariah was a young man when he was called in 520 BC, he would have lived on into the next century when the Greeks were emerging as a power to be reckoned with. He could well have seen them as the next empire after they had raided and burnt Sardis in 500 BC, and defeated the Persians at Marathon and Salamis in 490 and 480 BC. The Jewish nation was beginning to slide back into some of its old ways, as we know from Ezra and Nehemiah, and these chapters of Zechariah both warn and encourage.

The most noteworthy thing about these chapters is that whereas in Zechariah chapters 1-8 the Messiah is the temple builder, he is here the rejected Shepherd valued at thirty pieces of silver (Zechariah 11:7-15), the One who is pierced (12:10, where the Hebrew has 'look on me', i.e. on God who is speaking), and who consequently opens the fountain for sin and uncleanness (13:1). Finally there is the coming of the Lord, which means the judgment of suffering for some and the opening up of blessing for others (chapter 14). In this final chapter it is hard to sort out symbolism from material reality.

3. [NT]A priest who was father of John the Baptist (Luke 1:5). The priests worked on a rota basis, and when he went in on his day to burn incense in the temple, he was confronted by the angel Gabriel and told that he would have a son who would be the Elijah promised in Malachi as the one who would prepare the way for the Messiah. Zechariah queries the message, since he and his wife were both old. As a priest, he might well have remembered Abraham. His doubt cost him his power of speech until the baby was born, and Luke 1:62 shows that he became deaf as well as dumb. The child arrived safely, and when he was named at his circumcision both mother and father insisted that he should be named John, as Gabriel had instructed them. At this point Zechariah was inspired by the Holy Spirit to utter the words that are commonly known as the Benedictus, in which he hailed the near appearance of the Messiah as the fulfilment of all the prophecies that had gone before, and declared that his own child would be the preparer of the way (Luke 1.67-79).

4. ᴼᵀThere is one other Zechariah, who creates a puzzle. In Luke 11:51 Jesus speaks of the Old Testament martyrs in the words, 'from the blood of Abel to the blood of Zechariah, who perished between the altar and the sanctuary.' In 2 Chronicles 24:20-22 the prophet Zechariah, son of Jehoiada the high priest, is stoned to death in the temple, and since Chronicles is the last book in the Hebrew Bible Jesus would be saying the equivalent of 'All the martyrs from Genesis to Revelation.' However, the parallel in Matthew 23:35 reads, 'the blood of Zechariah the son of Barachiah ...'

The prophet Zechariah, whose book is next to last of the minor prophets, was the son of Berechiah (1:1) and, while it is possible that he was martyred, there is no evidence for this, and Christ's words surely demand some well-known event. Hence it is best to suppose that the same copyist who fancied his memory for the Old Testament, and tried to supplement Matthew in 27:9 by adding the name of Jeremiah where Matthew had simply written 'the prophet', did the same here, and added 'the son of Berechiah', again out of his faulty memory. (See **Judas**)

ZEDEKIAH. *Jehovah is righteous*
1. The last king of Judah, placed on the throne by Nebuchadnezzar after he had taken Jehoiachin and all the best people to Babylon in 597 BC. Zedekiah was the youngest son of Josiah, and Nebuchadnezzar changed his name from Mattaniah, *Gift of Jehovah,* which does not make much sense in view of the two meanings (2 Kings 24:17-18). Jeremiah and Ezekiel expose the moral and spiritual degradation of Judah during his reign. Eventually he rebelled against Nebuchadnezzar, and after a siege

of nearly two years Jerusalem fell to the Babylonians in 587 BC. Zedekiah nearly escaped, but was rounded up and taken to Babylon after being blinded. The last thing his eyes saw was the execution of his two sons (2 Kings 25:4-7). In Jeremiah 32-38 we have vivid pictures of the incompetence of this thirty-year-old king, and chapter 38 is particularly revealing.

2. The most demonstrative of the court prophets who urged Ahab to do what he wanted to do, namely to recapture Ramoth-Gilead from the Syrians. He pranced about with a pair of iron horns (1 Kings 22:11), and showed his contempt for Micaiah the only genuine prophet by giving him a stinging blow on the cheek (22:24). Micaiah declared that he would know the truth on the day when he crept away to hide himself as a discredited prophet (22:25).

3. One of two prophets deported to Babylon, who kept saying that the exiles who had come with Jehoiachin in 597 BC could look forward to a speedy return. Jeremiah, on the contrary, urged them to settle down and start building and farming and live a normal family life (Jeremiah 29:5-7). The exile would indeed end, but not yet. Zedekiah and his fellow prophet were arrested by the Babylonian authorities and put to death by burning (29:21-23), presumably because they were stirring up trouble. Jeremiah indicates that they were not only revolutionaries but were thoroughly immoral men as well (29:23).

ZELOPHEHAD. Possibly, *A shadow*, or *shelter, from fear*
A member of the tribe of Manasseh, and father of five daughters who were all unmarried at the time of his death. These daughters raised a matter of great importance with Moses (Numbers 27:1-11; 36:1-12). In the first place, could they inherit and carry on their father's name? The answer was Yes. But what if they married? The answer was that they must marry within their tribe, so that possessions did not pass from one tribe to another.

ZEPHANIAH. *Jehovah has hidden,* perhaps because he was born of godly parents during the days of persecution under

Manasseh.

Author of the book that bears his name, and which relates him almost certainly to King Hezekiah (Zephaniah 1:1). He prophesied probably in the early days of Josiah, soon after 640 BC, before the evils of Manasseh's reign had been swept away. Very possibly he helped to inspire Josiah's first reformation (2 Chronicles 34:3-7). He was a contemporary of Jeremiah.

His book denounces idolaters, especially idolatrous priests, and those leaders who maintained that God would not intervene for good or ill, to reward or punish (Zephaniah 1). His second chapter speaks of disasters that will fall upon other nations, whereas the third returns to Jerusalem, again revealing the rottenness that must be done away, and then passing to the future when God's people will be brought back to him, and others from the nations will come to him after passing through the fires, which may be fires of purification as well as judgment.

ZERUBBABEL

A Babylonian name of uncertain meaning. He was the son of Shealtiel (Ezra 3:2) and so grandson of King Jehoiachin (Matthew 1:12. In 1 Chronicles 3:19 the Hebrew, though not the Septuagint, makes him the son of Shealtiel's brother, Pedaiah, perhaps by a levirate marriage.) It is significant that in Haggai 2:23 Zerubbabel is taken up as a precious signet ring for God's finger, the reversal of Jeremiah 22:24 where his grandfather is the signet that is torn off God's hand and cast into exile.

Zerubbabel returned from exile in 537 BC with Sheshbazzar, who may have been his uncle. The two have sometimes been identified as one and the same person, but in Ezra 5:14 Sheshbazzar is referred to as one who is no longer alive, while Zerubbabel was extremely active. He and Joshua the high priest were the active leaders and set up the altar on the temple ruins, and then began to build the temple again (Ezra 3), but unfortunately the opposition of the people around proved too much for them after they refused the help of the half-and-half worshippers of Jehovah (4:1-4).

In 520 BC the prophets Haggai and Zechariah induced them to make a fresh start, and in four years the work was finished (Ezra 5 and 6). The celebrations at the dedication of the temple were open not only to those who had returned from exile, but also to all members of the northern kingdom of Israel who had not gone into exile, but who now, if not before, made a deliberate break with the polytheistic semi-Jehovah worship of the people who had been introduced into Palestine, and the rather similar worship of their own nation (Ezra 6:21; 2 Kings 17:14-18; 29-34) Zerubbabel became governor after the death of Sheshbazzar (Haggai 2:2).

ZERUIAH
Mother of Abishai, Asahel, and Joab (2 Samuel 2:18). For her relationship to David see **Nahash**.

ZIBA
His story is told under **Mephibosheth**.

ZILLAH
One of Lamech's two wives, the other being Adah. She was the mother of Tubal-cain and a daughter, Naamah, but the whole family were brilliant (Genesis 4:19-22).

ZIMRI
A general who assassinated King Elah while the latter was blind drunk. He reigned for no more than a week, but during that time managed to eliminate every one of the ex-king's relatives and friends before becoming the target of Omri, another army revolutionary. When he saw that all was lost, he shut himself in the palace and burnt it to the ground. If Zimri had lived, the record indicates that he would have followed the degraded morality and spirituality of his predecessors (1 Kings 16:8-20).

ZIPPORAH. *Bird*
Daughter of Jethro, priest of Midian, and wife of Moses (Exodus

2:15-22). She disliked what she regarded as the messy business of circumcision when she saw her first son circumcised, and was strong-minded enough to refuse to allow it for her second son. It was, however, vital that Moses, who was to enforce the fresh covenant on Sinai, should himself keep the covenant of circumcision made with Abraham (Genesis 17, especially verse 14).

On the way to Egypt, God brought Zipporah to her senses by her seeing Moses struck down with a sudden illness, which she realized was from God. So in the end she circumcised the child herself, touched Moses' feet with the foreskin she had cut off, and reproached him bitterly for the bloody act to which she had been driven through her marriage to him. But the Bible points out that it was only when Moses suddenly recovered that she expressed her relief by going for him (Exodus 4:24-26). Moses sent her and his sons back to her father, and they joined him again after the escape from Egypt (18:1-9).

ZOPHAR

One of Job's three friends. He is described as a Naamathite, and presumably came from east of the Jordan (Job 2:11). Each friend has his own character and approach. Zophar is the man of popular misconception who believes all he has been told about suffering being the result of sin. He utters his clichés in chapters 11 and 20, but fails to come up for the third round of speeches. (See **Job, Bildad, Eliphaz.**)

ALSO FROM WHITE TREE PUBLISHING

English Hexapla – The Gospel of John

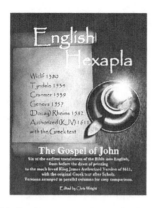

Published to coincide with the 400th anniversary of the Authorized King James Version of the Bible, this book contains the full text of Bagster's assembled work for the Gospel of John. On each page in parallel columns are the words of the six most important translations of the New Testament into English, made between 1380 and 1611. Below the English is the original Greek text after Scholz. To enhance the reading experience, there is an introduction telling how we got our English Bibles, with significant pages from early Bibles shown at the end of the book.

Here is an opportunity to read English that once split the Church by giving ordinary people the power to discover God's word for themselves. Now you can step back in time and discover those words and spellings for yourself, as they first appeared hundreds of years ago.

Wyclif 1380, Tyndale 1534, Cranmer 1539, Geneva 1557, Douay Rheims 1582, Authorized (KJV) 1611.

English Hexapla – The Gospel of John
Published by White Tree Publishing
ISBN: 978-0-9525956-1-8
Size 7.5 x 9.7 inches paperback
UK £6.95, €7.95, US $9.95.

MARY JONES AND HER BIBLE

Endorsed by Bible Society

AN ADVENTURE BOOK

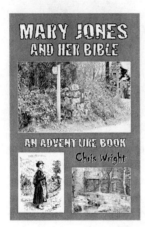

Mary Jones saved for six years to buy a Bible of her own. In 1800, when she was 15, she thought she had saved enough, so she walked barefoot for 26 miles (more than 40km) over a mountain pass and through deep valleys in Wales to get one. That's when she discovered there were none for sale!

You can travel with Mary Jones today in this book by following clues, or just reading the story. Either way, you will get to Bala where Mary went, and if you're really quick you may be able to discover a Bible just like Mary's in the market!

The true story of Mary Jones has captured the imagination for more than 200 years. For this book, Chris Wright has looked into the old records and discovered even more of the story, which is now in this unforgettable account of Mary Jones and her Bible. Solving puzzles is part of the fun, but the whole story is in here to read and enjoy whether you try the puzzles or not. Just turn the page, and the adventure continues. It's time to get on the trail of Mary Jones!

A true story with optional puzzles.
(Some are easy, some tricky, and some amusing.)
Published by Christian publishers White Tree Publishing
ISBN 978-0-9525956-2-5
5.5 x 8.5 inches paperback
UK £6.95, €8.95, US $12.95
156 pages of story, photographs, line drawings and puzzles.
The full story of Mary Jones's and her Bible
with a clear Christian message.

Lightning Source UK Ltd.
Milton Keynes UK

178593UK00001B/20/P